When the Dodgers Were Bridegrooms

When the Dodgers Were Bridegrooms

Gunner McGunnigle and Brooklyn's Back-to-Back Pennants of 1889 and 1890

RONALD G. SHAFER

McFarland & Company, Inc., Publishers
Jefferson, North Carolina, and London

Library of Congress Online Catalog data

Shafer, Ronald G.
When the Dodgers were bridegrooms : Gunner McGunnigle and Brooklyn's back-to-back pennants of 1889 and 1890 / Ronald G. Shafer.
p. cm.
Includes bibliographical references and index.

ISBN 978-0-7864-5899-8
softcover : 50# alkaline paper ∞

1. McGunnigle, William Henry, 1855–1899. 2. Brooklyn Dodgers (Baseball team)—History. 3. Los Angeles Dodgers (Baseball team)—History. I. Title.
GV875.B7S425 2011 2011010258

British Library cataloguing data are available

On the cover: Studio portrait of the 1889 Brooklyn baseball team (Library of Congress)

Manufactured in the United States of America

McFarland & Company, Inc., Publishers
Box 611, Jefferson, North Carolina 28640
www.mcfarlandpub.com

This book is dedicated to my wife, Mary Rogers, and our children, Daniel Rogers, Kaitlin Rogers and Kathryn Shafer Rivers, her husband, Howard Rivers, and our wonderful granddaughter, Kaylie Ryan Rivers. It also is written in memory of Barbara Lucas Shafer and Ryan Shafer, a great baseball fan.

Table of Contents

Preface

This book began as a birthday present to my wife, Mary Lynch Rogers, the great-granddaughter of William "Gunner" McGunnigle. The family story about her great-grandfather Bill McGunnigle was that he was a famous nineteenth-century baseball player who invented the catcher's mitt and managed the Brooklyn Bridegrooms. I am a longtime baseball fan who grew up following the Cleveland Indians — until they traded Rocky Colavito — and then the Cincinnati Reds. But I had never heard of McGunnigle or a team called the Bridegrooms. I surmised that he probably was a locally known amateur player who managed some obscure team in Brooklyn. So for one of Mary's birthdays, I Googled McGunnigle so that I could write a short history of her great-granddaddy.

To my surprise, I discovered that Bill McGunnigle was a famous and inventive baseball player in the late 1800s. He played in the major leagues briefly for the Buffalo Bisons when the team was a member of the National League. What's more, the Brooklyn Bridegrooms that he managed not only was a major league team (later to be known as the Dodgers); it won two pennants.

My interest in McGunnigle increased when my wife and I attended a Washington Nationals game with baseball expert Bruce Brown and his wife, Roslyn. Bruce is chair of the Washington, D.C., Bob Davids Chapter of the Society for American Baseball Research, or SABR, an international group of ardent baseball fans and researchers. He easily answered every obscure baseball question I threw at him. But Mary stumped him when she asked if he had ever heard of McGunnigle and the Bridegrooms. I figured if so little was known about a once-famous baseball man and his team, the forerunner of a legendary baseball franchise, maybe there was a book here somewhere.

I joined SABR and attended its 2009 convention in Washington, D.C., where I presented a proposal for a book on Gunner McGunnigle to McFarland. The McFarland folks suggested, and I agreed, that a book on both McGunnigle *and* Brooklyn's first major league pennants would be of broader interest.

As my research intensified, I made more discoveries. I found that a clever and fascinating man named Charles Byrne, more than any other individual, was responsible for starting the Dodgers franchise. What's more, he had a fierce rival named Chris Von der Ahe, a German-born saloon owner with a reputation for outlandish behavior. His St. Louis Browns, now the St. Louis Cardinals, won four straight pennants. I also discovered a colorful crew of Brooklyn players featuring such nicknames as "Adonis," "Needles," "Germany," and "Oyster," who carved the team's early baseball history.

To my knowledge, this is the first book entirely devoted to the first major league pennants of the Brooklyn club that became the Dodgers. (James Terry's Long Before the Dodgers does cover the franchise's start-up, in brief, but the book's focus is squarely on the Brooklyn teams that preceded it.) My purpose not only is to tell the story of Brooklyn's team but to show the contributions of its early players and owners to baseball. Most have long been forgotten, but it was these men who shaped the early game of baseball into America's national pastime.

In writing the book, I relied as much as possible on primary sources, such as the newspapers of the day and books of remembrances by early players and executives. Many people helped along the way. I want to give special thanks to my wife's niece, Monet Solberg, who wrote a paper on Bill McGunnigle for a class at the College of William and Mary and shared her research with me. Much information on McGunnigle's life came from the writings of the late Bob Kane, a SABR member and the town historian of Brockton, Massachusetts, which plans to dedicate memorials to McGunnigle and other city heroes, including boxing champion Rocky Marciano. Many current SABR members also were generous with their help.

Great thanks go to the armies of unknown people who have put nineteenth-century publications on the Internet. I could sit at my home computer and read old articles from the *Brooklyn Eagle* at the Brooklyn Public Library, *Sporting Life, The New York Times and The Sporting News,* via a link provided to SABR members. I also spent hours at libraries squinting at microfilm of old newspapers such as the *New York Clipper.* Thanks to those who helped me at the Williamsburg, Virginia, Library as well as at the Loudoun County, Virginia, Library, the Library of Congress in Washington, D.C., the Fall River, Massachusetts, Library and the SABR Lending Library. I also wish to thank Freddy Berowski and John Horne at the National Baseball Hall of Fame's A. Bartlett Giamatti Research Center, and Mark Rucker at Transcendental Graphics.

As I wrote the manuscript, I called on friends to check my facts and writing. Thanks to Bruce Brown for reading parts of the book to check its historical accuracy. Thanks, too, to fellow writers James M. Perry, a former colleague at the *Wall Street Journal*, and freelancer Judith Windeler in London. Most of all, I want to thank my toughest editor and biggest supporter, my wife, Mary.

Chapter One

A Team Grows in Brooklyn

Charles H. Byrne, the urbane president of the Brooklyn Base Ball Club, was steaming. Byrne, a small, personable man with a circular face, neatly cropped hair and a "black and shimmering mustache," was fed up with the insults, the accusations and the whining. The object of his annoyance was the cantankerous owner of the St. Louis Base Ball Club, Chris Von der Ahe, a big, stocky man with a scruffy, auburn mustache sprouting beneath his red bulbous nose. Responding to Von der Ahe's latest gripe, Byrne declared: "It is simply a case of abnormal enlargement of the cranium in a mentally small man supplemented by an acute attack of disappointment."[1]

In truth, it was Byrne who was increasingly disappointed in the late summer of 1887 as Von der Ahe's St. Louis Browns were again crushing the Brooklyn magnate's dream of capturing the major-league American Association pennant. The Browns were the original "nasty boys" of baseball. Led by hard-nosed player-manager Charles Comiskey, the team was infamous for bulldozing opponents and umpires into submission. This was a reflection of its combative, German-born owner, who after a loss would scream at errant players: "Vy did you drop dat ball, eh?"[2]

By contrast, Charley Byrne was a benevolent boss who paid his players well for that era and treated them with civility. Byrne was a talkative, intelligent and educated man with a quick sense of humor — and chronic indigestion. He was dignified and even-tempered, but his anger would flare when he was pushed too far. He was a dapper dresser: "Charley Byrne would be immaculate if there was a frost in Hades," one writer noted.[3] Byrne also was an aggressive businessman who usually got what he wanted.

Born in September of 1843 to Irish parents in New York City, Byrne graduated from St. Francis Xavier College, attended law school and worked as a sportswriter before heading west to Omaha, Nebraska. In the mining region there he clerked for a railroad company before being elected deputy sheriff. After his term was up, Byrne returned to New York, where he earned a small fortune dealing in the city's booming real estate market.

As an affluent New Yorker in the early 1880s, Byrne was one of the city's most eligible bachelors. He was short but strongly built. His countenance, by one account, projected "unusual strength and energy, but his smile is engaging."[4] He believed in honor, courage and civility. His philosophy, he once said, was that "it is always good policy to be polite to your fellow man, and the same holds good in the case of mules."[5]

"Why, that's Charley Byrne, a man who has done more than anyone else to give Brooklyn the position it occupies as a centre of professional base ball"—*Sporting Life* (Library of Congress).

Charley Byrne lived the good life—dining in New York's finest restaurants, enjoying Cuban cigars and soaking in the city's culture. His main interests were the arts and theater, especially the opera. His friends were actors and playwrights. He could converse with them for hours about popular plays or music from his favorite operas. Until the autumn of 1882, Byrne cared far more about *La bohème* than about "base ball" (it was two words back then).

Then he met hustling George J. Taylor, a man with a dream. Taylor was the 30-year-old night editor at the

New York Herald with a bushy handlebar mustache and a keen interest in baseball. When Taylor's doctor suggested that the chain-smoking newsman find a healthier occupation, he decided to pursue his dream: to form a new professional team to bring the game back to Brooklyn, once known as "the city of base ball." In the fall of 1882, Taylor had obtained the backing of a Wall Street financier and a lease on property in South Brooklyn at Fifth Avenue and Third Street. His plan was to build a ballpark over a skating pond but the investor got cold feet and backed out, leaving Taylor the lease. The newsman went to see a lawyer, John Brice, who had an office on Liberty Street near Broadway in New York. Brice introduced Taylor to 40-year-old Charley Byrne, who rented a desk at the office. Taylor, like Byrne, was a graduate of St. Francis Xavier College.[6]

The idea of starting a professional baseball team in Brooklyn stirred Byrne's interest. As a real estate investor, he knew that Brooklyn was on the rise. Called the "City of Churches" because of its more than 270 places of worship, Brooklyn had nearly doubled in population in the past decade, to more than 565,000 people. That made it the third largest city among the 38 states, trailing only Philadelphia and New York, which was No. 1 with more than 1.2 million souls. A second wave of immigrants — mainly Irish, German and East European — was fueling growth in both cities, with 40 percent of New York's residents and a third of Brooklyn's being foreign born.[7]

As the 1883–84 Brooklyn manager, former newsman George Taylor "worked on the sound principle that a good reporter could cover any assignment and was not in the least worried about running a team"— Charles Ebbets (*New York Clipper*).

Brooklyn's crowded, dusty streets bustled with

activity as pedestrians dodged the horse-drawn streetcars of the Brooklyn City Railway Company. This was what the leading author of the day, Mark Twain, called "The Gilded Age," a time of booming economic and population growth, with the two cities on the Atlantic Ocean leading the way. New York on the island of Manhattan had already become the world's financial center. Brooklyn on Long Island was a leading hub of sugar and oil refining with shipping docks, the Brooklyn Navy Yard and houses for the thousands who commuted daily to jobs in New York on the hundreds of boats run by 13 ferry lines across the East River. One 37-year-old journalist in 1856 was even moved to wax poetic about his commute:

> Crowds of men and women attired in the usual costumes,
> How curious you are to me!
> On the ferry-boats the hundreds and hundreds that cross,
> returning home, are more curious to me than you suppose,
> And you that shall cross from the shore to shore years
> hence are more to me, and more in my meditations, than
> you might suppose.[8]

The author of *Crossing Brooklyn Ferry* was then–Brooklyn resident Walt Whitman, who, in addition to being a poet, was a baseball fan.

Charley Byrne also was well aware that in 1883 a mammoth bridge, under construction for 12 years, was slated to join the two great cities. This growing throng of people would be looking for something to do. If you built a ballpark, they might come. As a former sportswriter, Byrne knew that Brooklyn was the cradle of baseball. In the 1850s and 1860s, three legendary Brooklyn teams dominated the championships of the amateur National Association of Base Ball Players. One was the Excelsiors of South Brooklyn, a gentlemen's club previously known as the Jolley Bachelor's Club. Another was the working-class Eckfords, a team of shipwrights and mechanics named after a late Brooklyn shipbuilder, Henry Eckford. The third squad was the powerful Atlantics, the "Bedford Boys" from what was then the Bedford district of Irish immigrants and today is Bedford-Stuyvesant.

Brooklyn was home to the game's first enclosed baseball fields where admission was charged — the Union Grounds in the Williamsburg section and the hallowed Capitoline in nearby Bedford. It was at the Capitoline that one of baseball's most historic games was played on June 14, 1870,

The powerful Brooklyn Atlantics were the champions of the amateur National Association of Base Ball Players from 1864 to 1867 (Library of Congress).

between the Brooklyn Atlantics and the visiting Cincinnati Red Stockings, baseball's first all professional team. More than 20,000 "cranks," or fans, had jammed into the stadium to see the local boys take on the "Reds," who had played 81 straight games without a loss over two seasons. When player-manager Bob "Death to All Flying Things" Ferguson raced home with the winning run in the 11th inning, Brooklyn had made baseball history.

But that was years ago. Brooklyn hadn't had its own baseball team since 1875, when the old National Association of Professional Ball Players collapsed after five struggling seasons. Byrne sensed pent-up demand by Brooklynites for their own team if one were put together properly. Baseball had evolved from its beginnings as a gentleman's sport played for recreation in the 1840s to a competitive and entertaining pastime. The game resembled today's fast-pitch softball. The pitcher threw underhand 50 feet from the batter (instead of 60 feet, 6 inches, as would be permanently established in 1893). Twirlers had learned to put speed, curves and even some spit on the ball. There was no pitcher's mound; instead hurlers threw from flat ground in a clearly marked pitcher's "box," leading to the term "knocked out of the box." Pitchers, however, rarely were replaced during a game, and most hurled complete games every day or two. Batters ordered that a ball be pitched "high" or "low." Home runs were rare, usually the result of a ball being hit between the outfielders into crowds of spectators and horse-drawn carriages surrounding the open outfield. If a home-team batter hit the ball, the sphere would mysteriously disappear amid a sea of shoes and hooves. If an opponent made the hit, the crowd would block the ball so the outfielder could retrieve it.

In the field, players caught the ball barehanded, except the catcher and first baseman, who had begun to wear rudimentary gloves. The catcher usually stood back far enough to catch a pitched ball on the first bounce. He would put on a mask and move up behind the batter with runners on base. A backstop's hands suffered heavy punishment. One old catcher's fingers "were battered into so many angles that when he spread them out they resembled pretzels," recalled Adrian "Cap" Anson, Chicago's great captain and player-manager.[9]

Yes, baseball could be big in Brooklyn, Byrne figured. He also knew that, though he was well off, he didn't have the kind of money it would take to build a baseball park and form a team. But he knew somebody who did. He went to see his brother-in-law, Joseph J. Doyle, proprietor of a popular casino on Ann Street in New York. The 45-year-old Doyle, known as "Uncle Joe" to his face and "Fat Joe" behind his ample back, was a jovial man with a jolly sense of humor, but he also was a shrewd businessman. He, too, saw the potential of professional baseball in Brooklyn and joined in.

Fat Joe, however, began sweating when the costs of just the initial grading and preparations for the ballpark exceeded $12,000. He decided that Taylor needed another "angel," a richer one. Joe went to his friend, 50-year-old Ferdinand "Gus" Abell, who owned a large casino in Narragansett, Rhode Island, as well as a house in New York City. Abell resisted. He knew plenty about gambling and horse racing, but little about baseball. Finally, Doyle persuaded him, and Abell's deep pockets joined up.

Abell was a courtly, unassuming man who loved to talk about raising crops on his farm on Cape Cod in West Yarmouth, Massachusetts. He had a wry sense of humor. He once said, "Whenever I go to a baseball meeting, I never forget to check my money and valuables at the hotel office before

Brooklyn co-owner Ferdinand "Gus" Abell once said, "I have been in the base ball business for 18 years, and in all that time have never known the magnates to do anything honestly or fairly" (*Sporting Life*).

entering the session chamber."[10] One reason the three men would work so well together was that all loved a good laugh, even if the laugh was on them.

Gus Abell and Joe Doyle became the chief financial backers for the operation; Charley Byrne probably never had more than a 20 percent interest in the club.[11] But Abell and Doyle knew Byrne was the man to run the club with his intelligence, diplomacy and knack for public relations. If someone would ask Doyle about the team, he would point to his brother-in-law and say, "You will have to go to him, he is the Brooklyn talking-machine."[12] Building a successful baseball team from scratch would be a formidable task, but Charley Byrne began to toil day and night to bring a big league championship to Brooklyn.

By late winter of 1882 work began in earnest on the ballpark, which would end up costing $30,000, a huge sum in those days. Byrne decided to call it Washington Park because it was built on the site where troops under General George Washington fought the first clash of the Revolutionary War on August 27, 1776, in the Battle of Long Island. As Washington ordered the outmanned American troops to make a hasty retreat across the East River, 250 soldiers from a Maryland regiment bravely held off the invading British army from inside an old stone house before being overwhelmed. The Old Stone House was retained as a "ladies house," because Byrne planned to encourage attendance of women at home games.

A 13-foot-high fence went up around the entire block. Work began on a wooden grandstand that would seat 2,500 people as well as an open "free stand" for 2,000 more in the wooden bleachers, called "bleaching boards" because the wood bleached in the hot sun. Still more standees and horse-drawn carriages could be accommodated beyond the outfield. The carriages would enter through a gate under a 30-foot-high arch. The goal was to have the park ready in time for the start of the rapidly approaching 1883 baseball season. But there were still a few things to be done — such as finding players to play there.

Byrne's goal from the start was to raise the level of the game in order to attract respectable people to the ballpark. The old professional league, which the players ran themselves between 1871 and 1875, failed largely because the stands were filled with gamblers and drunks. The players, too, often were street toughs and drinkers; sometimes when the bases were loaded, so was the pitcher. "Many games had fist fights, and almost every team had its 'lushers,'" said Albert Goodwill Spalding, the star pitcher for the league's four-time champions Boston Red Stockings, the forerunner of the Boston Braves and Atlanta Braves. "A game characterized by such scenes, whose spectators consisted for the most part of gamblers, rowdies and their natural associates, could not possibly attract honest men or decent women to its exhibitions."[13]

To avoid that image, Byrne and Taylor set strict requirements when they began to recruit players. As the *New York Clipper* noted: "The Brooklyn management will under no circumstances employ any player where integrity of character is not a feature of his recommendations, nor anyone who has not a clean record of temperate habits. They want men of intelligence and not corner-lot roughs who happen to possess some skill as players but whose habits and ways make them unfit for thorough teamwork."[14]

The effort won high praise from the local *Brooklyn Eagle*: "It is well to state that the club is in the hands of gentlemen of means ample enough to carry the enterprise through to a successful issue. Moreover, the management is of a kind that will insure the club's being run on a basis of honorable professional planning in every respect, and it will be one which will not include the customary corner lot rough element from which source too much of the professional recruiting is already done." Taylor, who would be the team manager, said: "No contract breakers, drunkards or crooks will be allowed in the ranks of our club, no matter how skillful as ball players they may be. We have opened up a new mine of professional talent and we feel that it will pan out well."[15] The team received more than 40 applicants, and 16 men were picked for the new Brooklyn squad.

The team still needed a league to play in. By 1883, there were two major leagues. In 1876, William Hulbert, the owner of the Chicago White Stockings in the old professional league, launched the National League that was run by businessmen and catered to a higher class of fans. He had the help of Al Spalding, who Hulbert purchased from Boston along with three other star players. The "League" charged 50 cents admission, banned Sunday baseball and barred beer and liquor. It also cracked down on gambling at games. In addition to the Chicago White Stockings, the teams in the league's first year were the Boston Red Caps, Cincinnati Red Stockings, St. Louis Brown Stockings, Louisville Grays, Philadelphia Athletics, Hartford Dark Blues and New York Mutuals, who were booted out when they failed to take their last road trip. The White Stockings, the great-grand daddy of today's Chicago Cubs, took the first pennant led by player-manager Spalding, who won 46 games.

The League had a monopoly on big league baseball until 1882, when a group of businessmen, including St. Louis saloon owner Chris Von der Ahe, started the rival American Association. Many of the club owners, like Von der Ahe, were in the beer business. They aimed their league at the working people, charging 25 cents, playing games on Sunday and selling booze. It quickly became known as the "Beer and Whiskey Circuit." At first the two leagues clashed over players but they soon reached a truce with the first National Agreement not to raid each other's players. Under the plan, teams also could "reserve" up to 11 players who could not sign with other teams. This was aimed at ending the problem of "revolvers," players who would switch teams when a better offer came along.

At this point, both Brooklyn and New York were without teams. But to the chagrin of Brooklynites, in 1883 the city across the river was slated to have squads in both leagues: the New York Gothams in the National League and the New York Metropolitans in the American Association. Both teams were owned by tobacco man Thomas B. Day and his Metropolitan Exhibition Company of New York.

Charley Byrne was anxious to get Brooklyn's oar in the baseball waters of the major leagues. The established National League was more in keeping with his image, but he knew the new American Association was a more likely bet. The association had no openings this close to the start of the 1883 season. It was still starting a minor league alliance called the Interstate Base Ball Association, and Brooklyn applied. At a March 31, 1883, meeting in Wilmington, Delaware, the new association accepted Brooklyn and Trenton, New Jersey, while rejecting Albany, New York. The league wasn't exactly filled with major metropolises. The other teams were Trenton, the Merritts of Camden, New Jersey, and the Quicksteps of Wilmington, Delaware, plus three Pennsylvania teams — Harrisburg, the Actives of Reading and the Anthracites of Pottsville. (It isn't known if there was a team called the Bituminouses.)

Okay, it wasn't the big leagues. But it was baseball, and excitement grew in Brooklyn as the season neared. "For years this city contained the championship clubs and the most noted players of the country," the *Brooklyn Eagle* said. "But events transpired which materially changed this pleasant aspect of base ball affairs, and eventually our city lost its supremacy in the national game. The time has come, however, for the revival of the good old days, and now the promise is that Brooklyn will, in the near future, resume its old time prominence in base ball."[16]

Byrne and Taylor worked feverishly to get their new team ready. The squad opened its maiden season on May 1, 1883, with two road games at Wilmington, losing the first 9 to 6 and winning the second 8 to 2. With Washington Park not ready for the first home game on May 9, the contest was scheduled at Newark. At the last minute, Byrne was notified that the Newark park had been booked for a circus the same day, and he frantically switched the game to a free field on the Parade Grounds at Prospect Park, Brooklyn's counter to Manhattan's Central Park. Despite the confusion, more than 1,000 people showed up to watch the first home game in the team's history.

The game was played against Harrisburg, a team of the very kind of street toughs that Brooklyn had tried to avoid. As the *Eagle* reported:

> There have been some pretty rough nines seen at the park grounds in its history, but a worse lot of "kickers" or a more undisciplined and badly managed professional nine has never played in Brooklyn than the mixed lot of professional roughs who opposed the Brooklyn team in this match. A man named Myers who, it is alleged, barely escaped expulsion from the American Association for nonpayment of money to the association, is the manager of the nine, and another man named Shketzline of Philadelphia, is the captain, while Schappert of Brooklyn is the pitcher; and these three made themselves offensively conspicuous by their "kicking" in every inning of the contest.

The trio immediately began kicking against the umpire's decisions. (There was only one umpire in those days.) "You make me sick," declared

Schappert when the umpire called his pitches a ball. "You're the worst I ever saw," bellowed manager Myers, "you ought to be ashamed of yourself." Pitcher Schappert threw the ball overhand in violation of the rules. Meanwhile, young Tommy Burns chirped noisily from his left-field position. Brooklyn maintained its cool against the bullies and won the game 7 to 1 behind 25-year-old pitcher Jim "the Troy Terrier" Egan (who a year later would die from "brain fever").[17]

The real focus of Byrne and the Brooklynites was on the first game at Washington Park, which took place on Saturday, May 12. As the *Eagle* reported:

> Yesterday was a gala day in the history of base ball in this city. Washington Park, on Fifth avenue, was thrown open for base ball purposes under the auspicious of the Brooklyn Base Ball Association. The ground has been arranged with great care, and in the opinion of good judges was recognized as one of the finest diamonds in the state. The president, Mr. Charles Byrne, is well known in this city, and he has shown an energy and most liberal spirit of enterprise in the matter which give promise of a full attainment of the ends desired by the association.

The game drew a standing-room crowd of more than 6,000 people. "Camp stools and chairs on the grounds were used on every available spot, while many spectators were standing near the boundary fence which surrounded the field," the *Eagle* reported. It was an astounding turnout. By contrast, the opening game of the National League's New York Gothams at New York's Polo Grounds drew 5,000 people.

The ceremonies began at 3 o'clock as the 23rd Regiment band began playing in front of the grandstand. The visiting Trenton team appeared first, wearing gray uniforms with red stockings. Then the crowd roared as the Brooklyn team ran out to the field donned in gray uniforms with blue lettering and dazzling polka dot stockings. That's right: polka dot! The game started promptly at 4:00 P.M. The teams tossed a coin with the winner deciding whether to bat first or go in the field. Trenton won the toss and went to bat in order to get the first crack at the only ball that would be used in the game. They promptly scored three runs as nervous Brooklyn fielders bobbled hit balls for errors. Brooklyn came back with two runs in its first turn and settled down in the field. By the fifth inning, the home team had moved far ahead and won its first game at Washington Park 13 to 6 as Eagan scattered 10 hits.[18]

Most teams then, including Brooklyn, didn't have official nicknames.

Contrary to some baseball histories, this Brooklyn team was never called the "Atlantics" or "Grays," and not until much later would it be known informally as the "Trolley Dodgers." If it had any nickname at all, it was the "Polka Dots" because of those wild and crazy stockings.

That same day, May 12, the Brooklyn club also made what would turn out to be one of its most important acquisitions. It hired Charles Hercules Ebbets, a 23-year-old architect and an accomplished bowler, as assistant secretary, bookkeeper and handyman in charge of ticket taking and whatever else Byrne wanted him to do. He would go on to become a major figure in the team's history.

The excitement over the new baseball team was exceeded only by the frenzy over the May 24, 1883, opening of the great Brooklyn Bridge, linking Brooklyn and Manhattan. It was the largest suspension bridge in the world, stretching more than 1.13 miles with 3,600 miles of steel-wired cables. Its Gothic-style towers soared more than 276 feet above the East River. The bridge had taken 13 years to build at a cost of $15 million and the deaths of a score of workers. It was considered the greatest engineering feat of the century.

More than one million people gathered for the opening and the first crossing at 1:00 P.M. as bells tolled across the city. President Chester Arthur was there. A "Prince Albert coat closely buttoned, gold eye glasses peeping from between its folds, a standing collar and scarf of quiet colors made up the principal apparel of the first gentleman of the land," the *Brooklyn Eagle* reported. New York Governor Grover Cleveland also attended. "He is a

Trenton	*R.*	*1B.*	*PO.*	*A.*	*E.*	Brooklyn	*R.*	*1B.*	*PO.*	*A.*	*E.*
Thatcher, ss	2	2	3	2	1	Walker, 1b	3	1	10	1	0
Quintan, c	2	3	8	0	0	Farrow, c	3	1	10	1	0
Harkins, p	0	1	1	1	2	Manning, 2b	1	0	4	1	2
Cronin, 2b	1	1	0	1	4	Schenck, 3b	1	1	1	3	0
Goodman, 1b	0	0	8	0	0	Eagan [Egan], p	1	2	0	1	2
Dwyer, rf	0	1	0	0	1	Williams, cf	0	1	0	0	2
Bastain [Bastian], 3b	0	0	0	2	1	Geer, ss	0	0	0	4	0
Heath, lf	0	1	2	1	2	Lough [Luff], lf	2	1	2	0	0
Denham, cf	1	1	2	0	1	Dolan, rf	2	1	0	0	0
Total	6	10	24	7	12	Total	13	8	27	10	6

The box score from the first home game in the 1883 team's first game on May 12, 1883, in the *Brooklyn Eagle.*

man of large frame, and appears as if he could enjoy a good dinner. His smooth, dark hair and mustache lift his features into prominent relief and sharply define a face that indicates strong common sense and honesty of purpose, combined with firmness that is likely to resist to the verge of stubbornness. Governor Cleveland dresses like a well to do Presbyterian elder, with as little ornament or ostentation of any sort."[19] The next year Cleveland would be elected president of the United States.

The celebration climaxed that evening with a giant display of 14 tons of fireworks, with 10,000 separate pieces, that engulfed the bridge in shimmering lights. The grand finale featured 500 rockets fired off at one time. "They went off with a force which fairly shook the great bridge, and when they had reached the upper air they exploded with a sound which resembled the thunder of a cannonade. They broke into millions of stars and a shower of golden rain which descended upon the bridge and the river. As the last star disappeared in the water and the last spark died away in the air, the whistles of the ferry boats were heard saluting the new bridge."[20]

The new bridge quickly paid dividends for the Brooklyn baseball team, as New Yorkers streamed over the structure to see the squad play exhibition games against the New York Mets. Meantime, Bryne kept his promise to attract females as Brooklyn became one of the first teams to start a regular Ladies Day, with women admitted free when accompanied by a male patron. In a July 1 game against the Anthracites from Pottsville, the *Eagle* reported: "It was Ladies Day at Washington Park yesterday, and the grand stand presented a very attractive appearance in consequence. Indeed the fair sex are beginning to get very much interested in the game, and they throng to the stands on these special occasions." Brooklyn lost the game 2 to 1 as manager Taylor sat nervously "smoking cigarettes at the rate of a dozen an hour."[21] But the female attention wasn't on baseball; it was on the young Brooklyn pitcher, 19-year-old William Terry, who recently had been signed as a pitcher and outfielder after a tryout. The handsome Terry was tall and slim with a flowing mustache that curled up at each end. He stood 5'11" and weighed 180 pounds. The clubhouse report was that "the more clothes he sheds, the larger he becomes."[22]

Terry soon became baseball's first matinee idol, earning the marvelous nickname "Adonis." Brooklyn scheduled him to pitch almost every Ladies Day game, and women flocked to see him. "Terry's quiet, gentlemanly behavior on and off the field, combined with his good looks, has made

A week after the Brooklyn Bridge opened on May 24, 1883, 12 people were killed and scores injured when many in a crowd of thousands crossing the bridge stampeded to exit on the New York side after a rumor spread that the bridge was collapsing (Library of Congress).

him the pet of the fair patrons of the game. One enthusiastic fair one the other day, when Terry made an important three-base hit, exclaimed, 'Oh, I think he's too splendid for anything.'"[23]

While Brooklyn was drawing large crowds, it was stuck in the middle of pack in the Interstate Association standings, with the Merritts of Camden residing in first place. In mid–July, Byrne heard rumors that the Merritts team was about to fold. He rushed to Camden and arranged a private meeting with team majority owner Senator Albert Merritt, the club's board of directors and several players. On the evening of July 20, the directors met to formally disband the squad because of financial woes. Waiting outside was Brooklyn manager George Taylor along with managers from teams

Adonis Terry was one of a few pitchers to throw from three different regulation pitching distances — 50 feet; 55 feet, 6 inches; and 60 feet, 6 inches. He won 198 games and lost 195 between 1884 and 1897 (National Baseball Hall of Fame Library).

in New York, Louisville, Philadelphia and elsewhere, eager to get the pick of the disbanded team. But Byrne had already gotten the "inside track," and Taylor signed the cream of the Camden players, "greatly to the discomfiture of the rival managers, who had to pay exorbitant salaries for the few men they did get," said the *Brooklyn Eagle*. The coup showed that Byrne was "one of the most capable executives ever known in the baseball fraternity."[24] Brooklyn signed six of Camden's top players: pitcher Sam Kimber, shortstop Frank Fennelly, first baseman Charlie Householder, second sacker Billy Greenwood, catcher Jack Corcoran and outfielder Bill Kienzel.

In its first game with the new players, Brooklyn knocked off a strong Wilmington Quicksteps team 2 to 1 behind Kimber's five-hit pitching. Fans applauded the newcomers, and the reaction was "Brooklyn's got a good nine now." Indeed it did. Brooklyn won 11 of its next 12 games, and by early September roared into first place. On September 27, Kimber pitched the first no-hitter in team history, blanking the Reading Actives 13 to 0. On September 29, Brooklyn defeated second-place Harrisburg to capture the title. The score was 11 to 6, with young Terry pitching the win, giving Brooklyn a minor-league championship in its first year back in baseball with a record of 66 wins and 40 losses. The team also won 20 of 30 exhibition games, including several with major league squads.

Baseball observers were impressed by the team's success in 1883. The *Morning Journal* noted:

> It can be truly said that an element greatly to the advantage of base ball has entered into the sport in the persons of the managers of the Brooklyn club. These gentlemen started their enterprises last Spring almost at the eleventh hour, and in the short space of five weeks fitted up their grounds, on which they expended $30,000, and got together, considering that they had to take players that had been largely overlooked by the older organizations, the nucleus of a strong team. The thousands who visited Washington Park last season were struck with the excellent management everywhere apparent and the perfect order that was maintained. During the whole season not a disturbance of even the most trivial nature occurred to mar the pleasure of the spectators, among whom were always many ladies moving in the highest circles in the City of Churches. This is the right element to have in base ball, and in the years to come its influence will be felt to the advantage and prosperity of the sport.[25]

The team broke even financially and proved that Brooklyn would support a ball team. Said the *Eagle*: "To President Charles H. Byrne is largely due the successful issue of the managerial campaign of the club. In every respect has he shown himself to be the best president a professional base ball club ever had. He has been ably assisted by his club manager, Mr. George Taylor, and the patrons of the game in this city may safely look forward to a still more successful season for the Brooklyn's representative club in 1884."[26]

With one championship in his quiver, Charley Byrne was ready to take Brooklyn to the major leagues. He caught a break in 1884. Hoping to capitalize on the players' resentment regarding baseball's reserve rule that tied them to one team, St. Louis businessman Henry Lucas formed an outlaw league, the Union Association. To avoid losing potential franchise cities, the American Association expanded from eight teams to 12, adding Brooklyn, Toledo, Washington, D.C., and Indianapolis. A potential snag emerged in March when the New York Mets tried to bar Brooklyn from playing home exhibition games against National League teams, fearing the contests might compete for fans with a New York game. At an American Association meeting in Baltimore, the Mets' glib manager, James Mutrie, argued New York's case against Charley Byrne. The outcome was described by the *Cincinnati Commercial*: "When Jim Mutrie and President Byrne engaged in a forensic wrestle at Baltimore the other day, delegates opened the windows. Jim is devilishly cute but he has no business fooling with Byrne's logical buzz saw."[27] Owners not only brought Brooklyn into the association but elected Byrne to the league's board of directors and put him in charge of drawing up season schedules.

Brooklyn played its first big league game on May 5, 1884, with George Taylor as its first manager. More than 4,000 people, including "the largest assemblage of the fair sex ever seen at a ball match in Brooklyn," turned out at Washington Park to see the home "boys in blue" trounce the Washington Nationals 11 to 3.[28] The crowds kept coming as Brooklyn's owners personally courted the fans. All three men cheerfully greeted patrons at Washington Park, with bachelor Byrne especially attentive to the ladies. Good-natured Joe Doyle rooted for the home team like any other fan and deflected any criticism of the team to Byrne, saying with a laugh, "Well, there's the man who is responsible for it." Some of Byrne's friends liked "to rub the fur just far enough the wrong way to see a flash come into his eyes."[29]

Charley Byrne generally was a calm man, but he could get fired up about baseball. One night at a local newsroom, Byrne was having a vigorous discussion with some sportswriters. "A handsome lady walked in" to place a religious ad in the paper. "While paying for it, she heard the rumpus and quietly walking over to the Brooklyn president, she tapped him on the shoulder and handed him a little slip of paper," *Sporting Life* reported. When Byrne opened the paper, the six words in black type that stood out were: "What becomes of us after death?" He immediately took on a more reverent tone.[30] Byrne worked tirelessly, arriving at his corner office in Washington Park at 6:00 or 7:00 in the morning. The light wouldn't go off until long after dark. He schmoozed sportswriters, giving interviews or offering news tips privately. He also wrote articles under pen names to promote his team and baseball.

But the refugees from the Interstate Association soon found themselves in over their head in the big leagues. By June, the team had fallen deep in the American Association standings. President Byrne was getting anonymous letters of complaint. Said one writer: "Why do you keep changing the order of your team's striking the way you do?"[31]

Brooklyn settled into a battle with the Toledo Blue Stockings for eighth place. Despite its lowly position, Toledo was drawing attention. As the *Washington Post* noted before a June game in the capital: "This afternoon the Washingtons will meet the celebrated Toledo team with their famous battery of Tony Mullane and Walker. The latter is a colored man, and no doubt many will attend the game to see 'our colored brother' in a new role."[32] The catcher was 26-year-old Moses "Fleet" Walker, who on May 1, 1884, became the first documented African American to play major league baseball. And he played well, as the follow-up *Post* story reported: "It was the general expectation yesterday that the Washingtons would again defeat the Toledos, but such was not the case. Mullane was put in to pitch for the Toledos, and proved very effective. Walker, the colored catcher, supported him in fine style. Toledo won 6–1."[33]

Newark fans celebrated Fleet Walker in this poem: *There is a catcher named Walker, Who behind the bat is a corker, He throws to a base, With ease and grace, And steals 'round the bags like a stalker* (National Baseball Hall of Fame Library).

Walker—a tall, thin and intelligent man—had first gained attention playing ball at the University of Michigan, where he attended law school. He was "a plucky catcher, a hard hitter and a daring and successful base runner."[34] He hit .263 in 42 games for Toledo in 1884. (His brother Welday also played for the team for a while.) Fleet Walker was tough. Spurning the buckskin gloves that some catchers had begun wearing, he caught fastball pitchers with his bare hands. He had the respect of his white teammates, but not their support. Star pitcher Tony Mullane said Walker "was the best catcher I ever worked with, but I disliked a Negro and whenever I had to pitch to him I used to pitch anything I wanted without looking at his signals."[35]

Walker was cut from the team late in the season, supposedly because of injuries. However, his release probably had more to do with a letter sent to Toledo's manager just before a late-season road trip to Richmond, Virginia. It read: "We the undersigned do hereby warn you not to put up Walker, the negro catcher, the evenings you play in Richmond, as we could mention the names of 75 determined men who have sworn to mob Walker if he comes on the ground in a suit. We hope you will listen to our words of warning, so that there will be no trouble; but if you do not there certainly will be. We only write this to prevent much bloodshed, as you alone can prevent."[36]

Walker continued to play in the minor league International League until 1889, teaming with star black pitcher George Stovey. Some major leaguers — including Cap Anson, one of baseball's greatest stars and biggest bigots — refused to play exhibition games against black players. After 1889, the International League banned African American players, and the ban became an unwritten "gentlemen's agreement" for all of baseball until the great Jackie Robinson played for the Brooklyn Dodgers in 1947.

After Walker left, Toledo and Brooklyn continued to battle into the fall. On October 4, Brooklyn's 31-year-old Sam Kimber became the first pitcher to hurl 11 innings in a game without giving up a hit. But Brooklyn failed to score against Toledo's Mullane, who gave up just three hits, and the game was called because of darkness with the score 0 to 0. "The game was a battle of the pitchers, in which each man went in for speed as his strong point, both striving to intimidate the batsmen."[37] Toledo took eighth place, edging Brooklyn, which finished 33 1/2 games behind the pennant-winning New York Mets. Nevertheless, Brooklyn's first season of major league ball was a financial success as the team made about a $10,000 profit.

Rumors started to spread that Brooklyn would jump to the National League. Byrne denied the rumors. Privately, he vowed not to consider the idea until Brooklyn won the American Association pennant. That was easier dreamed than done. No Brooklyn hitters came close to the league leaders, such as New York Mets first baseman Dave Orr, who led in batting with a .354 average, or Cincinnati's "Long John" Reilly, who hit a league-leading 11 home runs. Adonis Terry led Brooklyn's pitchers with 19 wins and 35 losses, far below Louisville's Guy Hecker, who won 52 games.

It was clear to observers that Brooklyn had to dig up some better players. But as fall turned into winter with no changes in sight, many Brooklyn backers were wondering if Charley Byrne had gotten the message.

Chapter Two

Der Boss President

If there was anyone more determined to win the American Association pennant than Charley Byrne, it was Chris Von der Ahe, the president of the St. Louis Browns. Von der Ahe, after all, was one of the founders of the association in 1882 and one of its leading magnates. Yet, here it was 1885, and he had yet to win the championship.

Christian Friedrick Wilhelm Von der Ahe was an American success story. He was born November 7, 1851, in Hille, Germany, in what was then Prussia, near the border with the Netherlands. The son of a prominent grain dealer, Chris came to New York alone as a teenager but soon moved to St. Louis, where he became a grocery store clerk. In 1870, he married Missouri-born Emma Hoffman, and the same year their only child, Edward, was born.

Within a few years, Von der Åhe owned the grocery store and added a saloon in the back. Business was good, and he soon moved his operations to property he purchased at the northwest corner of nearby Grand Boulevard and St. Louis Avenue, where he also built a house for his family. Down the street was a run-down, open baseball field and German shooting park called Grand Avenue Park, which was leased by a local sportsman, August "Gus" Solari. Von der Ahe became involved with baseball as early as 1877, when he was vice president of the Grand Avenue Club that ran the park.[1] In 1878, the National League St. Louis Brown Stockings folded and some members formed a semi-pro team that played games at the park. The manager, veteran ball player Edgar Cuthbert, became a part-time bartender at Von der Ahe's Golden Lion saloon.

In spring of 1881, several locals, including journalist brothers Alfred and William Spink and Congressman James O'Neill, formed the Sportsman's Park and Club Association with plans to field a new Brown Stockings

St. Louis Browns owner Chris Von der Ahe in 1889 banned shirt pockets in team uniforms after right fielder Cliff Carroll juggled a hit ball and lost it in his shirt pocket while a runner scored (Library of Congress).

squad. Cuthbert tried to persuade his boss to invest in the team. Von der Ahe didn't know much about baseball, but he did notice the ring of cash registers when there were games at the park. "It was Eddie who talked me into baseball," Von der Ahe later recalled.[2] "The Dutchman," as most first-generation German-Americans were called, became the biggest investor in the group, which sold stock at $10 a share for a total of $1,800. The club, with Chris as president and head of concessions, took over the Grand Avenue facility, built a double-decker stadium called Sportsman's Park and fielded a successful semi-pro team. Von der Ahe's triumph so angered the jealous Gus Solari that he had a high fence erected around the park to block the view from Chris's house.[3]

At the end of the 1881 season, Von der Ahe moved to take over the team. He announced to the club's investors that the stock had been sold. "Who bought it, Chris?" asked one investor. "Neffer mindt who pought it," said Von der Ahe. "Here is der check of Chris Von der Ahe for $1,800."[4] His new team would be called the Browns. And Von der Ahe became the self-professed "Der poss of der Prowns."

The new Browns team began playing in the American Association's first season, in 1882. With a major league attraction, the money flowed like the German beer that added to the gate receipts. Patrons guzzled brew at their seats, standing at bars with foot railings or relaxing in a beer garden behind right field, where a ball bouncing off the beer steins was still in play. After the games, the cranks flocked to Chris's saloon. "Five tousand tamn fools, und one wise man is me — Chris Von der Ahe," he would chortle. At the games, Der Boss would sit in his private box with big binoculars focused on his players. He would blow a whistle "for the players, for the special cops and for a beer."[5]

Von der Ahe quickly became an icon in the national game. He was a blunt, mercurial man who would scream angrily one minute then turn into a genial German the next. He would fine his players at the drop of a hat, then buy them a new suit of clothes. He could be a tightwad in pay negotiations but a soft touch for a former player with a sob story. Von der Ahe "speaks his mind," said *Sporting Life,* "but nobody ever gets offended at what Chris says for it's Chris, you know, and anybody who knows him knows he has a heart inside his vest as big as his head, which is not at all shrunken."[6] In 1885, Von der Ahe put up outside Sportsman's Park a larger-than-life statue of his favorite person — himself. The statue later was moved to Bellefontaine Cemetery in St. Louis, where it still stands today.

With his naiveté and broken English, Von der Ahe was a ripe target for sportswriters, who quoted his odd sayings like a nineteenth-century Yogi Berra. As with the New York Yankees catcher, it wasn't always clear which stories were true and which were apocryphal. A favorite tale was about the time a fan called the ballpark after a game and got Von der Ahe on the phone. "I left an umbrella at your park today. Have you seen it?" the caller asked. Chris held an umbrella up to the phone, and said, "Vos dis idt?"[7]

His players loved to play jokes on Der Boss, led by third baseman Arlie Latham, baseball's court jester. "Dot feller Latams will be the death of me yet," Chris would moan. One day in his room on the fifth floor of New York's Fifth Avenue Hotel, Von der Ahe was lecturing his players on the evils of alcohol when Latham laughed out loud. "Dot laff gosts you vun hundred, Ladain," Von der Ahe shouted. "Honest, boss," Latham said, "I was laughing at a boy that passed the window and made a face at me." "Dot's all right, den, Lad," said Von der Ahe, who only later realized the impossibility of Latham's assertion.[8]

Latham told of the time Von der Ahe heard "a commotion outside his private office, with his name being called out in less than a flattering manner. Dashing to the door, Chris yelled, 'Hey you, Latams. Dot vill cost you fifty dollars.'" Others outside the room told him that Latham wasn't there. "Vell, vere the devil is he? If he isn't dere, he is up to some of his jokes, and dot fifty dollars fine stands for him and his tricks." When Latham confronted Der Boss later, "I yelled blue murder, but he remained firm. So I said, 'All right, Chris, but I have no money. Now if you give me $50 in cash, we'll be even.'" Von der Ahe did.[9]

Von der Ahe certainly was colorful, but he was no buffoon. He made a fortune on the property he bought on Grand Avenue, where he built rows of houses. "When I went into the base ball business I was pretty well fixed financially, and my friends told me that I was a fool for having anything to do with the national game," said Von der Ahe, who reporters quoted without the mangled English when they weren't making fun of him.[10] His friends were wrong. Within eight years, Chris's $1,800 investment in the Browns had earned him $500,000 at a time when a half-million dollars was a lot of money. He wasn't shy about showing it off. He would put each day's game receipts into a wheelbarrow and parade down the street to the bank.

The Dutchman spent money as fast as he made it. One night after a big holiday game in Cincinnati, Von der Ahe went to retrieve St. Louis's share of the receipts, which were being held in two satchels in a hotel safe. When he asked for one of the satchels, the clerk refused to give him the money without a receipt from the club's treasurer. Von der Ahe fired the treasurer and wrote a receipt for all the money. He grabbed both satchels, called for a carriage and went out and spent the money that night.[11]

While Von der Ahe knew more about beer and pretzels than he did baseball, he recognized talent when he saw it. In 1884, he decided to make his lanky, 24-year-old first baseman, Charles Comiskey, the team's manager and captain. Comiskey, the son of an Irish politician in Chicago, was a born leader, and he was tough. If a player didn't respond to his orders on the field, Comiskey would walk over to him and slug him in the jaw. "Commy" was a bully but a brainy one. He studied opponents and the game. He perfected the art of playing off the bag to field grounders instead of staying anchored to first base, and taught his pitchers to cover first base. He hassled umpires and opposing players. Von der Ahe loved it. If the umpire fined Commy or his players, Der Boss happily paid the fines.

By 1885, Von der Ahe was surrounding Comiskey and Latham with other talented players. He acquired Curtis Welch, a rough-playing, hard-drinking center fielder from Toledo, and a promising outfielder, James

"Tip" O'Neill. But the major prizes were two pitchers acquired late in the 1884 season from the minor leagues, stringbean Dave Foutz and wiry little Bobby Caruthers. The Brown Stockings, which eventually would become the St. Louis Cardinals, even added a little color as team members wore floppy caps with bright red vertical stripes, making them look more like ice cream vendors than ball players. This could be the year that the American Association "rag" would fly over Sportsman's Park, Von der Ahe thought. Most baseball observers, however, figured the Browns would finish in the middle of the pack.

St. Louis Browns captain Charles Comiskey wasn't apologetic about his rough play. "I go on a field to win a game of ball by any hook or crook," he said. "It is the game we are after, not reputations of society dudes" (Library of Congress).

The big buzz was about the sensational doings in Brooklyn. At the end of 1884, Charley Byrne got wind that the Cleveland team was about to fold and resign from the National League. Working with Cleveland's owners and its manager, Charlie Hackett, Byrne secretly arranged to acquire seven of Cleveland's best players. The Brooklyn president hoped to repeat his 1883 miracle when he bought the Camden Merritts players and won the Interstate Association championship. There was just one catch. Under baseball rules, the players had to be released for 10 days so all teams could bid for them. Lawyer Byrne found a loophole. In late December, he hid the players, who had agreed to join Brooklyn, at a Cleveland hotel. When the 10-day period expired at precisely 12:10 A.M. on January 5, 1885, Brooklyn signed all of the players for a whopping $9,000–$5,000 to the Cleveland owners and $4,000 to the players as advance money. The surprising signing was "the biggest sensation ever made in baseball," the *New York Times* said.[12]

The announcement set off a firestorm. "The outraged and outwitted delegates from elsewhere discussed Messrs. Byrne and Abell in a manner that made the swearing of the army in Flanders sound like a Sunday school address — but that was the good it did them," said Charley Ebbets. "Much talk was heard of expelling Brooklyn, hanging the owners and decapitating the players, but everybody sat tight and nothing happened."[13]

The acquired players included two clever infielders who would be Brooklyn mainstays for years. One was quiet, blond-haired, 5' 7" George Pinkney, a 23-year-old third baseman who was "wonderfully quick in the field and a fine base runner." Pinkney came from a prominent family in Peoria, Illinois. His father was a judge on the Illinois State Supreme Court, and his brother was Peoria's district attorney.The other infielder was outgoing 6' George J. Smith, 22, from "Pittsburg" (before it had an "h" at the end). Known as "Germany" because that's where his parents were from, Smith was one of baseball's best fielding shortstops, being "quick as a cat and a remarkably fine thrower across the diamond." But he had a weakness for the bottle, a frequent flaw of players of the day.

Brooklyn's Germany Smith was one of baseball's widest-ranging shortstops and committed 1,007 errors during his career, one of the highest career totals on record (Transcendental Graphics).

The other players were pitcher John Harkins, first baseman Bill Phillips (another drinker), center fielder Pete Hotaling and catchers Alfred Bushong and Bill Krieg. On the advice of Hackett, Byrne kept the journeyman Krieg and let Bushong go to the St. Louis Browns. Byrne soon knew he had made a big mistake, as Bushong became one of the game's greatest catchers. As part of the big deal, Cleveland's former manager, 30-year-old Charlie Hackett, took over as Brooklyn's skipper, replacing George Taylor, who moved into the front office as team secretary. By the next year, Taylor would be out of baseball and back in journalism.

The sensational Cleveland deal earned Byrne a reputation as quite a deal maker. "While the patrons of the Brooklyn Base Ball Association have been expressing their surprise at the apparently easy method of taking things which the management of the Brooklyn Club seemed to have adopted in preparing for the campaign of 1885, events have shown that President Byrne has for two months past been quietly and most effectively laying his plans for a baseball coup d'tat, which now that it has been consummated shows him to be a master of the art of skillful diplomacy," said the *Brooklyn Eagle*.[14]

The little president was a man of many baseball innovations. Before the season began, the team revamped Washington Park, building a new grandstand and adding new facilities for women so the Old Stone House could be used as the players' dressing room. Byrne turned the old grandstand into one of baseball's first no-smoking sections for nonsmokers and ladies. "It will be a relief to numbers of the patrons to get rid of the smoking annoyance in the grand stand," the *Eagle* commented favorably.[15]

In April, Byrne announced another big change. "Every day will be ladies' day this season, and we hope to see the fair sex grace our grand stand with their welcome presence every match day. We have found by experience that where there is an assemblage of ladies at our matches we get more orderly gatherings."[16] The only trouble was that the ladies' favorite, Adonis Terry, couldn't pitch every day. Byrne also was credited with inventing the rain check, which allows a ticket holder to get into another game free if a game is rained out. A Philadelphia paper noted that the wisdom of the rain check "introduced by Mr. Byrne was made very evident last week at the Athletic grounds. Threatening and rainy weather prevailed all week, yet large crowds were present at each game. But for the rain checks not half the people would have taken the risk of seeing but a few innings and losing their money."[17]

On the field, baseball was undergoing a revolutionary rule change. In 1884, the National League began allowing pitchers to throw overhand. In mid–1885, the American Association also began overhand pitching. Most pitchers switched to overhand, though some stars, such as future

Hall of Famers James "Pud" Galvin and George "Old Hoss" Radbourn, continued to hurl from down under. Because the batters still could order a pitch to be low or high, it took seven "unfair" balls to walk versus three strikes for an out.

Byrne's bold acquisition of the Cleveland players seemed to have paid off, with a fast Brooklyn start giving evidence "that our city had at last secured a first class professional team to represent it in the American championship season," the *Eagle* concluded.[18] But by June the team had plummeted to seventh place, as the players failed to perform up to expectations. It may have been at this point that Byrne first said, "Some players resemble eggs in that they are not what they are cracked up to be."[19] Local fans began asking, "What is the matter with the Brooklyn team?" What was the matter was that two cliques on the team — the former Cleveland players and the returning Brooklyn players — were at each other's throats. Both sides blamed Manager Hackett and complained to Byrne. After a disastrous road trip, leaving the team with a record of 12 wins and 20 losses, on June 5 Hackett resigned under pressure from Byrne in response to the player complaints.

Pitcher John Francis "Phenomenal" Smith wasn't so phenomenal, compiling a record of 54 wins and 74 losses in eight major league seasons (Library of Congress).

Then on June 17 came one of the darkest days in Brooklyn baseball history. To try to spark the team, Byrne brought in a 19-year-old minor league lefty pitcher, John "Phenomenal"

Smith, from Allentown, Pennsylvania, to start against the St. Louis Browns. The veteran Brooklyn players were upset to see a "busher" put in, and Smith didn't help himself by declaring that he was so good that he didn't need any help in the field. As a result, the team purposely didn't give him any, making 11 infield errors, seven by the usually reliable Germany Smith. St. Louis won 18 to 5, and would have scored more except that disgusted Browns players purposely wandered off the bases to get tagged out. Von der Ahe declared — with expletives not deleted — that it was the most contemptible spectacle he had ever seen.

Byrne, viewing it all from his private box, was embarrassed and enraged. After the game, he went to the dressing room and calmly ordered the players to be in his office at 10:00 A.M. the next morning. "You have had your innings today, I will have mine tomorrow."

The next morning, the players arrived to see their usually calm chief with "blood in his eye." Pulling a player contract from his pocket, Byrne noted that it bound team members to give their best efforts. "On your return from the Western tour, when you were questioned as to the cause of the unwanted number of defeats the club has sustained, the reply was — and almost unanimously — that the fault lay at the door of the manager," who resigned. He continued:

> What has been the result? Simply a worse condition of affairs than before and finally the culmination of the trouble in the disgraceful, cowardly and dirty piece of work witnessed on the field at the hands of a minority of the team yesterday. From this it would appear that it was not the fault of the manager that the team failed out West. Now, what I want to say to you is this; From this time out every man of the team has got to play ball in everything that terms means, or I will know the reason why. Hereafter you will have to put forth your utmost ability, and give the club faithful and honest service on the field or be expelled from the ranks.

Byrne then issued fines totaling more than $500. To avoid further disruption, he sent Phenomenal Smith packing.[20]

After the tongue-lashing, Brooklyn came back to beat St. Louis two days in a row, 3 to 1 and 10 to 0. The pitcher both days was 27-year-old Henry Porter, a talented right-hander who won 33 games for Brooklyn that year. At first, co-owner Joe Doyle briefly tried his hand at managing, then the team played without any official skipper until Byrne named captain Jack Cassidy to the post. Finally, the Brooklyn president made a startling decision: He appointed himself as manager. The team responded to

Byrne's handling, recording its best two months of the season and finishing in a fifth-place tie with Louisville. But the finish wasn't enough to quiet critics who were pleased to see Brooklyn's effort to "buy" a pennant fail. Even worse, the club lost money.

Meantime, Chris Von der Ahe's St. Louis Browns took off, moving into first place. The Browns' rowdy play delighted the rowdy fans at Sportsman's Park. But not all of the action was limited to the ball field. In a June game in St. Louis, one of the spectators was a Miss Kitty Dewey, "a handsome blonde girl," who also happened to be Von der Ahe's mistress. She also happened to be sitting near Mrs. Von der Ahe, whose eyes remained fixed not on the field but on Miss Dewey. Mrs. Von der Ahe sat quietly until the Browns won the game. Then, "she arose from her seat and walked rapidly to where Miss Dewey sat." She stopped just behind her with her right hand concealing something in the folds of her dress. She said, "Miss Kitty, Miss Kitty, didn't I tell you not to put your foot in these grounds again?" Miss Dewey turned around quickly and "became as pale as a sheet," but "before she could rise or get out of the way, Mrs. Von der Ahe raised her right hand, which had a firm hold on the neck of a bottle of soda water and struck her over the head." Just then Chris Von der Ahe appeared and grabbed his wife, as his mistress made a hasty exit through the crowd.[21]

Despite such distractions, the Browns soared to Von der Ahe's first pennant, mainly on the strong right arms of twirlers Bob Caruthers and Dave Foutz, who between them won 73 of the Browns' 79 victories—Caruthers with 40 and Foutz with 33. Back in St. Louis, "Ancient Greece never welcomed an Olympic victor with more enthusiasm and rejoicing," as more than 1 million people lined the streets to see the champs in a long parade. "Last of all the happiest and most contented man on the ground was Chris Von der Ahe, whose face was a perpetual smile."[22]

The joyous Von der Ahe wasn't ready to stop there. In 1884, the National League champion Providence Grays and American Association leader New York Mets had played a winner-take-all, post-season series that Providence won 2 games to 1. Von der Ahe challenged 1885 National League winner, the Chicago White Stockings, now owned by Al Spalding, to what Von der Ahe called a "world championship series." Sportswriters quickly shortened the title to the "World's Series." Each owner put up $500, with the total $1,000 to go to the winning team. St. Louis claimed victory by winning 3 games to 2. But that didn't include the second game, which Chicago claimed by forfeit after Browns manager Comiskey pulled his team off the field. Von der Ahe contended that game two shouldn't count but reluctantly agreed to call the series a tie. Each owner kept his $500.

As Von der Ahe's team rose to new heights on the field, Charley Byrne's star was rising within the inner workings of the American Association. At a joint meeting of the association and the National League that December at the Continental Hotel in Philadelphia, the Brooklyn magnate was named as the sole Association member on the prestigious three-member arbitration committee that resolved disputes in both leagues. He also was named to a three-member Association committee overseeing the umpires as well as head of the scheduling committee.

"The one man of the Association who has shown himself capable of successfully meeting the League diplomats on their own ground, appears to be Mr. Byrne, of the Brooklyn Club," *Sporting Life* reported. "Mr. Byrne is an able speaker, whose language is of that convincing, practical character, and withal fluent and interesting, that carries his hearers with him except when their interests are thought to be opposed."[23]

After Brooklyn's strong close of the 1885 season, owner-manager Charley Byrne figured his team was ready to contend with Chris Von der Ahe's Browns for the 1886 flag. The previous year's team initially "failed to work together harmoniously, and discords arose which it seemed almost impossible to allay," Byrne told reporters. "It took time to crush out this evil, and late on in the season the club showed its mettle and played well."[24]

In 1886, Brooklyn began taking advantage of the American Association rule allowing Sunday baseball. Playing ball on the Sabbath was banned in Kings County, which included Brooklyn, so Byrne located a park just over the line in Queens County in Ridgewood. The park was only 20 minutes from the city by rail and sat on high ground, offering a view of Brooklyn and the towers of the great bridge. Precisely 8,372 people jammed into the park for the first Sunday game May 23 against the first-place St. Louis Browns. They had plenty to cheer about. The game went into the 10th inning tied 12 to 12 before Brooklyn pitcher John Harkins drove in the winning run.

On July 24th Brooklyn made team history again back in Washington Park. A crowd of 7,000 people roared as Adonis Terry took to the pitcher's box in the ninth inning with a 1 to 0 lead without having given up a single hit. Terry retired the first two batters. "Now came the irrepressible Latham, and everybody watched him as if the fate of the day demanded upon him and it did," the *Eagle* reported. Latham flew out to right, "the crowd rushed on the field for Terry, and he was cheered to the echo all the way to the club room, for he had won the honors of the season in being the first man to shut out the St. Louis champions in a match without their securing a solitary base hit in the entire game."[25] It was the first official no-hitter in Brooklyn's major league history.

Byrne and Von der Ahe continued to clash over St. Louis's bullying playing tactics. Rough play was common among all teams, including Brooklyn, but especially among western teams, led by the Browns. Infielders would bump, trip, grab and even sit on base runners. Some base runners would literally cut corners to score. The tactic was made famous by Chicago catcher Michael "King" Kelly, the most celebrated baseball player of the day whose sliding style inspired the popular song, "Slide, Kelly, Slide." If Kelly was on second base, and the batter hit a ground ball requiring the single umpire to focus on the throw to first base, Kelly would skip third and run directly home. Despite the opposing team's howls, the ump had to call Kelly safe at home because he didn't see the chicanery.

St. Louis developed an especially notorious style of coaching base runners. Typically, Comiskey coached at first base and Arlie Latham at third. Instead of just encouraging the runners, they mainly yelled insults at the opposing players. The witty Latham at least was entertaining and occasionally did somersaults. Sometimes the first- and third-base coach would go up on either side of the catcher and loudly question his ancestry. Comiskey also constantly "kicked," or complained, to the umpire. If all else failed, he would pull his team off the field.

The issue finally came to a head with two incidents, both, unsurprisingly, involving St. Louis. In the May 23 Sunday game at Brooklyn, Comiskey kept up a constant barrage against umpire "Honest John" Kelly. "You are no good," Comiskey said after one call. (At least, that's what Commy claimed he said.) Kelly fined him $25. "You are no good," Commy said again, and Kelly responded, "That will cost you another $25." Commy retorted, "You are no good, if it costs me a million." Comiskey ended up being fined $225 by the association, but he refused to pay. The Browns captain defended his style of play: "I go in and kick because I believe that unless you kick, you stand a good chance of losing every game that you play, and because I believe that kicking is half the game."[26]

The second incident took place on June 3 in Baltimore. "I need a ladder to catch your throws," third sacker Latham loudly griped to catcher Al Bushong. Then Latham booted a throw from center field, allowing a runner to score. At the end of the inning, on the players' bench, which in the days before dugouts sat out in the open, Bushong told the third baseman to play ball instead of playing to the grandstand. Latham leapt to his feet and called the catcher a barrage of obscene names. Bushong took it for a while, then "jumping up, he hit the dude in the neck."[27]

As a result of the two episodes, the American Association called a special meeting in Columbus, Ohio. Byrne was chairman of the presiding committee. He began by noting that the fines against Comiskey, Latham and Bushong hadn't been paid. Von der Ahe, seeing which way the wind was blowing, promptly wrote a check for $260 for the fines. Then Byrne offered a resolution to bar "offensive coaching," which a majority of owners approved. Charley Byrne thus created coaching boxes, requiring base coaches to stay at least 75 feet from home plate.

Then Byrne asked Baltimore owner Billy Barnie to tell about the trouble there. He said the St. Louis players had "used such vile language that it could be plainly heard in the grand stand" and urged that both Bushong and Latham be suspended. At this, Von der Ahe jumped up and said: "If you propose to win the championship from me in this way, you can consider me out of the fight [by taking his team out of the American Association]. You know that not a man, woman or child outside the players themselves saw the one blow struck by Bushong. They were hidden from the crowd by an awning."[28] In the end, association president Wheeler Wyckoff fined both men $100 but didn't suspend them.

As far as the western teams were concerned, the main villain of the piece wasn't the Browns, but Charley Byrne. Said the St. Louis-based *The Sporting News*: "At the meeting of the American Association held in Columbus last week one of the most despicable attempts to beat the St. Louis Browns out of the championship of the American Association was made." The paper singled out Byrne, taunting him as "His Highness" and the "Pooh-Bah" of the association.[29]

The issue continued to boil as Brooklyn headed on a western road trip. In Pittsburgh, whenever a Brooklyn fielder ran near the stands to catch a ball, the fans jumped up, waved their hats and shouted at the player to drop the ball. As the *Brooklyn Eagle* reported, "The manager of the Pittsburg Club, a man by the name of [Horace "the Hustler"] Phillips, whose reputation in the base ball world is very unsavory, had materially aided in the ill feeling by spreading the report that President Byrne, of the Brooklyn Club, had been buying up or intimidating umpires." Every unfavorable call by the umpire was met by shouts of "Thief," "Robber," and "How much did you get?" After the game, which Brooklyn lost 6 to 2, the ump had to have a police escort to his hotel.

The bad blood escalated at the next stop in Cincinnati. In the sixth inning of the July 11 game, Brooklyn catcher Bob Clark noticed a commotion in the stands and looked up to see a mob of drunks beating on his younger brother. Clark ran into the stands before being restrained by Brooklyn captain Ed Swartwood. Police restored order, and Brooklyn won the game 11 to 7. After the game, Clark went to Byrne to apologize. Byrne quickly stopped him, saying: "All right, Bob. You violated a rule, and I presume the association will punish you for it. But if you had not done just what you did, I should have punished you. You would not be fit to wear a Brooklyn Club uniform if you had not the manhood to defend your brother in a crisis like that. If they undertake to discipline you, I'll defend you the best I can."[30]

Brooklyn catcher Bob Clark made 54 errors in 53 games during the 1889 season. In that era, when catchers wore mitts that were little more than work gloves, many top backstops averaged an error a game (*New York Clipper*).

The *Cincinnati Enquirer* was less forgiving, blaming Byrne for the entire episode. "Mr. Byrne of the Brooklyn club is the prime cause of the trouble. For some time past he has been charged with crookedness and double-dealing. He tried to cripple the St. Louis club by attempting to have Bushong and Latham expelled, and has virtually forced that organization to open negotiations with the League."[31] (In fact, Byrne not only didn't try to get the St. Louis players expelled, he was instrumental in persuading the association president to only fine them.) Back home Byrne said, "Never in my life have I experienced such treatment as we received in the western base ball towns." To make matters worse, Brooklyn shortstop Germany Smith had gone out drinking with old pals in Pittsburgh and had refused to continue the road trip with the team.

Still, Brooklyn played well under Manager Byrne's benevolent hand. At his encouragement, the players opened bank accounts. "My boys are the happiest lot on the turf," Byrne said. "Every one of them has a bank account and keeps adding to it. When the cold winds come blowing, gentle Annie, my boys will be enjoying their hard earned money, while other ball players that I know will be living on snow balls and wishing that summer was at hand before the winter has fairly commenced."[32] The manager called his players "his lambs" and often handed out cigars after victories. He took his players to cultural events as a team. After one win in St. Louis, he took them all to see Gilbert and Sullivan's *Mikado*. In a season-ending surge, Brooklyn won 14 of 18 games to finish third, the team's best showing yet. What's more, the team's attendance of 185,000 was the third best in baseball. "Financially, the season has been a great success for the club," the *Brooklyn Eagle* reported.

Nobody could catch St. Louis. While the Roughhouse Gang intimidated teams with its tactics, they also played solid team baseball under Comiskey. This time pitchers Foutz and Caruthers recorded 71 of the team's 93 wins, with Foutz scoring 41 and Caruthers 30. A new pitcher, Nat Hudson, won another 16 games. The Chicago White Stockings again won the National League flag, setting up another post–season clash. Responding to Von der Ahe's challenge, Chicago owner A. G. Spalding urged a "winner take all" seven-game series. With the series tied, the seventh game went into the 10th inning, when St. Louis's Curt Welch raced for home on a wild pitch and won the game with his "$15,000 slide." The win earned St. Louis all of the receipts — actually $13,920, so Welch had a "$13,920 slide."

Baseball went under some big changes in early 1887. The leagues did away with the arcane rule of the batter calling for a high or low pitch. Concerned that overhand throwing had given pitchers the upper hand, the leagues sought to aid batters by moving the pitcher's box back to 55½ feet. Also, there would be five balls and four strikes. ("Strike four, you're out?") Weirdest of all, they decided to count bases on balls as base hits! That should fatten the old batting average. Then in February, Spalding stunned the baseball world by selling his star player, King Kelly, to the League's Boston Beaneaters for the unheard-of sum of $10,000. The staid Spalding was out to rid his team of drinkers, and Kelly was the king of the boozers, as well. When Spalding confronted Kelly with a detective report that he had been out in an after-hours bar drinking lemonade, the player indignantly retorted: "It was straight whiskey; I never drank lemonade at that hour in my life."[33]

After Brooklyn's strong finish in 1886, owner-manager Byrne was optimistic that 1887 would finally be the year for his team to win the pennant. The club renewed its lease on Washington Park until 1892 and also moved to a new park in Ridgewood for Sunday games. The new Ridgewood Park was built on the Wallace Grounds just west of the previous park on the site of an old horse market. The stands could hold 6,900 people, plus room for several thousand more to ring the outfield.

More than 10,000 people turned out at Washington Park on April 16 for Brooklyn's opener against the rival New York Mets. The home team marched onto the field in their new uniforms of bluish gray trimmed in red with red stockings. To the joy of the crowd, Henry Porter pitched all the way as Brooklyn won 14 to 10. The joy didn't last long. By the time the Browns visited Brooklyn in late May, Byrne's team had slipped to fourth place. At that point, Brooklyn's owners made a startlingly bold bid to strengthen the squad. Brooklyn director Joe Doyle ran into Chris Von der Ahe in a corridor of New York's Grand Central Hotel. As *Sporting Life* reported:

> "Chris," said Mr. Doyle, in an off-hand manner, patting the St. Louis owner on the back, "I will give you $5,000 for the release of one of your men."
> "Who is the man?" asked Von der Ahe, in utter surprise. "Bushong?"
> "No, sir."
> "Caruthers?"
> "Wrong again."
> "Foutz?"
> "Try once more."
> "Oh, yes, I know now," exclaimed Von der Ahe, with a twinkle in his eyes, and drawing the Brooklyn stockholder closer to him he murmured "Hudson."

"Wrong again," was the response.

"Who is he, then?" asked the perplexed president.

"Comiskey, your first baseman. I will give you $5,000 for him at half an hour's notice if you will agree to release him from his contract so that he can join the Brooklyn team."

"I will not accept the offer," was Von der Ahe's reply. "No amount of money can purchase him from the Browns."[34]

Brooklyn could have used Commy in the series. The Browns reeled off four straight wins, knocking Brooklyn all the way to sixth place in the eight-team association. When St. Louis returned to Brooklyn on July 24, both teams were in bad moods. The Browns didn't arrive at Ridgewood for a Sunday game until 4:00 P.M. because its horse-drawn carriage had broken down on the road. What's more, the regular umpire didn't show up, and the job fell to a much-maligned backup named Mitchell. Brooklyn went up 3 to 0 after four innings, behind Adonis Terry, but St. Louis erupted for four runs in the fifth inning. Then the Browns' feisty little second baseman, Yank Robinson, bunted his way on and went to second on a bad throw by the catcher. The next batter, Arlie Latham, laced a grounder to Pinkney at third base. While Umpire Mitchell was watching Pinkney's throw to first, Robinson played the Kelly trick, cutting directly to home plate to score what would turn out to be the winning run. The Brooklyn fans went berserk. No sooner did Robinson return to the St. Louis bench then Brooklyn's Byrne plopped down beside him. "That was a d____ dirty trick of you, Robinson, trying to win a game that way." Robinson answered: "Are you hiring me?" By now Von der Ahe was on the scene: "Now look here, Byrne, you manage your men and I'll attend to mine. If the umpire didn't see the play that was his fault not ours. Now you get off our bench and leave us alone, or I'll see that you do."[35]

Matters went from bizarre to worse the next day. Byrne fired off a letter to association President Wyckoff, supposedly with Von der Ahe's support, demanding a new umpire. But the new ump didn't show, and in stepped another backup. All was relatively quiet until Brooklyn came up in the top of the ninth, trailing 2 to 1. After first baseman Bill Phillips singled in the tying run, Germany Smith slapped a grounder toward second. Phillips jumped over the ball, causing second sacker Robinson to yell "obstruction." The ball rolled away, allowing Phillips to reach second. The umpire ruled Phillips out for interference, but to the consternation of the Browns he let Smith stay at second base. Smith promptly scored the winning run.

Von der Ahe, whose team was being pressed by second-place Baltimore, sent a letter to Wyckoff, claiming that he never agreed to a new umpire as Byrne had said and again threatening to move his team to the National League. Soon after Von der Ahe held a secret meeting of owners to try to oust Wyckoff, whom he claimed was a "tool" for Byrne. The meeting, to which Brooklyn wasn't invited, failed because of a lack of a quorum. It was at this point that Byrne attributed Von der Ahe's outbursts to "a case of abnormal enlargement of the cranium in a mentally small man supplemented by an acute attack of disappointment." Chris wasn't cowed. "Byrne said I was a big man with a little head, and I say he is the little man with the big head."[36]

"What has gotten into the American Association club magnates that they cannot keep their tempers?" the *Brooklyn Eagle* asked. "It must be the hot weather. One cannot account for it otherwise."[37]

For Charley Byrne, it wasn't the heat, it was the humiliation of again losing to that "wooden shoed Dutchman" in St. Louis. Brooklyn continued to sink. First baseman Phillips was suspended for drinking. Shortstop Smith was out much of the time with an injury. By September, Brooklyn fell back into sixth place to stay. Concluded *Sporting Life* about the team: "The plain truth is the whole crowd, with three or four honorable exceptions, laid down like a lot of whipped dogs." Von der Ahe's Browns won a third straight championship. Under the strange rule of counting walks as hits, outfielder Tip O'Neill batted .435 (aided by 50 walks) as he scored baseball's first Triple Crown with 14 homers and 123 runs batted in. The leagues quickly dropped the "absurd" rule of counting walks as hits.

That fall, the National League held its first meeting with the National Brotherhood of Professional Base Ball Players, a union that had been officially formed the previous year. But the players' complaint that they were bought and sold like slaves gained scant public sympathy. Noted one *Buffalo Commercial* reporter:

> It is a pity about those overworked ball players. To think of their having to play four and sometimes five two-hour games of base ball a week for six months, and then only to receive a paltry sum average $2,000 to $2,500 each for the summer's work. It is outrageous. True they are taken traveling all over the country in Pullman cars and lodged at the best hotels free of expenses to themselves, but what of that? These senseless excursions take up time that they could spend at earning $10 a week loading steamboats or working on a farm from 6 in the morning until the same hour at night.[38]

It was true that major league baseball players made far more than the average American worker, but their pay was nothing like the millions of dollars earned by today's players. A player's salary of $2,500 in 1887, adjusted for inflation, would be the equivalent of about $59,000 today.

The union's gripes were overshadowed by headlines about the Brotherhood's founder, New York Giants star shortstop, 31-year-old John Montgomery Ward. The movie-star handsome Ward, who had attended Penn State University and earned a law degree from Columbia University, was preoccupied with another union: his wedding to the leading lady of the New York stage, 26-year-old Helen Dauvray. "I met him socially," the actress stressed. But she also was an avid baseball follower, attending many Giants games to cheer on her "Monte." At one game, *Sporting Life* reported, "whenever he made a brilliant play, her plump little hands would patter with ecstasy."[39] She was so enamored with the game that in May she announced plans to present a "Grecian Loving cup" valued at $500 to the winner of the "World's Series." The "Dauvray Cup" was to be made of "solid silver with a suitable inscription on one side. On the other will be the figure of a batter."[40]

The contenders for the cup in 1887 were St. Louis and the National League pennant-winner, the Detroit Wolverines. The teams scheduled a moveable baseball feast of 15 games in cities from St. Louis to New York. Even after Detroit took an insurmountable lead of 8 games to 2, the games went on into the cold of late October. Only 800 shivering spectators turned out for the final contest in St. Louis as the Browns

New York Giants shortstop John Montgomery Ward attended Penn State University at age 13. At age 19 as a pitcher he led the Providence Grays to the National League pennant with 47 wins, and the next year pitched the second perfect game no-hitter in major league history (*New York Clipper*).

lost the series 11 games to 4. Despite his third pennant, Von der Ahe ended the season in a foul mood.

Helen Dauvray became a Broadway star in the 1885 hit *One of the Girls.* She later married an admiral and is buried at Arlington Cemetery in Arlington, Virginia (*New York Clipper*).

Not as foul as Charley Byrne, who was in a grand funk—even though Brooklyn had drawn a league-leading 285,000 people. Uncharacteristically, Byrne publicly criticized his players and even blamed himself, sort of. "The more I think over it, the stronger the conviction comes to me that I am at fault more than any one else," he told a reporter. "We employed a body of men who claimed to be ball players, paid them such salaries as first-class ball players receive, and we assumed they would do their work to the best of their ability. It did not occur to me that it was necessary to rule men with an iron hand to get them to do honest work for good pay." Asked whether this scenario would continue, the reporter said Byrne responded "with a harshness I never saw him manifest before." He snapped: "Well, hardly. The Brooklyn public have stood by us most generously, in spite of our defeats. We will give them a team that can play ball next year, or we will tear down our fences and use our stands for kindling wood."[41]

Byrne vowed to buy new players and even fired himself as skipper to hire a real baseball man as manager. He knew just the man: the brainy center fielder of the champion Detroit Wolverines, Ned Hanlon. In the offseason, Hanlon ran a hat shop on Fulton Street in Brooklyn. Gus Abell went over and offered him $5,000 as a player-manager. Hanlon jumped at the offer, but Detroit refused to let him go.[42] Byrne then headed for New England, where he had his eye on an unexpected choice: a pioneer baseball player and an innovative manager of several minor league pennant-winners.

His name was Bill McGunnigle.

Chapter Three

Gunner McGunnigle

William Henry McGunnigle was part of an Irish baseball brigade that significantly shaped the national game in the late nineteenth-century. "Give me a good Irish infield" of "quick-thinking sons of Celt, and I'll show you a good team," said New York Giants manager Bill Joyce.[1] They had names like Boyle, Keefe, Kelly, McCarthy, McGraw, O'Brien, O'Neill and Reilly. These sons of Irish immigrants found a life their parents never dreamed of when they left Ireland to come to America.

Bill McGunnigle's father, James. F. McGunnigle, was growing up in County Donegal, Ireland, when a virulent blight wiped out the potato crops across the country, setting off the Great Famine. In 1847, when James was 13, his parents, William and Bridget, joined the early wave of the more than two million people who fled the Emerald Island between 1846 and 1855.[2] The McGunnigles were among the 1.5 million Hibernians who emigrated to America, settling with thousands of countrymen in Boston's crowded North End. The newcomers faced widespread discrimination. Jobs were hard to come by as employers put up signs saying, "No Irish Need Apply." William McGunnigle was able to work as a shoemaker to help raise his family of 11 children in his new country.

When James McGunnigle was nearly 20, he fell in love with an Irish lass. On February 23, 1854, he eloped with Hannah Murphy to Brooklyn, New York, where they were married in the Saints Peter and Paul Church.[3] The couple returned to Boston, where Billy McGunnigle was born on New Year's Day of 1855. The family soon moved about 20 miles south to East Stoughton (now Avon), next to Brockton, then the shoemaking capital of the world, where James learned the shoemaking trade. As young Billy grew up, he began playing the game of baseball on the green fields of East

Stoughton, a game that was rapidly spreading in popularity from the East Coast to as far west as Chicago and beyond.

Also spreading was a bitter divide between the industrial North of the United States and the agrarian South with its institution of slavery. In April 1861, less than a month after Illinois Congressman Abraham Lincoln was inaugurated as president, the Confederates fired on Fort Sumter, South Carolina, igniting the Civil War. At the forefront of those who answered President Lincoln's call for volunteers to fight the South were thousands of Irish Americans. In East Stoughton, 27-year-old James McGunnigle cut the proclamation from a newspaper and went through the town and neighboring villages soliciting volunteers to join a "Stoughton Guard" of the "Fighting Irish Ninth" of the Massachusetts Infantry Volunteer Regiment.[4] He got 21 signatures, including those of his brothers, Hugh, 23, and William, 16. On June 11, 1861, when Billy was six years old, his father went off to war.

The long and bloody Civil War would cost more than 640,000 lives, and feisty James McGunnigle, "a rough-hewn, outspoken" man, was in the thick of the fighting. On July 1, 1862, in a battle at Malvern Hill, Virginia, south of Richmond, a rebel musket ball slammed into Lieutenant McGunnigle's collarbone, where it stayed. Initially, he was officially listed as dead, but he was only wounded and recovered. Doctors decided it would be too risky to try to take the bullet out, and it remained in his body for the rest of his life. He was promoted to captain and sent home to recuperate.

Back in East Stoughton, friends presented McGunnigle with an 1850 model field officer's sword and a gold watch. The next day he was at the train depot, heading back to the front, when he showed the watch to a friend who told him the timepiece was too frail to take into battle. "Take mine instead," the friend offered. "It will do you a lot more good." McGunnigle accepted the heavy hunting watch.[5]

Captain McGunnigle and his troops were at Gettysburg in early July of 1863 as Union forces turned back the charge led by General Robert E. Lee. Then on May 12, 1864, he was under fire again in the Battle of Wilderness at Spotsylvania, near Fredericksburg, Virginia, under Union General Ulysses S. Grant. Shortly after 8:00 A.M., his squad came under heavy rebel attack. McGunningle, riding his horse, was urging his men on when he felt a sharp pain in his chest. He had been hit again, but there was just a small trickle of blood. This time the bullet was stopped by the shattered watch in his breast pocket. The army decided that McGunnigle had had enough and ordered him home. Before he left, his men presented him with a gold medal with a Maltese cross on the front. When James McGunnigle returned to East Stoughton on July 24, 1864, son Billy was nine years old. The war finally ended in June of 1865 when the South surrendered.

As much of the post-war economy struggled, New England hummed with textile and shoe factories. Typically, young men quit school, went to work in the factories, married young, had lots of kids and rarely ventured far from home. Billy, who inherited his father's dashing, dark-haired good looks, seemed destined for the same life. After the eighth grade, he dropped out of school and began working in the local shoe factory to help support the family, which now counted six children. On November 24, 1874, he married Mary McCullough, the pretty daughter of Irish immigrants. But Billy had another love, the game of baseball, and it would change his life.

Billy was in the crowd for an 1873 game between the nearby towns of Brockton and Grafton when Brockton's catcher was injured. Brockton's captain, Owen Canary, asked if anyone could catch. "A young fellow of eighteen came out of the woods with a gun on his shoulder and asked for a chance to catch the pitching of Joe Hallett, local twirler for the Brockton nine," said Canary. "I gave it to him, and he made good."[6] Billy's strong throwing arm earned him a new nickname: "Gunner." In 1874, Gunner joined the Howard Juniors, an amateur team in Brockton, and led them to the Junior Championship of Massachusetts. "He was delighted and inspired when he hit his first home run in Brockton, ran crazily around the bases and turned a somersault as he crossed home plate to win the game. He decided that baseball was the game for him."[7]

By this time, towns were looking to hire professionals to boost their amateur teams. One of them was the club in Fall River, Massachusetts, a booming textile town near the Rhode Island border. When the Howard Juniors played there in the spring of 1875, the Fall River folks found their man. They recruited Bill McGunnigle to be the team's first and only professional player. For Gunner, who was making $5 a week working 10 hours a day, six days a week in the shoe factory, it was an offer he couldn't believe. "A man could enjoy this kind of work," he said.[8]

On July 4, 1875, Gunner made his debut as a catcher in the gray and red uniform of Fall River in a 10 to 5 win over the Egglestons of Boston.

At 5'9" and 155 pounds, young McGunnigle hardly fit the bulky image of a catcher. But the position called for a player nimble of foot and mind with a strong arm. Gunner filled the bill. Although just 19, McGunnigle was mature for his age and a natural leader. He was quiet and courteous around strangers, but he was a strong-willed competitor who was always looking for an edge that would help him win. "He was the brainiest man the game ever knew," said teammate Owen Canary.[9]

Gunner put his name in the baseball record book in his first year. "The catcher's mitt was first used in 1875 by William McGunnigle of the Fall River team," according to *Reach's Official 1895 Baseball Guide*.[10] "His hands became very sore" from catching barehanded. As a result, before a game with Harvard College, Gunner borrowed a pair of thick bricklayer's gloves from a family member. He tried them out during practice but found they restricted his throwing. So he got out a jack knife and cut the fingers off the right-hand glove. The mitt "was an immediate success," the *New York Sun* said, that "will save the broken fingers known until now."[11]

McGunnigle wasn't the first catcher to wear a glove. That player was recorded as Doug Allison of the Cincinnati Red Stockings. The *Cincinnati Commercial* on June 29, 1870, noted: Allison caught "in a pair of buckskin mittens to protect his hands." Although Allison and some other early catchers wore light kid gloves, "I never saw them wear anything stronger in the matter of hand covering than that," recalled pioneer player Ed Cuthbert.[12] Most catchers shunned any glove at all because they didn't want to have their "manliness"

While playing for Buffalo, Bill McGunnigle won the Clipper Prize from the *New York Clipper* newspaper for 1878 as the best fielding right fielder in the International League. The Clipper Prize was a solid-gold medal with a figure of a baseball player encircled by a wreath (*New York Clipper*).

questioned. But in the Harvard game, opposing backstop Jim Tyng borrowed McGunnigle's gloves after the third inning. Tyng later bought a pair for himself and lined them with lead. By the late 1870s, catchers commonly wore thick, workman-like gloves made specifically for baseball.

(Harvard's Tyng made history in 1877, when he became the first catcher to wear a mask in a game, against Live Oaks in Lynn, Massachusetts. The mask, resembling a birdcage, was designed and patented by Harvard third baseman Fred Thayer. "For the first year, if I remember rightly, hardly anyone beside myself used the mask," Tyng later recalled, "but broken noses and damaged eyes soon brought conviction that catching with steel bars was preferable to unnecessarily exposing one's features as a target for erratic foul tips.")[13]

Fall River played in the New England Association, a loose federation of teams that competed against one another and also scheduled games with any other team that would play them. In July, the professional champion Boston Red Stockings came to town, led by star pitcher Al Spalding. Fall River hung close until Boston broke open the game to win 10 to 1. Spalding praised the Fall River team, saying "the boys are pretty smart." Gunner went 2-for-3 as the leadoff hitter. Fall River went on to finish second in the league.

Before the 1876 season rolled around, young McGunnigle had more big ideas. The team had been purchased by a new owner, and Gunner pleaded with him to bring in more pro players. The National League began that year and is now seen by some baseball historians as the only major league of its day. But players of that era considered "the League" to be no better than any other league. McGunnigle argued that "Fall River was just as ripe for pro ball as Boston" or any other big city.[14] The new owner agreed.

In a year when Alexander Graham Bell was inventing the telephone, General George Custer was getting wiped out at Little Big Horn, and Rutherford B. Hayes was being elected president, young Gunner McGunnigle helped put together a powerhouse professional baseball team. The new team included Gunner's old teammate, Owen Canary, and future major league infielders Roger Connor, Steve Libby and Arthur Whitney. The club hired a flamboyant young shortstop, Jim Mutrie, as manager, at $60 a month. The speedy McGunnigle began playing the outfield, dazzling fans with spectacular, barehanded catches. Fall River roared to the New England championship.

In 1877, many of the team's star players were lured away. McGunnigle and Mutrie remained, and the team picked up talented third baseman Ned Hanlon. During a game at Portland, Maine, another prospect emerged. The home team was short a player, and a "big-strapping, barefooted fellow, who was the personification of rural simplification, stepped forward and said he would play if they wanted him to," the Portland newspaper reported. His name was George Gore, and he was sent to play left field. "The Fall Rivers had a pitcher that day who was considered a perfect terror, and the Portlands went down before him like grain in the face of a high wind. When, however, it came Gore's turn at the bat he swung the bat around with giant strength, met the ball and lifted it far over the center fielder's head, to the great astonishment of everybody, including the Fall Rivers themselves. He was the hero of the day."[15] After the game, Mutrie recruited Gore for the Fall River team at $8 a week. George "Piano Legs" Gore played 33 games and hit .319. He went on to become one of baseball's most feared hitters.

New York Giants outfielder George "Piano Legs" Gore became a New York policeman and later a businessman in Nutley, New Jersey. He died in 1933 at age 76 (Library of Congress).

Fall River was in the pennant race again, and the ambitious McGunnigle looked for more ways to advance. He kept his eye on the pitchers, thinking he too could do that. Between games, "Mack" practiced his underhand twirling. Then, on August 2, he got his chance against the first-place team from

Lowell, Massachusetts, known as the "Lowell Ladies Men." As the *Fall River Daily Herald* reported, "Mack made his debut at pitch yesterday and wonderfully well did he do. Swift deliveries, mixed with slows, and in curves and out curves, rising and drop balls bothered the Lowells yesterday, and that only six hits were made by them tell the story."[16]

After Fall River finished second in 1877, McGunnigle decided it was time to move on, much to the regret of local fans. "He is the greatest right fielder we ever saw," said the *Daily Herald*.[17] McGunnigle was perhaps the most famous person in Fall River until 1892 when young Lizzie Borden, as the song says, "took an axe and gave her mother 40 whacks. And when she saw what she had done, she gave her father 41." (Lizzie, by the way, was acquitted.)

McGunnigle turned his eyes to the Queen City of Buffalo, New York, a growing industrial city of about 150,000 people on the shores of Lake Erie. Buffalo played in the International Association, so-called because the teams included the 1877 pennant-winning Tecumseh club from London, Ontario, Canada. In early 1878, McGunnigle wrote to H.S. Sprague, owner of the Buffalo team, about his pre-season workouts: "I am at work (in the shoe factory) every day and I don't have tim to eercise anny. but I am going to try to get a month if I can I have joined the Brocton gymnasium it aint a very good one (although) it is long enough to pitch and catch in."[18]

Fortunately, Gunner's ball playing was better than his spelling, and he was hired for $700. Buffalo was building a strong team. Its star player was a stocky, 22-year-old pitcher named Jim "Pud" Galvin. The "Pud" stood for pudding, which was what quivering batters seemed to be reduced to when facing Galvin's underhand fireballs. "In Galvin," the *Buffalo Express* said, "Buffalo has the speediest pitcher in the profession. The pace of his balls is certainly a marvel and it is wonderful how he can find catchers willing to face him."[19] In those days, teams carried only two pitchers. The main hurler pitched almost every game without relief. The second "change pitcher" filled in every once in a while to give the main man a breather. McGunnigle became Buffalo's change pitcher and on other days played right field.

The scrappy Buffalo squad drew thousands of fans to the team's new ballpark on the city's west side. One big fan, literally, was Grover Cleveland, a prominent lawyer who soon would become mayor of Buffalo and then governor of New York. The team got off to a fast start in a duel for the pennant with the Syracuse Stars. Buffalo also squared off against a parade of teams from other leagues, including the National League.

Dashing Billy McGunnigle, now sometimes called "Mac," quickly became a fan favorite. "This handsome young man has no superior in the country as a right fielder, prancing over his territory with a nervous energy which is destruction to everything sent his way," the *Buffalo Express* said.[20] Mac's specialty was charging like a shortstop to field a ball hit "safely" to right field and gunning the batter out at first base. "I have seen McGunnigle throw out as many as seven men in one game from right field to first base," said Buffalo teammate Sam Crane.[21] That season the *New York Clipper* newspaper began the Clipper Prize that, like today's Gold Glove Award, was given to the best fielding player at each position in the International Association. Gunner won the award, a gold medal, for right field, with *the Clipper* emphasizing his throwing 28 runners out at first, "his work in this respect being the best on record."[22]

Unfortunately, Mac was a good-field, no-hit player, and he was benched in mid-summer for his weak hitting. A proud man, he asked for his release, but the club directors refused to give it to him. "McGunnigle is an excellent player and has by his hard work and gentlemanly conduct in the city won many friends," the *Buffalo Express* said. "We hope McGunnigle will stay."[23] He did. In a September game against Manchester, he returned to right field, and, as the *Express* reported, "surpassed anything that has been done in that field in this city this year. Nobody was able to send anything in that direction that was not cared for by Mac's magnificent catches or lightening throws to first."[24] His batting also perked up, and he ended the year hitting .240.

The tight pennant race between Buffalo and the Syracuse Stars was muddled by the departure of several teams from the league. Buffalo finished the season with a record of 32 wins and 12 losses, but "the Twinklers" had fewer losses with a 27 and 10 record. League officials didn't decide until February, when they declared Buffalo the winner. Including games against non-league opponents, Buffalo won 81 games and lost 31, with Jim Galvin picking up 72 wins. Many baseball experts consider the 1878 Buffalo team to be one of the best minor league teams of the nineteenth century.

Because Buffalo won 10 of 17 games against National League teams, McGunnigle and his mates figured they were every bit as good as players in "the League." They got their chance to prove it in 1879, when Buffalo and Syracuse were accepted into the National League. The "Bisons," as they were now called, proved their case as they fought for first place with the Providence Grays, Boston Red Caps and manager Cap Anson's Chicago White Stockings. In the big leagues, McGunnigle continued to shine in the field. In a win over Troy, the *Chicago Tribune* reported, "McGunnigle affected some astonishing fly-catches in right."[25]

Once again, Mac couldn't hit a beach ball with his bat and again was benched. Again he asked for his release, but was refused. He rode the bench until August, when Jim Galvin was injured. Mac took to the pitcher's box and blanked Cleveland. The next day he pitched again. "Will McGunnigle tower up again today?" a paper asked. "He towered up," pitching a 2 to 1 win.[26]

Setbacks seemed to make the feisty McGunningle even more determined to fight back, noted an observer in Troy, New York, after Mac pitched a one-hit win there. "It must be that he was provoked at the way the Troys batted him in former games and determined to make up for it yesterday as he succeeded admirably. The way he pitched the ball, and the way Troy did not bat the ball, and it is without any hesitancy whatsoever that we say his pitching yesterday was the finest we have seen here this year."[27]

The innovative McGunnigle apparently found a new pitch, third baseman Hardy Richardson later claimed. Mac, he said, "conceived the idea that by putting a thimble on one of his fingers he could produce a peculiar twist to the ball. McGunnigle caused the ball to leave his hand over the thimble and discovered that this motion produced a twist on the sphere which was much superior to that obtained by ordinary means." One day, with "McGunnigle and his trusty thimble doing the pitching," Richardson said, "we had our opponents beat for fair. Along about the fourth inning, McCormick, who was pitching for Cleveland, called the attention of the umpire to the appearance of the ball, which, he claimed, commenced to resemble an angora cat, such was the fizz that the thimble was raising on the ball. The umpire promptly investigated with the result that McGunnigle was compelled to discard the thimble. The Cleveland batters thereafter had no trouble hitting the ball and they won the game with ease."[28]

The accuracy of the story might be of some doubt since it referred to McGunnigle as "Fred," but if Billy was indeed outed and forced to discard his trusty thimble, he still managed to roll up stellar pitching numbers

Young Bill McGunnigle was described as a "Buffalo Frenchman with oiled side-burns and padded nethers, who cavorted in right field." The photograph was taken in 1878, not 1887 (National Baseball Hall of Fame Library).

without it. In September he pitched two straight wins over Chicago, enabling Buffalo to edge the White Stockings for a respectable third-place finish. McGunnigle hit an anemic .170 for the season but rolled up a pitching record of 9 and 5 with a 2.62 earned run average. That was good enough for Buffalo to sign him for the next season. Over the winter McGunnigle and his wife, Mary, stayed in the city, while Gunner worked at Staley's Shoe and Boot Store on Main Street. The McGunnigles' second child, William, was born in Buffalo in 1880 and their third, Mary, arrived in 1882. Like their father, both children were born on New Year's Day.

The club made 25-year-old Gunner the captain-manager for the 1880 season. He also took part in another baseball innovation. Buffalo became the first team to alternate pitchers, with McGunnigle pitching one game and newcomer Tom Poorman hurling the next. The change was born out of necessity. Gentleman Jim Galvin — who had won 37 games in 1879 — left to play for the San Francisco team in the California League, a new minor league.

The experiment started off well enough. On Opening Day, McGunnigle pitched Buffalo to a 7 to 4 win over Cleveland. But the Bisons soon tumbled badly. After Buffalo's bad start, the owners said, "Send for Galvin," and asked his wife to get him back. Galvin took a train from San Francisco a short distance, then, to avoid detectives who been sent by his California team to retrieve him, jumped off and walked 23 miles in the desert.[29] But he was a shell of his former self that season. After 17 games, Buffalo released McGunnigle from the team and named 24-year-old second baseman Sam Crane the new manager. The team continued its slide, finishing in next-to-last place.

Bill McGunnigle mysteriously disappeared from baseball. He turned up in June of 1880 as the losing pitcher for Rochester in the International League, with the *Washington Post* noting that he "pitched with a lame arm." He would play only three more games in the major leagues — one with the Worcester Ruby Legs in 1880 and a double-header with Cleveland in 1882. His short big league career ended with a .173 batting average, and a pitching record of 11 wins and 8 losses. Mac focused on his business endeavors, which he said were "progressing so finely that he prefers to remain at that rather than again enter the arena." The personable McGunnigle was at times a shoe salesman and a cigar salesman.

McGunnigle had not given up on baseball. On November 14, 1882, an item in the *New York Clipper* noted: "William H. McGunnigle, whose lame arm has kept him from playing during the last two seasons, has got well at last and proposes reentering the professional arena in 1883." As the new Brooklyn team was being formed in New York, Mac was recruited by a new baseball league in the Midwest. The Northwestern League was the first league officially formed as a minor league training ground for future big leaguers. Represented were teams from Saginaw, Bay City and Grand Rapids in Michigan, Toledo, Ohio, Fort Wayne, Indiana, and Springfield, Peoria and Quincy in Illinois. McGunnigle was signed to captain the squad in Saginaw, where he would team with future Hall of Fame pitcher John Clarkson, shortstop Yank Robinson and manager Art Whitney, his old Fall River teammate.

The new league ran into controversy before the first season even began. In March, Peoria tried to "forbid the employment of colored players" to prevent the Toledo Blue Stockings from playing its star catcher, Moses "Fleet" Walker, but the motion "met with such disapprobation" that it was withdrawn.[30] Walker became a leading player for Toledo that year.

The new league did adopt some rules to keep its ball players on the straight and narrow, such as rule 8: "Players are forbidden all public or private association with harlots, or with gamblers, or men known to bet on games of ball."[31]

McGunnigle's team was called the Saginaw Old Golds. Players wore white flannel uniforms with gold trimmings and cardigans to match old gold stockings. The "effervescent" McGunnigle became one of Saginaw's top players. He also had a couple of close brushes with personal disaster, according to news reports. While boating with three teammates on a lake in Peoria, "a cyclone struck them, and they were all thrown into the water."[32] In Saginaw, "McGunnigle, the efficient right fielder of the home team, had a narrow escape from instant death last evening, from a severe shock of electricity."[33] After Saginaw topped Springfield the next day, the paper reported, "That electric shock seemed to have infused new life into Mac's batting powers."[34] Led by Clarkson and McGunnigle, Saginaw battled Toledo for the pennant, before the Blue Stockings took first place by two games. But when Toledo early the next year chose to join the major league American Association, the Northwestern League awarded the pennant to Saginaw. Mac had another championship.

In its second year, an expanded Northwestern League ran into financial difficulties. To raise money, Saginaw peddled McGunnigle to the league's Bay City squad and later sold ace pitcher John Clarkson to the National League Chicago White Stockings. At Bay City, where he also was captain, Mac joined future Brooklyn pitchers Dave Foutz and Henry Porter as well as hard-hitting James "Cuddy" Cudworth, who would become his best friend. The potent Bay City "Chocolates" were vying for first place in late July when it, too, hit the financial skids. After the club sold off Foutz to the St. Louis Browns, the team disbanded. McGunnigle already had been moved to the league's Muskegon, Michigan, team, where he gained a reputation as a complainer, or "kicker." McGunnigle, said one news report, "is playing left field for the Muskegons and leads the blatting list — not the batting. His blatting propensities remain intact."[35] Shortly thereafter, Muskegon and the entire league folded.

McGunnigle was out of baseball again, but baseball was not out of his blood. In 1885, he returned home to Brockton, a city of 20,000 people. Now 30 years old, and sporting long sideburns and a handlebar mustache, he was a confident and self-educated man. In private, he was "a story teller in several dialects, had a good singing voice and a hearty appreciation of friendships. His family cherished him and his numerous friends took great delight in his company."[36] His pals included heavyweight boxing champion John L. Sullivan. Mac was a snappy dresser, preferring natty light trousers and cutaway jackets.

McGunnigle was determined to enter a team from the Shoe City in the new Eastern New England League, and he approached his goal with the same zeal he showed on the field, despite such obstacles as little money and no ballpark. "Having undertaken to organize a club in this city, he has injected a surprising amount of energy and push into the enterprise," the *Brockton Weekly Gazette* said, so that such obstacles "have been literally carried by storm." The paper added: "It is a noteworthy fact, and one which augurs well for the new team, that every club with which McGunnigle has been connected has won a championship."[37] Mac used what money he had to became part-owner of the new team and began building a ballpark at Grove and Main streets. He signed players, including his Bay City buddy Jim Cudworth. Mac himself would be the leadoff hitter and playing manager. He dressed the team up in short-sleeved maroon shirts and old-gold stockings and belts. Across the chest of the shirts was "Brockton" in gold letters. Soon the roar of fans could be heard at the new Brockton ballpark.

That year all of baseball began allowing pitchers to throw overhand. But the pitcher's box remained 50 feet from home plate, and hit batters didn't get to take first base. It was headhunting season for hard-throwing hurlers. On July 22 in Brockton, McGunnigle stepped into the batter's box to face pitcher Dick Conway of the Lawrence, Massachusetts, team. The result was reported in the *Brockton Weekly Gazette:* McGunnigle dodged the first pitch, a fastball thrown squarely at his head. "The second was directly in the direction of the first, and the batter only saved himself by dropping suddenly on all fours to the ground." When "a third ball sped from the pitcher's hand like a bullet from a gun ... the unfortunate batsman could not avoid the ball in time. And it struck him with a crash, which was heard in every part of the grounds. Poor 'Mac' fell like an animal beneath the butcher's axe, and his quivering form was drawn up in agony as he lay upon the ground."[38]

The *Boston Globe*, in writing about the incident, said "The only topic on the street tonight is the question of whether it was Conway's idea to frighten the batsman or if he was trying to get the balls as close to the batsman as possible."[39] Mac was hurt badly but came back within a week against Newburyport. When he came to bat for the first time in the second inning, the umpire stopped the game and a Brockton citizen stepped forward to present McGunnigle on behalf of the town "an elegant watch, chain and charms in a fine case lined with a cashier's check for $92.75. The surprise of the doughty Mac was such as to forbid his making an adequate response," the *Boston Globe* said.[40]

After McGunnigle recovered, the notorious incident eventually led to a family poem that Mac's daughter Mary passed on to her children:

Casey on the pitcher's mound
McGunnigle at the bat
Casey let the ball go
And knocked McGunnigle flat.[41]

Meantime, McGunnigle honed his skills as a manager. He blew a tin whistle to get his players' attention. He closely studied pitchers and catchers, becoming a master at stealing signs. He was the first manager to signal players by waving a scorecard, bats or hats from the bench. "As a player McGunnigle was picturesque, and as a captain probably never had a superior," the *Brockton Times* said. He became known for running in from the outfield to "'lay down the law.' He was a strict manager, yet a kind one, and brought out the best in many men who now figure as stars of the diamond."[42]

McGunnigle led the Shoe City team to first place when the season ended in October — at least Brocktonites thought he did. "The Brocktons have won the pennant," said the *Brockton Gazette*. "Whether they will get it or not is the question." Second-place Lawrence was allowed to play some postponed games after the season ended, and the two teams ended up tied. The league ordered a three-game playoff. Lawrence won the first two games and the official title. To McGunnigle and Brockton, the 1885 championship would always rightfully belong to the Shoe City. Mac returned the next year but gave up his part-ownership in the "Brockton Shoe Nine." The team ran into financial trouble and played poorly. When the owners ordered McGunnigle to fine the players, he refused to do so and quit the team, leaving to play for the New England League's Haverhill squad.

In 1877, the New England League's Lowell team hired McGunnigle as its player-manager. Lowell's prospects didn't seem so hot. The team was known as a "bunch of bummers who liked their drink," and fans hooted the players at the first home game. Led by player-manager McGunnigle and his buddy Cudworth, the team took off. Before long, the Lowell Browns became a favorite of fans at home and the bane of fans in opposing towns. One day while the team was on the road, Mac was getting a shave in a barbershop when the talk turned to the Lowell nine. "That darned McGunnigle," the barber said. "If I had him here, I'd cut his big throat." Mac chose to keep mum.[43]

Lowell muscled up even more when McGunnigle picked up outfielder Hugh Duffy, a future Hall of Famer. Duffy played 78 games and batted .428. In a key series sweep against Manchester, Duffy hit three homers over the fence, along with a triple. By season's end, Lowell ended up in a five-game playoff for the championship with the Portland team. In the first game at Portland, Lowell came out on top 6 to 5 "largely due to the superb work of Manager McGunnigle in the box," the *Boston Globe* reported. Back in Lowell, the Browns captured the second game in 10 innings. The final game was played in Boston, where Lowell won the championship. The team returned to a giant celebration in Lowell, where the players yelled, "McGunnigle's a king."[44]

Gunner's triumphs gained wider attention. McGunnigle "as a manager, player and general on the field is head and shoulders above anything in the league and excelled by precious few in the country," said *Sporting Life*.[45] In the minds of the baseball public, the *Boston Globe* said, McGunnigle's name "is a household word."

The pennant-winning manager caught the attention of Brooklyn president Charley Byrne, who made McGunnigle an offer he thought Mac couldn't refuse—$2,000 to manage the Brooklyn team. Mac was interested, but he had agreed to manage Lowell in 1888. "McGunnigle acted very honorably in his dealings both with Lowell and Brooklyn," the *Brooklyn Eagle* reported. He went to the Lowell officials, who matched Byrne's offer but agreed to let Mac go. Byrne raised his bid to $2,500, and Gunner was off to the big leagues again, this time as a manager. "I will say right here," Byrne said, "that Manager McGunnigle will have full charge of the team and will place it to suit himself."[46]

"Yes, I am of course gratified to be entrusted with the management of such a team, and I shall try my best to win the pennant for the gentlemen who have engaged me," McGunnigle said. "They are very agreeable gentlemen, and I feel that I shall have no occasion to find fault with them. I wish I could feel sure that they will have no more cause to be dissatisfied with me."[47]

Baseball columnist Oliver Perry (O.P.) Caylor sarcastically observed of Byrne's decision to turn his managing duties over to the new man: "What a sigh of relief the other club officials [in the American Association] will heave to know that McGunnigle has removed the team pressure from Charley's brain to such an extent that he can run the Association single-handed and alone."[48]

Chapter Four

Stars for Sale

Brooklyn president Charley Byrne was the George Steinbrenner of his day when it came to trying to buy a pennant-winner. Actually, it is more accurate to say that New York Yankees owner Steinbrenner was the Charley Byrne of modern baseball, as it was the Brooklyn president who set the big-bucks mold. Before the 1888 season, Byrne's wheeling and dealing had heads spinning from New York to San Francisco.

The Brooklyn magnate began his buying spree before the end of the 1887 season by purchasing the entire New York Metropolitan franchise lock, stock and jockstraps from Staten Island businessman Erustus Wiman. Investors led by Wiman had purchased the Mets only two years earlier for $25,000 from New York Gothams owner John Day's Metropolitan Exhibition Company amid great controversy. Day's American Association colleagues had accused him of using the Mets as a farm team for his National League squad. In early 1885, he switched Mets manager Jim Mutrie to be the skipper of the Gothams. Then he wanted to transfer star pitcher Tim Keefe and outfielder Tom "Dude" Esterbrook to the league team but ran into that pesky rule barring players from being signed until 10 days after their release. Mutrie, therefore, took the two men on holiday at the Hamilton Hotel in Bermuda to wait out the 10-day period. On the trip, the three men used aliases, with Esterbrook going by "T. Flanagan."[1] After 10 days, the two players signed on with the Gothams. Outraged owners banished Mutrie from the association. Soon after, the association went to court to try to block Day's sale of the Mets to Wiman's Staten Island group. When the court backed the sale, Wiman joined the American Association, where he was about as welcome as a woman suffragist at a voting place.

Wiman was out to boost his business interests. He owned the Staten Island ferry and the Staten Island Cricket Club field just 300 yards from the ferry stop, which is where he built a new ballpark. Besides baseball, the field brought in such performers as a Wild West show, a circus and a show called *The Fall of Babylon*. But baseball didn't draw well at the remote location, and by 1887 the team was in deep financial trouble. Wiman began secret talks with New York Gothams owner Day, who was interested in buying the team back if the price was low enough.

"Accidentally, I learned what the New York people were doing" to buy back the team, Byrne said. "I determined to secure it myself." He telegraphed his two partners, Gus Abell and Joe Doyle, who were on vacation. "They came on at once and decided with me that it was of vital importance to local base ball interests for us to secure the franchise." The Brooklyn trio began secret negotiations with Wiman, and within 24 hours on October 1, 1887, closed a deal to buy the club for $25,000. The Metropolitan stockholders elected Abell as the new president and Byrne as secretary. "Had the New York people known what we were doing, we no doubt could not have secured the franchise," Byrne said. Brooklyn's plan was to keep the cream of the Mets players and sell the rest to a new American Association franchise, which turned out to be the Kansas City Cowboys. The Brooklyn owners were bent on building the best team that money could buy, even if they had to invest another $10,000.[2]

First baseman Dave Orr had a lifetime batting average of .342, the same as Babe Ruth. Many believe Orr should be in the Baseball Hall of Fame (Library of Congress).

The biggest catch in the Mets purchase, literally, was 28-year-old first baseman Dave

Orr, who stood 5'll" and weighed 250 pounds. The affable Orr was the association's 1884 batting champ. The other prize was strapping, 24-year-old outfielder Darby O'Brien, 6'1" and 186 pounds. O'Brien, like Brooklyn third sacker George Pinkney, hailed from Peoria, Illinois. He was a spirited, fun-loving player who during game rain delays loved to slide head first through the mud. Brooklyn also picked up 22-year-old pitcher Al Mays, who won 17 games and lost 35 for the Mets in 1887.

Then Byrne, adopting a philosophy of "if you can't beat 'em, buy 'em," turned to an unlikely source — his rival, the boss of the St. Louis Browns. Chris "What have you done for me lately" Von der Ahe was conducting a fire sale of the Browns' high-priced players after the team's disappointing loss to Detroit in the World's Series. The first to go were center fielder Curt Welch and shortstop Bill Gleason to the Philadelphia Athletics. Then Der Boss sat down with Byrne and Gus Abell in New York to discuss the sale of the Browns' Big Three: Bob Caruthers, Dave Foutz and Al Bushong. "I had to deal with Von der Ahe, and no one on earth could say with certainty what course he would pursue in the matter," Abell said. "Chris would not sell the three men in one transaction. The total cost was $19,000, but I had to buy each one separately."[3] (In fact, this wasn't the first time Brooklyn had tried to buy St. Louis players. It was later reported that at the end of the 1886 season, just before Von der Ahe set sail on his yearly European trip, Byrne offered to purchase the entire St. Louis team for $100,000 cash and all of the Brooklyn squad. Von der Ahe declined.[4])

Brooklyn outfielder Darby O'Brien off the field sometimes carried snakes in his pocket and loved to pull them out to startle people (*New York Clipper*).

Al Bushong was the first to sign, on November 24, 1887, in San Francisco, where the Browns were on a post-season tour of exhibition games. The veteran catcher was nicknamed "Doc" because he had a degree from the University of Pennsylvania School of Dentistry. The tall, thin Bushong was an intelligent and level-headed man. Though an average batter, the brainy Bushong was a superb catcher and handler of young pitchers. Byrne had long regretted letting the catcher get away in the 1885 Cleveland deal. "Every visit that the Brooklyn Club made here last season, President Byrne was always at its head, and he has watched Bushong work behind the bat with a wishful eye," *Sporting Life* said. "He wished to see the 'Doctor' on the team that represents the City of Churches, and he has not been any way backward in expressing his desires."[5]

Many baseball historians credit Bushong with inventing the padded "pillow" catcher's mitt to replace the work-glove mitts that Bill McGunnigle had used. Doc Bushong, "the famous catcher of the old St. Louis Browns, was very careful about his fingers, as he intended practicing dentistry after his days as a ballplayer were over," the *New York Times* said in 1915. "He wore the largest glove he could find, and had added pads until it looked like a pillow. The Doctor was proud of this affair, and would not allow anyone to use it."[6]

Other historians credit Joe Gunson, who claimed to have come up with a mitt in the minors before advancing to the majors. As Gunson explained it:

> While I was catching for the Kansas City Blues in the Western League, in 1888, there were two games scheduled for Decoration Day. Our other catcher was injured, and I had a crippled finger on my left hand. I stitched together the fingers of my left-hand glove, thus practically making a 'mitt'; and then I caught both games. It worked so well that I got to work. Took an old paint-pot wire handle, the old flannel belts from our castoff jackets, rolled the cloth around the ends of the finger and padded the thumb. Then I put sheepskin with the wool on it in the palm and covered it with buckskin, thus completing the mitt, and the suffering and punishment we endured at the then fifty-foot pitching level was over.[7]

Gunson claimed that when he showed the glove around, the idea was stolen by ne'er-do-well catcher Harry Decker, who patented a mitt before Gunson was able to do so. The "Decker's Safety Catchers Mitt" sold for years, though Decker wound up in the San Quentin prison for forgery. Eventually, New York backstop Buck Ewing started using a mitt as big as a suitcase. Even third basemen tried the big glove until 1895 when baseball limited the mitts to catchers.

The record shows that Doc Bushong was using a pillow glove long before Gunson claimed to be inventing his. An October 13, 1887, article in the *Brooklyn Eagle* tells of Bushong losing his "old glove," and "he feels pretty badly over the matter.... it was padded and fixed up until it was as soft to his hand as a pillow, and it was his best friend while he was up under the bat. It will take him some time to become accustomed to a new glove, and it will be several seasons before he can get as many patches on the one he wears now as he had on the old one. The latter would have been a good attraction at a dime museum. It resembled something that had been fired from a cannon."[8] By 1889 *Sporting Life* reported that "Doc Bushong catches balls nowadays with a spring mattress on his left hand."[9]

Bushong and teammate Charley Comiskey, by the way, were among the first players to endorse products. One 1887 ad featured Bushong's picture with the caption: "While playing in one of the games in St. Louis this Spring, I caught cold, and my limbs considerably stiffened up. I soon got over it, however, thanks to Merrell's Penetrating Oil, I am in better shape than I ever was before."[10]

Brooklyn catcher Doc Bushong believed that a mustache was good luck for a baseball player, saying "I am an advocate of hairy lips in the profession" (Library of Congress).

With Bushong in tow, the next piece to fall in place for Brooklyn was Dave Foutz, who signed on December 8, also in San Francisco. The tall, skinny Foutz, at 6'2" and only 170 pounds, had trouble bending his knees, producing an image that earned him such names as "Scissors," "Needles" and "the Human Hairpin." The multitalented Foutz had pitched 25 wins for St. Louis in 1887 and also hit .357 while knocking in

108 runs. A writer for the *Louisville Courier-Journal* described Foutz's pitching motion this way: "His 'Needles' Foutz doubles himself up in a knot and suddenly straightens out his tall form and fires the ball sharply at the batter. He usually wipes the dirt on his hips, deliberately fixes his finger on the ball, then exchanges winks and nods with the catcher, when he throws. Foutz always smiles when he does well and closely watches the course of the ball as it leaves his hand."[11] Brooklynites lauded the Foutz deal. "The leading topic of contemporaneous human interest in this city is the acquisition of Dave Foutz by the Brooklyn Base Ball Club. This man's ability as pitcher, first baseman or right fielder closely approaches genius," *the Brooklyn Eagle* said. And at $5,000 he was a bargain, because Brooklyn "must have the pennant next year if it costs nine times $5,000."[12]

The final and biggest prize was Bob Caruthers, and he wouldn't be easy to land. He was known as "Parisian Bob," because early in 1885 he held out by going to Paris with Bushong and refusing to sign until Von der Ahe would pay $3,200—which Chris finally did. In addition, other teams were after him, especially Cincinnati. The 23-year-old Caruthers was only 5'7" and weighed 168 pounds. But he was a wiry and crafty right-handed pitcher, a capable outfielder and a solid hitter, batting both right and left. In 1887, he won 29 games and, like Foutz, hit .357. As a pitcher, he stressed control over strikeouts. "Caruthers first advances his right leg, fumbles the ball on his hip a second and then with a sour look throws to the batter. He pitches

Dave "Scissors" Foutz while pitching for the St. Louis Browns in 1886 picked a runner off first base by dashing from the mound and tagging the runner out. Foutz pitched 11 shutouts that year (Library of Congress.)

without effort and seemingly does not care whether the batter hits the ball or not."[13]

Byrne hired St. Louis sportswriter Joe Pritchard to persuade Caruthers to sign with Brooklyn. The rotund Pritchard had the deal all locked by late November, or so he thought until he went to meet with Caruthers in St. Louis. As Pritchard wrote:

> Last Thursday morning I walked into the Liclede Hotel to have a talk with Bob Caruthers in regard to the great pitcher signing a Brooklyn contract. I was under the impression that the coast would be clear, as I knew that everything had been amicably settled between Presidents Byrne and Von der Ahe, but to my great surprise Manager Gus Schmelz, of Cincinnati, had Caruthers cornered, and he was telling the Chicagoan how invalids become healthy when they settle in the Paris of America.
>
> He also told Bob, at least I imagined so, that the players on the Cincinnati team received all the way from $500 to $2,000 at the end of the season as a present from the club's president, and the silver dollars that were thrown at a player's feet after having made a home run were often piled higher than Long John Reilly's head. It was undoubtedly the place for the hard-hitting pitcher to go, as his home runs would foot up thousands of dollars during the championship season. He was also promised a banquet every time the club returned from a trip. All of this "boiled down sugar" better known as "taffy" caused Caruthers to think favorably of Cincinnati, and he told Gus that he would be pleased to play ball under him. My arrival broke up the little mutual admiration *tête-à-tête,* and I took the great pitcher under my wing and proceeded to tell him all about the City of Churches. Had President Byrne been within hearing distance I am positive that he would have made me a present of the Brooklyn Club franchise, grand stand and all.

Dave Foutz in action (Transcendental Graphics).

After a few days, Caruthers agreed to go with Brooklyn. Then his brother, James, "came down from Chicago and begged him to quit the diamond" and return home to the Windy City, Pritchard said. The brotherly plea failed, and Bobby seemed ready to sign ... but wait. "No, I will not sign any paper till after I have heard from my mother," Caruthers declared. Said Pritchard: "This was a rather a queer way to act, to say the least, after having promised to sign as soon as we could come to an understanding." Then came a wire from Mrs. Caruthers: "Do not sign an agreement under any circumstances." This was followed by another telegram from big brother: "Take mother's advice." What's a mama's boy to do? Caruthers decided to stop the whole proceedings and go back to Chicago.[14]

Informed of these developments, Byrne decided there was only one thing to do: Jump on a train to the Windy City to see Caruthers himself. He met up with Pritchard, and early on a Monday morning they went to see the great pitcher at his hotel. "Byrne is very gentlemanly and is a good talker. Caruthers received his visitors pleasantly, and the men at once proceeded to talk business," *Sporting Life* reported. "The young man went over the old ground about wanting a big salary and a percentage of the release bonus. He added, of course, that he was not compelled to play base ball for a living and that his mother would be greatly pleased in case he would retire." Byrne seemed bored. He figured it was all a big bluff. He had never met a ball player who could afford to turn his back on the game. Caruthers finally said: "Let us not discuss it any longer now. If you gentlemen will take supper with me, I think we can get back to the question."[15]

Pitcher Bob Caruthers' career record of 218 wins and 99 losses is one of the highest of any pitcher not in the Baseball Hall of Fame (Library of Congress).

Byrne wrote down the mother's address. That evening, he and Pritchard got into a horse-drawn cab, and Byrne gave the address to the driver. The two passengers didn't know much about Chicago. To their great surprise, the cab drove up in front of an elegant mansion on LaSalle Avenue. Byrne thought perhaps the driver had made a mistake, but he and Pritchard got out. They rang the door bell and were ushered in by a butler, who assured them they had the right house.

For once, Byrne had failed to do his homework. Robert Lee Caruthers was born with a silver spoon in his mouth in Memphis, Tennessee, where his father, James P. Caruthers, was a district judge. His mother had inherited a substantial amount of money and Chicago real estate from her dad. In 1876, the family moved to Chicago, where Mr. and Mrs. Caruthers started a profitable hardware company before the judge died in 1886. Mrs. Caruthers was against Bobby playing ball when he was a boy because he was so small and "delicate." His father, however, believed the exercise would help his son stay healthy. Bobby became so good at baseball that in 1883 he was signed at age 18 for $75 a month to play for Grand Rapids in the Northwestern League. The next year, the league's Minneapolis team grabbed him for $175 a month. Then in late 1884, St. Louis's Chris Von der Ahe outbid Chicago's A. G. Spalding to nab Caruthers for $250 a month. Now he was demanding $5,000 a year, the highest in the American Association. It wasn't that he needed the money; his grandfather had left him $30,000 and his mother 10 times that amount.

Charley Byrne had his work cut out for him. "Mrs. Caruthers, who is a very refined lady, greeted the two gentlemen cordially," *Sporting Life* said. "She did not know they were baseball men, Bobby having merely told her that he had invited two friends up to dine with him. Inside of ten minutes Byrne realized that Caruthers had not been bluffing. He set to work to win Mrs. Caruthers over and after a while it leaked out that he was a base ball manager."[16]

By now Byrne realized what he was up against in trying to land Caruthers. "I found his mother a most charming lady of much cultivation," Byrne said. She wanted Robert to join his brother in the family business. "She had already invested considerable capital in the hardware business in giving her eldest son a start and she was prepared to invest a still larger amount whenever her youngest son was willing to enter into partnership with his brother.

"It took me a long time to overcome her objections, especially as she has ample means and as the base ball playing keeps her son away from her for some months of the year," Byrne said. "She admitted that the compensation offered was very liberal and much larger than he could hope to obtain in any other profession and she gave quiet consent to let her son go with us."[17] Mom drove a hard bargain. The next morning Caruthers went to Byrne's room at the Clifton House hotel and signed a contract for $5,500 (the equivalent of about $130,000 today), with $1,500 up front. Brooklyn paid St. Louis $8,500 for his release, of which Caruthers collected a percentage. As soon as Caruthers had put his John Hancock on the contract, the Brooklyn owner presented him with a $200 diamond stick pin. Byrne promptly sent a telegram to the *Brooklyn Eagle* about his coup. "As you knew that I would succeed, I need only say that Caruthers has signed with Brooklyn."[18]

The stunning deals made Byrne the talk of the baseball world. "What a pushing, energetic and enterprising club president Charley Byrne, of the Brooklyn Club, is," wrote veteran sportswriter Henry Chadwick. "In base ball enterprises he seems to know no such word as fail. Certainly, if pluck and energy, combined with liberal outlays of money, can achieve success in securing first-class players with which to improve his team, Charley is going to get it."[19] Even the St. Louis-based *The Sporting News* was impressed. "At last Brooklyn is to have a team it will be proud of. Byrne, Doyle and Abell are men of recognized business ability and their untiring work will undoubtedly be rewarded fittingly."[20] Not everyone approved. The *Philadelphia Record* tersely remarked: "The management of the Brooklyn Club must be in the baseball business for glory, not money. Something like $40,000 has been paid out in deals since the close of the last playing season."[21]

Byrne was able to make the sensational deals with St. Louis after temporarily patching relations with Chris Von der Ahe. After the summer flare-up when the Browns owner vowed to oust American Association president Wheeler Wyckoff or he would quit the association, Chris had taken up a new demand. At that time, visiting teams got a flat $65 for each game. Von der Ahe wanted teams to split game receipts. Both he and Byrne had long opposed revenue sharing because their teams drew bigger home crowds than most squads. But attendance had dipped in St. Louis, while the champion Browns were a big draw in opposing cities. To Von der Ahe, sharing the receipts of other teams' home games suddenly seemed like a wunderbar idea.

Byrne had called a special meeting of the American Association for late August in New York, where he planned to propose a number of policy changes. Shortly before the scheduled meeting, he was passing by Westerman's Saloon when he saw Von der Ahe's horse and buggy parked outside. The Brooklyn owner went into the saloon, walked up behind the Browns owner sitting at a table and gave him a friendly slap on the back. "How are you, Chris?" he said.

Von der Ahe was surprised, but seeing Byrne's smiling face, he held out his hand. "Hello, Byrne, what'll you have?"

"It's my treat," the Brooklyn magnate said.

"Brooklyn money is no good here," said Chris. "Nominate your medicine, and I'll do the banker's act." The two men had drinks, broke out some cigars, and soon several other baseball officials who were there joined the two men. During the conversation, Byrne said he had come around to Von der Ahe's views on dividing receipts and would propose a change at the coming meeting.[22]

The August meeting was postponed until September 5, when American Association owners gathered at the Fifth Avenue Hotel in New York. There Byrne pushed through the most sweeping changes in the association's history. "The special meeting of the American Association last Monday may, in future times, be referred to as the most important convention in the history of base ball," *Sporting Life* said.[23] Indeed, many of the Byrne reforms, including systems for teams to establish a reserve corps of players and for drafting upcoming players, continue in some form today. The goal was to try to put teams on a more equal footing, especially at the box office. Von der Ahe and some other owners had argued for giving visiting teams up to 50 percent of home-gate receipts. Byrne pushed through a compromise giving visiting teams 30 percent of receipts for all games except holidays, or a minimum of $130 per game — double the previous $65 guarantee.

Finally, in a move aimed directly at Browns captain Charley Comiskey, Byrne proposed a $1,500 fine if a team was pulled off the field before a game was over. The owners, including Von der Ahe, adopted all of Byrne's proposals unanimously.[24] Then in a December meeting, the Brooklyn owner was instrumental in another major change designed to offset the loss of revenue for home teams: increasing the basic admission price to 50 cents, the same as the National League.

Byrne's triumphs placed him as a top power in the American Association, earning the diminutive Brooklyn owner the name of "the Napoleon of Base Ball." Said *Sporting Life:*

> Mr. Byrne has become the ruling mind in the affairs of the Association. In fact, MR. BYRNE IS THE ASSOCIATION. As a natural sequence of superior general abilities, he is president, secretary, board of directors and all the Committees. He is 'Captain, cook and all the crew on board the Mary Jane.' The other members of the ring fondly delude themselves with the belief that they are participating partners, and their thinking so is one of the greatest tributes to the peculiar abilities of Mr. Byrne. Either by study or by intuition this admirable diplomat becomes thoroughly conversant with the subtlest governing characteristics of his colleagues, and he manipulates this knowledge so delicately, and yet so skillfully, that there is responding result without even the manipulation or the *true* product being observed by the objects of it."[25]

Byrne's critics in St. Louis took a darker view of the Brooklyn president's rise to power. "His smooth, oily ways are captivating and his glib tongue wields a power to manipulate at will," said the *St. Louis Post Dispatch*. "Byrne is anxious to win the American Association pennant and little things like altering a few desultory facts to accomplish his ends does not in the least bother him."[26]

Von der Ahe remained an important voice in the association, but unlike the hard-working Byrne, the Dutchman had little patience for policy details. He spent much of his time at owner meetings entertaining colleagues with dirty jokes. Columnist O.P. Caylor noted that at the September meeting, Von der Ahe's female "traveling companion at the time absorbed most of his attention."[27] Even though some of Byrne's moves, particularly the fine for leaving the field, were aimed at St. Louis, Von der Ahe came away from the September meeting satisfied. "I will remain in the Association. Every club in the Association has agreed to give me a percentage of the receipts. That is all I have ever asked for."[28]

As for the sell-off of his top players, the Browns owner took the high road, saying that he had the good of the American Association in mind. "I have come to the conclusion that it does not pay to have a club far superior to every other," he said. "Our games are nearly all one-sided and as a result the attendance has diminished to a marked degree. By placing all the teams on a level, I think that interest in the game will be increased.

We will make more money, and the contests will give better satisfaction to the patrons. Of course, the St. Louis Club will try and win the championship again, but there is nothing in glory; we must do something to swell the attendance. Winning championships is one thing and losing money is another."[29]

As they say in Brooklyn, if you believe that, we have a bridge to sell you. Von der Ahe had several other reasons to dispose of his high-priced players. Though the Dutchman had a huge ego, he was a small man in the class department and quickly turned on the very men who had brought him three championships. After pitcher Dave Foutz's finger was broken by a ball hit back to the box, his teammates "lost all confidence in him and it was the general opinion that his arm was gone," Der Boss confided. "The Brooklyn managers thought well of him, however,—so well that they sent me this telegram offering me six thousand dollars for his release. Had I not been thoroughly convinced that Foutz had seen his best days, I would not have released him for any money." (What nobody knew at the time was that Foutz had been lying about his age; he was 31 instead of the 26 he claimed.)

As for Doc Bushong, Von der Ahe figured the 32-year-old catcher's best days also were behind him after the catcher, too, suffered a broken finger. He added: "Ever since last summer when he had that quarrel with Latham there has been a coolness between the two and Bushong has acted as though he cared little for the success of the team. I let him go to Brooklyn, who paid me a bonus of $5,000 for his release." And Bobby Caruthers, his star pitcher? "I offered him to Brooklyn only for the reason that he has caused me so much trouble every spring" with his salary demands, said Von der Ahe, who also blamed the pitcher for the World's Series loss because of his "card playing proclivities" and late-night carousing in the billiard halls.[30] (Bobby was an excellent pool player.)

The reality was that Caruthers had grown tired of Von der Ahe's tantrums. "I will not be seen with a pair of brown stockings on and the word St. Louis on the front of my shirt," he said. "I don't think that I have been treated right by the Brown Stocking management and I will never throw another ball for the club. No, sir. Never again."[31]

Von der Ahe was able to deal his ace pitcher because he still had a King to play—Silver King, a 19-year-old former bricklayer who had won 32 games in 1887. The German name of the pitcher, who had silvery hair, was Charles Frederiek Koenig, but "Silver King" sounded much cooler. The bottom line was that Der Boss collected a hefty price for the former players, money he could use to buy more men at less pay or for whatever he wanted. *The Sporting News* publisher Al Spink noted that Von der Ahe apparently cleared enough "to build a block of stone-front houses on St. Louis Avenuc, just west of Grand."[32]

St. Louis pitcher Silver King quit the game in 1896 at age 28 and went into the brick contracting business in the Mound City (Library of Congress).

Von der Ahe's fire sale set off huge opposition in St. Louis. Even Charley Comiskey was agitated. "I look upon the release of these men as a very unwise move, and I don't know what Mr. Von der Ahe could have been thinking about," the Browns manager said. "He is the hardest loser in the country, and I dislike to lose game after game, but I think we will get our stomach full during the coming season. I have a pretty hard row to hoe, but I believe that I can pull through."

"Comiskey actually shed tears when he learned of these changes were to take place," Bushong said. "He has been our captain and manager for several years, and the boys all like him and it will be a little tough to creep in under a new captain's wings."

"What team do I think will win the championship next season?" Bushong asked in response to the question. "If the Brooklyn Club does not win the pennant next season, then just put me down as a know-nothing when it comes to base ball. I am just as sure that Brooklyn will win the pennant as I am sure that twice two is four."[33]

Chapter Five

Here Come the Bridegrooms

After gobbling up the best players that money could buy, Charley Byrne figured he finally had put the pieces in place to bring Brooklyn its first pennant in 1888. But some questioned whether a "picked" squad of stars could play in harmony as a team, especially under a new manager. Brooklyn's new skipper, Gunner McGunnigle, at age 33, was barely older than some of his players. Moreover, he was a non-playing manager, leaving the team without a manager-captain on the field. Frank Brunnell, the sports editor of the *Cleveland Plain Dealer*, said of Brooklyn: "Strongest team in association, but unruly and unsteady. Three cliques within; no captain or second baseman."[1]

Newcomer Dave Foutz, who had played in Bay City, Michigan, when Gunner McGunnigle was the captain, saw reason for hope. Foutz predicted that McGunnigle would be a successful manager "if he is given full swing, as he knows how to take care of a lot of men. He is kind to the boys, and at the same time firm" but "not bossy." Foutz added: "I think we ought to land in first place. The material is there, and all we want is team work, and without that our name will be mud."[2]

Another kind of harmony already was spreading among many of the team's players — marital harmony. On February 1, 1888, a notice appeared in the papers that right fielder Ed Silch had married Miss Rose Neary at St. Michael's Church in Brooklyn. In March, another article reported that in Chicago, Robert S. Caruthers had tied the knot with Miss Mamie Danns, a "highly educated" and "very handsome" woman and the daughter of an IRS official.[3] A *Sporting Life* article noted that pitcher Al Mays, third baseman George Pinkney and shortstop George Smith also had gotten hitched since the close of the season, and "Dave Orr may be added to the list shortly." Concluded the correspondent: "Now isn't this a 'bridegroom' team?"[4]

The name caught on, and soon the "Brooklyns" unofficially became known as the "Bridegrooms." Newspaper writers loved alliteration, and now they could write of "Bryne's Brooklyn Bridegrooms." Their mouths watered for the first meeting between the Bridegrooms and "Billie Barnie's Baltimore" team. In all, the *Brooklyn Eagle* reported, "Eleven of the Brooklyn team are blessed with charming wives, and they have something to work for beside their own individual pleasure. Most of these Benedicts are yearling bridegrooms. The other five are unlucky bachelors who are likely to be caught out by some Brooklyn belles this season."[5] The previously wedded list included a big catch — Adonis Terry, who early in 1888 became a father of a baby boy. So "Bridegrooms" it was, though not all of the players were thrilled with the moniker. Doc Bushong wrote to a friend: "Do you fancy the name? I don't."[6]

Brooklyn's baseball bliss was undercut by a bubbling backlash against Charley Byrne, who had played a key role in doubling the American Association's basic admission price to 50 cents in 1888. As one writer to the *Brooklyn Eagle* complained about Byrne: "He has promised for the last two years to give the patrons of Washington Park better ball and he did not do so. He offered the excuse that he could not get better men. Now this year he has engaged better players and he wants the public to pay for them right away. If Manager Byrne prizes his team so high and has combined to charge 50 cents with the other managers of the association, I hope he will find out that it will not be such a success as he thought it would be."[7]

"We voted for the increase because we deemed it not only a wise and business like change, but it really became a matter of self preservation," Byrne responded. "The Brooklyn Club today can state without fear of contradictions that to strengthen its team for next year it has paid out more money than has ever been paid by an individual club since professional base ball was established and its salary list will be larger than paid by any club in the country, with the possible exception of the Detroit champions."[8]

Whatever the price of admission, Brooklyn fans were buzzing about the new team. Rain, not higher ticket prices, held the crowd to 2,586 on

April 18 when the Bridegrooms opened the season against Cleveland. The gates at Washington Park opened at 2:00 P.M. as Conterno's Forty-Seventh Regiment Band entertained. Co-owners Byrne, Abell and Doyle stood just inside the entrance welcoming patrons and soothing bigwigs who under the new revenue-sharing rule no longer received free tickets. At 3:40 P.M. a bell rang, and the crowd roared as the Brooklyn team marched onto the field in their new uniforms, led by new manager McGunnigle. The Bridegrooms was one of three teams that year to introduce pinstripe uniforms. Their caps were maroon and white in alternate stripes, with shirts and pants covered by checks in the same color. The *Eagle* deemed the new duds quite "handsome." The *New York Times* sniffed that the Brooklyn players "might have been mistaken for a troupe of acrobats, so gorgeously hued was their apparel."[9]

Brooklyn manager Bill McGunnigle was a fancy dresser and did not wear a uniform during games. "One of the most interesting sights of the game," a sportswriter once wrote, "was Billy McGunnigle. Arrayed in a beautiful pair of lavender trousers and weighed down with a solid gold watch, he capered near the bench" (National Baseball Hall of Fame Library).

Gunner McGunnigle, unlike most managers, didn't wear a uniform. The natty, mustachioed Mac was attired in a dark suit, a bright tie, a shirt with a high white starched collar, a derby hat and black patent leather shoes. "It's only a good looking man like yours truly who could wear patent leathers on the field and get away with it without getting shot at," Gunner once joked to a reporter.[10] Sometimes McGunnigle wore baseball shoes with removable spikes, a shoe that he had invented. In those days, most ballparks didn't have dressing rooms for visiting players and umpires, which required them to change at the hotel before games. Their spiked shoes, hotel managers complained, tore up the carpets. McGunnigle and Samuel Kingston, a Brockton shoemaker, came up with and patented the "Detachable Sole-Plate and Spike for Boots and Shoes" (patent number 383,133). American Association umpires wore the shoes during the 1888 season.[11]

McGunnigle mapped a four-man pitching rotation for his first season — Bobby Caruthers, Adonis Terry, Al Mays and 21-year-old rookie Mickey Hughes. Dave Foutz would be a part-time hurler but mainly play right field. First baseman Dave Orr was picked as captain. Caruthers was the starting pitcher for the first game. At 4:00 P.M. umpire Frank Gaffney, dressed in a blue uniform with an Irish green cap, called, "Play ball," and a new era in Brooklyn baseball began. Brooklyn third baseman George Pinkney opened the game with a liner that was too hot for the bare-handed pitcher to handle. After "Pink" reached third on a passed ball and stolen base, he scored the game's first run when the shortstop couldn't field second sacker Bill McClellan's hot grounder. Caruthers reached base on yet another error, and Darby O'Brien's single to left sent both base runners home, giving Brooklyn a 3 to 0 lead to the crowd's great delight.

Caruthers gave up two quick hits, but new catcher Doc Bushong threw out both runners trying to steal. In its opening game, Brooklyn roared to a 10 to 1 win.[12] The team followed this up with a 14 to 3 win the next day behind Adonis Terry, the only remaining player from Brooklyn's first team in 1883. Brooklyn made it three straight behind Al Mays. Then on Sunday at Ridgewood, McGunnigle sent out 5' 6" Mickey Hughes, who shut out Cleveland 3 to 0.

The locals were impressed with the Brooklyn players. "They are working together very harmoniously, and certainly Manager McGunnigle is winning the good opinions of the men by the quiet, effective methods he adopts with them and the attention he gives to their welfare," the *Brooklyn Eagle* said. "They are all well aware of the fact that they are employed by a club which has obtained an enviable name for the liberal treatment accorded to its team players who have given the club faithful service, and also that with the players the club now has on the team there is the material at hand to win the pennant race."[13]

Brooklyn fans were just getting to know McGunnigle. He was quiet in public but quite a talker on the bench, sometimes driving his players to near distraction with batting tips. "A party who claims to have heard manager McGunnigle's directions to his team on the bench is of the opinion that he interferes too much with their freedom of movement in batting," *Sporting Life* reported. He provides so much detailed instruction for the proper technique, "until the poor fellows had to work out problems in logarithms before they could tell just what to do with any particular curve."[14]

Beneath Gunner's quiet exterior breathed a competitive fire — and a stubborn streak. Most managers were also players, such as Charley Comiskey of the St. Louis Browns and Chicago's Cap Anson. Some players and umpires questioned just how much power a bench manager had on the field, as McGunnigle discovered in an early May game in Philadelphia when former Browns player Curt Welch pulled the old Kelly trick of cutting home from second base. The home crowd was "laughing and shouting at Welch's cuteness in cutting third base" when McGunnigle yelled out to pitcher Dave Foutz, "Dave, throw that ball to third." Foutz threw the ball to Pinkney, who stepped on third. The umpire promptly called Welch out. Philadelphia contended that McGunnigle had no right to coach from the players' bench, and team captain Harry Stovey demanded that Gunner be removed from the bench. Umpire Bob Ferguson — the same man who had scored the winning run in the old Brooklyn Atlantics game against the Cincinnati Red Stockings — agreed. "Ferguson talked soothingly to Manager McGunnigle, the crowd yelled and the players talked among themselves, but McGunnigle would not move. After ten minutes delay the game proceeded, with McGunnigle still holding the fort."[15]

By late May, Brooklyn was locked in a tight race with Cincinnati for first place. Despite grumblings about the 50-cent admission, the team was drawing large home crowds. On May 27, the 4,875 who turned out at Ridgewood got their money's worth. Brooklyn was up 4 to 0 in the top of the ninth inning with Louisville coming to bat. Adonis Terry, with his "well disguised change of pace bothering Louisville batsmen greatly," had yet to give up a hit. With two out, Louisville's most feared hitter, Pete Browning, stepped to the plate. He hit an easy grounder back to Terry, who recorded his second no-hitter in three years.[16]

Brooklyn had reeled off six straight wins when first-place Cincinnati came to town for a May 29 double-header. Long before the 10 A.M. game time the free seats on the right side of Washington Park were all occupied, and the grandstand was nearly filled. More than 5,000 people were in the stands when Umpire Gaffney, this time dressed in a brown uniform, began play. It took 11 innings, but Brooklyn won 4 to 3 behind Terry, who also batted in the winning run. The Bridegrooms were on a roll. On June 2, another 5,000 were on hand to see Brooklyn score its eighth straight win behind Caruthers, as catcher Doc Bushong "astonished the crowd with two two-baggers and a single."[17] Brooklyn was now in first place. The "picked" squad of stars was playing like a close-knit team.

Still, Manager McGunnigle fretted about the fielding of second baseman Bill McClellan, one of the last of the left-handed second sackers. That led Charley Byrne to acquire a surprising choice for the spot — Boston's "Black Jack" Burdock. True, Burdock was one of baseball's most brilliant fielders, but he was 36 years old and a known drinker. "If anybody had said to me a year or two ago that I would ever buy Burdock, I would have thought he was crazy," the Brooklyn president said. "Burdock has been in Boston 11 years. He was once the idol of the town. Then when he fell off a bit in his play, perhaps through indiscretions, the very people who once praised him the most denounced him the worst. He has a wife and five children at Brooklyn, and for several years he has asked me to buy his release. 'All I want is a chance,' is what he said, and 'a chance' is what he shall have."[18] Added the *New York*

Second baseman "Black Jack" Burdock played in the major leagues for 18 seasons until he was 39 years old. He lived in Brooklyn, where he died in 1931 at age 79 (Library of Congress).

Times: "It is hoped that 'Burdy' has seen the folly of his ways and will in the future behave himself. He is a good ball player, but ball playing and barleycorn don't mix well."[19]

"Burdy" made his debut July 3 as Brooklyn won at Cincinnati, saving two runs with a stop that "was greatly admired." He also soon began showing off his other side. On July 21, after Brooklyn beat Philadelphia, Byrne called for Burdock to come up to his office. There he introduced him to a Detective McGrath, who proceeded to arrest the player. The charge? Miss Tillie Brown, of 365 Fifth Avenue, had accused a very drunk Burdock of "outraging public decency" by trying to kiss her.[20] Eventually, a judge acquitted Burdock of the charges when Miss Brown didn't show up in court, but urged him to stop drinking and play ball.

While Brooklyn fans were continuing to pour into Washington Park despite the 50-cent admission, Charley Byrne was bothered by one fallout from the revenue sharing plan: the banning of free admission for women. At a special meeting in St. Louis in July, Byrne, with strong support from Chris Von der Ahe, won approval for teams to admit ladies free on Mondays and for 25 cents for weekday games. The move did not win the approval of the male chauvinists of the day, however. One of them was Cincinnati columnist O.P. Caylor, who also had been involved in founding the American Association and had been a manager for three seasons with the Cincinnati Reds and New York Mets.

Caylor called the Ladies Day change a "neat advertising scheme" for Charley Byrne, adding:

> It may be gallant and all that. But, to be practical and business-like, suppose we ask why ladies should be admitted to ball games for a less price than gentlemen? Every lady who goes to see a game occupies a seat and sometimes slightly bulges over onto that seat next to her. She usually wears a lighthouse hat and shuts off the view of the fellow behind her as effectively as a post or column, and even more so, for the post or column does not keep bobbing about from side to side, keeping time with the fellow who is trying to dodge it. If the lady enjoys the game she enjoys it more than half a dollar's worth, and as she doesn't have the great privilege of huzzahing and yelling herself hoarse at a good play or calling the umpire a thief and a robber, she should be allowed to express her intense enjoyment by the price she pays for the privileges. As for those ladies who attend games and don't know a base hit from a score board and put in the time telling her escort about horrid Miss Smith, or asking whether the bat is made out of rubber or whalebone such ladies, we say, ought to be charged a dollar for her privileges.[21]

As it turned out, some American Association teams that competed in the same city with National League squads, such as Philadelphia, needed more than discounts for ladies to keep fans coming to the park. By August, the association decided to return to the basic admission of 25 cents to better compete against the 50-cent National League. The receipt-sharing also was reduced.

Meantime, the "silver plated" Bridegrooms headed to St. Louis for the first time since acquiring former Browns stars Caruthers, Foutz and Bushong. The Mound City welcomed their former heroes home as they rode in a grand parade in their honor, complete with about 20 horse-drawn carriages and a brass band. The "Big Three" returned the favor by leading Brooklyn to four straight wins over the retooled Browns. More than 6,000 people turned out for the first game to see Caruthers beat his old team 6 to 2 as Dave Foutz banged three hits. The Bridegrooms won the second game 6 to 3 as St. Louis couldn't solve Mickey Hughes's "puzzling delivery." Caruthers came back to pitch two more wins in two days as St. Louis fans hooted controversial calls by umpire Bob Ferguson.

Der Boss Chris Von der Ahe was apoplectic. As usual, he tried to blame his Brooklyn rival, Charley Byrne. "With each defeat the 'genial German' had been growing more furious and after the fourth straight last Tuesday he fairly boiled over," *Sporting Life* reported. "He publicly accused Umpire Ferguson, an honest, incorruptible man, of intentionally umpiring to favor Brooklyn; charged Byrne with tampering with the Browns and announced he would not play the Browns in Brooklyn unless another umpire than Ferguson acted." Von der Ahe claimed that Ferguson, a lifelong resident of Brooklyn, favored his hometown team. "He has given men bases on balls when they should have been called out on strikes, and he has given Brooklyn the benefit of every doubt," said Von der Ahe. He contended that Brooklyn's Byrne had used his position as head of the schedule committee to ensure that Ferguson umpired Brooklyn's games, "and there is no telling where he [Byrne] will stop unless he is called down."[22]

The tampering charge involved star St. Louis outfielder Tip O'Neill. While the Browns were in Brooklyn, Tip told his old teammate Doc Bushong that he wanted to get away from St. Louis, too. "Well," Bushong responded, "if you want to get away, and can get your release, Brooklyn can use you." When Brooklyn co-owner Gus Abell saw newspaper articles that St. Louis was considering sending O'Neill to Philadelphia in order to get Curt Welch back, Abell suggested to Bushong that he write his old teammate about coming to Brooklyn. Byrne also wired Von der Ahe that Brooklyn would be interested in acquiring O'Neill if he were to be released.[23]

After the losses to Brooklyn, Der Boss laid off O'Neill without pay, and for good measure fined workhorse twirler Silver King $100 for not pitching well. "I think O'Neill wants to go to Brooklyn, and Bushong and other members of that team have been working on him for some time, and ever since O'Neill has been wanting to quit playing ball entirely," Von der Ahe said. "He's been playing for his release but he'll never get it. I wouldn't let him go to Brooklyn for any consideration."[24]

St. Louis outfielder Tip O'Neill (misspelled O'Neil on card) was born in Canada. After his playing days he owned a saloon in Montreal. He died in a streetcar accident in 1915 at age 57. U.S. Democratic House Speaker Thomas "Tip" O'Neill of Massachusetts took his nickname from the baseball-playing O'Neill (Library of Congress).

Charley Byrne strongly denied the tampering charges. "Ordinarily I would make no answer to any charge or insinuation the St. Louis president would make, especially while he is suffering from the late defeats," Byrne said. "Everybody knows Chris—how impulsive and unreasonable he is in defeat, how generous, patronizing and altogether lovely in the hour of victory. However, there are many people apt to take as the Gospel truth a charge published by a journal, particularly if the charge is one affecting a person's reputation, that to remain silent means a confession of guilt. The Brooklyn Club has not tampered with Mr. O'Neill of the St. Louis Club."

As for Von der Ahe's complaints about the umpire, Byrne added: "I thought the time had come when blaming an umpire for a defeat had passed. What in the name of heaven does Von der Ahe expect anyhow? He has disposed of the best men his team ever had, received gladly a large money consideration thereafter and has not spent a dollar on strengthening his team or to fill the vacancies he made, and yet when he doesn't win every game, as of old, he charges his defeats to every considerable thing but the proper one, viz, that his team is weaker than of old, and even the genius of a Comiskey cannot make it win."[25]

To many in the baseball world Von der Ahe's diatribes against Umpire Ferguson and Byrne were getting out of hand. "This undignified row in the American Association, started by hot-headed Mr. Von der Ahe's charges against Mr. Byrne, has grown in intensity," *Sporting Life* lamented. At a special meeting, the American Association's board of directors found no grounds to question Ferguson's integrity. While the "Brooklyn Club has been indiscreet" in instructing a player to communicate with another team's player, the directors also saw no need to take any action for "tampering."[26]

The fact was that both O'Neill and King had been ill, and the Von der Ahe charges of slacking were baseless. Maybe Der Boss was trying to light a fire under his team with his tantrums. If so, it worked. By late July, his Browns moved into first place while an ominous pattern began emerging with Byrne's Bridegrooms. The team's sick list was growing rapidly. Pitcher Al Mays was out with cholera, Dave Foutz had a bad knee, George Smith had a leg injury, and catcher Bill Holbert was suffering from heat exhaustion. Caruthers was in poor health, even stirring rumors that he had a heart problem. Moreover, now that the rules had been changed so that he no longer could order the pitcher to throw the "high" pitches he favored, his batting slumped.

In addition, captain Dave Orr had missed more than 30 games because of rheumatism. At least that's what he complained about. Just before a home series with first-place St. Louis, the team doctor went over to check on the big first baseman. Orr's landlady said her tenant wasn't at home but she thought he had gone over to the Coney Island amusement park area. When Orr called in the next day to say he was too ill to play that day's game, Byrne hit the roof. "Just when we needed him, too. He played the same trick on the Mets, but he won't play it on us. We wanted him especially in these three games with St. Louis." Byrne suspended Orr without pay "until he concludes to play ball and discontinue monkey-shines." Darby O'Brien was named the new captain.[27]

To fill the gap, Byrne made yet another acquisition, purchasing 24-year-old Tom Burns from Baltimore for $3,500. Burns was the same loud-mouthed outfielder who had played for the Harrisburg toughs against Brooklyn in the team's first year in the Interstate Association in 1883. Burns, known as "Oyster" because he sold shellfish in the offseason, seemed an unlikely choice for a team seeking "harmony." He had a loud, irritating voice and a personality to match. Said one of his Baltimore teammates: "Personally, I like Burns, but it was a good thing that he was released. He was a disturber and one of the worst that ever played ball. His disposition was very bad, and he made it unpleasant for any of the boys that crested him. He is what you would call a bulldozer. McGunnigle may be able to handle Burns, but I doubt it."[28] At the same time, the stocky Burns was a powerful left-handed hitter who could play both the outfield and infield. And he had a fire that Byrne figured could help ignite the Brooklyn team.

As the team prepared for a do-or-die western road trip in early August, Manager McGunnigle was seething over press reports that he was merely an empty suit on the bench, and that Charley Byrne really ran the team. "I have seen it in print, and I understand that it started in the West, that I am only a figure-head in the Brooklyn Club, and simply carry out Mr. Byrne's orders. This is false all the way through," he told reporters. "Mr. Byrne has always treated me courteously and never has interfered with my management of the nine. I say this more in justice to him than to gratify my personal pride."[29] In fact, Gunner was in full

Tom "Oyster" Burns was called "the noisiest man that ever played on the Brooklyn team. His voice reminds one of a buzz-saw" (*New York Clipper*).

control on the field. According to Brooklyn executive Charley Ebbets, McGunnigle "was really the first manager Brooklyn ever had. Prior to that Mr. Byrne had been the actual manager although others had worn the title."[30]

Brooklyn headed into St. Louis to face the first-place Browns, hoping to repeat its sweep of early June and get back on track. More than 5,000 people turned out at Sportsman's Park for the first game to see the Browns edge the Bridegrooms 1 to 0 with Silver King beating Mickey Hughes. Nat Hudson pitched a 7 to 0 shutout over Dave Foutz in the second game, and St. Louis swept the series as King again bested Hughes 4 to 2. For the Bridegrooms, the honeymoon clearly was over. "This ended the second tour West and Brooklyn returns home occupants of fourth place, with a terrible uphill fight before them from now until October to even secure second place in the race," the *Eagle* reported. "The trip was a test of McGunnigle's management, and the result is eight defeats out of twelve games."[31] Already names were being floated as possible replacements for Gunner in 1889.

By the start of a final September road trip, Brooklyn was down and almost out. On September 5, Terry threw one pitch against Louisville and left the game with a sore arm; he was expected to be out for the remainder of season. Shortstop Germany Smith broke his arm when a Cincinnati base runner jumped on him. Brooklyn left for the trip without Terry, Smith, Burns and Caruthers. The team was down to 12 players, including three catchers and three pitchers. Critics wondered why McGunnigle stuck with Burdock at second base. Though Burdy's fielding was second to none, he literally wasn't hitting his weight, which was only 158 pounds. He would end the season batting .122. There was even speculation that the team's blushing bridegrooms were expending too much of their energy at home in the bedroom than on the field.

After all the turmoil over peddling his star players, Von der Ahe cruised to an unprecedented fourth straight pennant, thanks in large part to the very players he had maligned. Outfielder Tip O'Neill led the league in batting with a .335 average. Pitcher Silver King won a league-high 45 games after hurling 64 complete games and pitching an astounding 585 innings. The St. Louis owner had rounded up enough decent players to enable Manager Comiskey to do his magic. It was Von der Ahe's greatest triumph yet. Best of all, it won him revenge against Charley Byrne. "They laughed at the Wooden-Shoed Dutchman," he said. "I sold my five best players and then turned around and picked up boys around town on the sandlots and won the pennant."[32]

As soon as the Browns' season ended in Cincinnati, the Dutchman pulled out all the stops. The New York team, now known as the Giants, won the National League pennant, and the first game of the World's Series was scheduled for the Polo Grounds. Von der Ahe wired Al Spinks, the sports editor of the *St. Louis Globe-Democrat*, asking him to arrange a special train to take all of Der Boss's friends and the press to New York with free fare, food and hotels. The Browns team would join up on the train in Columbus, Ohio. Be sure, he said, to "fix up the train in fine style and to see that there is plenty to eat and drink on board."

Spinks checked with the local agent for the Vandalia and Pennsylvania Railroad Line, who responded: "Why, Al, it's nonsense talking about a special train. One like Chris wants will cost $20,000 for the round trip." Informed of the advice, Von der Ahe responded: "Tell the damn passenger agent to mind his own business." So the "Champagne Special" was arranged, and rolled on to New York with a banner on the side reading, "St. Louis Browns — Four Time Pennant–Winners." New York prevailed in the World's Series, winning 6 games to 4. But this time, Von der Ahe wasn't all that upset. In fact, before the team and its fans returned home, he told every player and every man on the train to go to a New York tailor, get a new suit and send the bill to the boss of the St. Louis Browns.[33]

The Dutchman's greatest reward was seeing Brooklyn's Charley Byrne being made a laughingstock. One Louisville crank told Byrne, "You can spend $50,000 on players and buy all the stars in the Association and put them in your team. Then next year Charley Comiskey will come along with his gang of Job Lots and knock you out of the pennant again."[34] Needled the *Cincinnati Enquirer*: "It is reported that Charley Byrne will lecture this Fall. The title of the lecture will be 'How the St. Louis Dutchman sold me $20,000 worth of ball players and then beat me out of the championship with a King high, which he had held up his sleeve.'"[35]

Despite another failure to win the pennant, there was no gloom in Brooklyn. In late September, the squad of stars came together, playing as a team as Manager McGunnigle came to know his "boys" better. Dave Orr was back hitting the ball; he would lead the team with a .305 average. Little Mickey Hughes was winning while working with catcher Bob Clark as Doc Bushong struggled in a season that he hit only .209. Hughes "has turned out to be one the surprises of the season," the *New York Clipper* said. "If he keeps on improving, he will be one of the greatest pitchers in the business before the close of another season. He and [catcher] Bob Clark make a great pair."[36] Third baseman George Pinkney, the *Clipper* reported, "is proving himself to be one of the greatest third basemen in the profession. Some of his stops of hot hit balls are simply marvelous."[37]

(By the mid–1880s, many — but not all — infielders had begun wearing crude fielding gloves on both hands, basically thick leather work gloves with the fingers cut off. The first infielder to use a glove was Providence shortstop Arthur Irwin. During a game in 1884, Irwin broke a finger on his left hand. As a result, so he bought a buckskin glove that was too big for his hand and sewed the fingers together. He discovered he could field better even with his injured finger and kept using it after his finger healed.[38] Soon, he was marketing the glove for others to use. Even with the gloves, good infielders still made 90 to 100 errors in a season, compared with generally fewer than 20 today. Outfielders and pitchers continued to play without gloves.)

The Brooklyn comeback of 1888 continued, even though health issues forced Caruthers to end his season in early October, finishing with 29 wins and 15 losses. The Bridegrooms closed with 10 straight wins at home in October. On October 13, Brooklyn moved past Philadelphia into second place as Mickey Hughes beat the Athletics 4 to 2. Hughes ended his rookie year with 25 wins. Dave Foutz pitched three wins down the stretch, compiling a record of 12 and 7 for the year. He also batted .277 and knocked in 99 runs. Terry came back to win one more game, pitching a three-hitter to beat Baltimore 5 to 2, giving him a record of 13 wins and eight losses for the season. Third baseman Pinkney led the association in runs scored with 134. The feat won him the prize from Pike's haberdashery in Brooklyn for most runs scored on the team. His reward: "One-half dozen shirts, one-dozen handkerchiefs, one-dozen collars, one-dozen pairs of cuffs, one-dozen pair hose, one-dozen ties, two suits of underwear, one pair of suspenders, two pair kid gloves."[39]

Brooklyn finished in second place, its best showing since entering the American Association in 1884. What's more, the team finished first in one important category — home attendance, with more than 245,000 paying customers going through the turnstiles at Washington Park. The season was a very highly profitable one for the Brooklyn owners. But would the big finish be enough for Manager McGunnigle to keep his job? In late October, Byrne ended the suspense when he announced that McGunnigle would be retained to lead the 1889 team. "We have deemed it but just to give him another season's trial," the Brooklyn president said, noting that the many team injuries "were in no way his fault or due to his alleged mismanagement." Byrne also was swayed by the fact that the players unanimously wanted McGunnigle back. "I never saw a more gratified set of men than I had in this office today when the fact was given out that we had signed Mr. McGunnigle to manage the team for 1889," he said. "Deeds speak louder than words and the eagerness of our players to sign with us again for 1889 testified in an unquestionable manner" to their support for the manager.[40]

The decision generally won praise from baseball observers. "It was a very wise move on the part of the Brooklyn Club to engage Manager McGunnigle," the *New York Clipper* said. "He did exceedingly well during the past season. It is argued by the Brooklyn management that if he landed the team in second place the first year he should do even better with another trial. McGunnigle is on very friendly terms with all of the players who to a man were anxious to have him manage next year."[41]

Despite Von der Ahe's boasting, despite the carping about "silver plated" players, both Charley Byrne and Gunner McGunnigle suddenly had confidence that the American Association flag would soon fly over Washington Park. Not for the last time, the cry went up in Brooklyn, "Wait till next year!"

Chapter Six

A Bridge Too High?

As an ever-optimistic Irishman, Gunner McGunnigle had no doubt about the 1889 baseball season. The Brooklyn manager vowed to "make a head long plunge from the top of one of the towers of the Brooklyn Bridge into the East River" if the Bridegrooms didn't capture the pennant.[1]

This would be Gunner's second year as skipper of Brooklyn. For this competitive man, it was a chance to prove that he could lead a major league team to a championship. McGunnigle was a player's manager. He imposed few rules and expected his "boys" to behave harmoniously as a team. "I will acknowledge now that there was a little discord in the team last year. Some of the players did not work in harmony either with the players or manager," he said. "The result was, of course, disastrous to us. I saw that fueling and tried to block it, but failed. Certain changes have been made, and I can truthfully say there is no discord now. We have a great team, though not only of ball players, but of perfect gentleman."[2]

There certainly was reason to be rosy. Brooklyn was loaded with good pitching. McGunnigle planned to use a four-man pitching rotation of Bob Caruthers, Adonis Terry, Mickey Hughes and stocky Tom Lovett, a newcomer from the Western League signed by Charley Byrne for more than $3,000. To finally best the Browns, Byrne further opened the club's wallet to plug remaining weak spots. He shelled out $3,000 to Louisville to outbid other teams for the services of 26-year-old Hubbard "Hub" Collins to be the new second baseman, replacing Jack Burdock who had been released. The speedy, 5'8" Collins ironically was a huge fan of the Anheuser-Busch Brewing Company in St. Louis, and wore a gold and silver watch charm with the company's emblem — an A and an eagle. To fit in with the "Bridegrooms," Collins even got married in January of 1889.

Late in the 1888 season, Byrne also had snapped up John Corkhill, the star centerfielder of the Cincinnati Red Stockings. The 31-year-old Corkhill, known as "Pop" because of his receding hairline, was a former Philadelphia patrolman and was considered one of the best out fielders in baseball. To shore up the bench, Byrne acquired 29-year-old Joe Visner, who could play both outfield and catcher. Visner was a hard hitter, but his throwing as catcher was said to be a "trifle erratic." The Bridegrooms even adopted a live "little puny monkey" from a Brooklyn policeman as a good luck mascot. Shortstop Germany Smith was put in charge of the little fellow and planned to dress him in a tiny Brooklyn uniform.[3]

After his Coney Island contretemps, Dave Orr was shipped off to the new American Association team in Columbus, Ohio, along with pitcher Al Mays. Lanky Dave Foutz replaced Orr at first base. His teammates also unanimously picked him as team captain. This was far more than a ceremonial decision because the authority of a team captain on the field nearly matched that of the manager. Indeed, on some teams the manager and the captain were one and the same, as with Charley Comiskey in St. Louis and Cap Anson of the National League Chicago White Stockings. The captain was expected to help coach and even discipline his teammates, and he was the only team member who was allowed to "kick," or complain, to the umpire. Unlike the pugnacious Comiskey and Anson, Foutz was a gentlemanly man, who, though highly competitive, wasn't the type to get in the faces of his teammates. Foutz took his new duty seriously and predicted a winning campaign.

Brooklyn second-sacker Hub Collins led the American Association in doubles with 31 in 1888 and led the National League in runs scored with 148 in 1890 (*New York Clipper*).

Spring of 1889 was eventful around the world. A company that would become the Coca-Cola Company was incorporated in Atlanta, Georgia. Benjamin Harrison was sworn in as the twenty-second president of the United States. In New York, the *Wall Street Journal* began publication. The Oklahoma land rush began as thousands of horse-and-buggy settlers rushed to claim land in the Oklahoma Territory — only to find some already claimed by early birds known as "Sooners." The Eiffel Tower opened in Paris to jeers from the French people who initially considered the structure an eyesore. And, with scant notice, Adolph Hitler was born in Austria-Hungary.

In Brooklyn, all thoughts were on baseball. The *Brooklyn Eagle* stoked the hopes of hometown cranks sky-high with its pre-season hoopla. That the team "is better prepared to reach the championship goal which the club has been striving for since they entered the association arena in 1884 is another assured fact, the Brooklyn team for 1889 not only being stronger in batting ability and in base running, but in that most desirable essential, harmony in the ranks," the *Brooklyn Eagle* said.[4]

Early in the year, Charley Byrne traveled across the bridge to the Manhattan den of the New York Giants to try to arrange some exhibition games with the reigning world champions. Giants owner John Day was reluctant, figuring that his squad had nothing to gain, but added: "If you challenge my team, I will have to respond." Byrne did, and three games were arranged for mid–April with the winner of each contest to get all of the receipts from that match up. The move proved a real coup for Brooklyn when the Giants subsequently lost their lease on their home field at the Polo Grounds, which by April was being torn down. As a result, all three games were played in Brooklyn before large crowds at Washington Park.

The excitement reflected the rivalry between Brooklyn and New York, one in which the Brooklyn side suffered a definite inferiority complex. Though the Brooklyn Bridge had connected the two cities in 1883, a huge gap remained. Brooklyn had grown rapidly in the 1880s, to about 800,000 people, and was the nation's fourth-largest city. Top-ranked New York had swelled to more than 1.5 million residents[5] The culture and economic gaps were even wider. New York was the city of the upper class, home to Wall Street, Broadway and Park Avenue, the theater and the garment industry. Brooklyn was the city of working stiffs laboring in sugar refining plants, slaughterhouses, ironworks and dockyards. (In 1898, Brooklyn residents would narrowly vote to join New York as one big city, a move some Brooklynites still refer to as "the mistake of '98.") Fans from both sides of the Brooklyn Bridge swarmed to the pre-season games in early April in what would become a lasting rivalry between the Brooklyn team and the Giants.

On April 13, in the third game of the series, Brooklyn "achieved the most noteworthy victory in the history of the club," according to the *Brooklyn Eagle*. Never mind that it was a mere exhibition game. The Bridegrooms defeated the world champion New York Giants 4 to 0 even though the Giants fielded their top pitcher, Tim Keefe, and legendary catcher Buck Ewing. The cross-river rivalry drew more than 8,000 people, the biggest ever for a spring exhibition game in Brooklyn.[6] Forget that the Giants had clobbered the Bridegrooms in the first two games; the win in the third contest meant that for one glorious day Brooklyn reigned supreme over the champs from across the bridge in what might be a harbinger of a fall World's Series. The glorious scenario was now set. Brooklyn would roar through its opening road trip and then return in triumph to Washington Park in an inevitable march to the pennant. Unfortunately, somebody forgot to send the script to the opposing teams.

Brooklyn got off to a bad start on Good Friday in Philadelphia as the Athletics, led by captain Harry Stovey, bopped the Bridegrooms 4 to 1. Not to worry. Brooklyn recovered the next day, edging the Athletics 9 to 8 before a capacity crowd of more than 10,000 people. Then came the deluge. The rest of the series was told by the headlines in the *Brooklyn Eagle*: "WON BY THE ATHLETICS, The Brooklyns Hit Hard and Badly Beaten." "BAD BATTING Costs the Brooklyn Ball Players Another Game." The Bridegrooms moved on to Baltimore, but the headlines repeated the same sorry theme: "STILL LOSING, President Byrne No Doubt Sad That His Players Don't Do Better." Byrne was more worried than he let on. "Isn't there a song about a cat that always comes back?" he asked hopefully. But at this point, he figured there was nothing more that he could do to strengthen the team. He instead crossed his fingers in hopes that the team he had built would play up to its payroll.

But the bad news kept coming: "LOST ONE MORE, Brooklyn's Lengthening Record of Defeats." "STILL BAD LUCK, Another Defeat for the Brooklyn Team." The Bridegrooms finished the road trip with a record of one win and six losses. "The enthusiasts in other Association cities are laughing at Brooklyn's poor start in the race," said *Sporting Life*. "There can be no excuse for these repeated defeats. The Brooklyn public demand better ball, and President Byrne ought to see that they get it."[7] A former New York

Mets player on the Bridegrooms squad anonymously complained that the Bridegrooms weren't tough enough: "Unless you can command respect and obedience, you are a mere tadpole in the puddle. We started out with the idea of respecting the rights of everybody and stepped on nobody's toes. We have not deviated from that path."[8]

The Bridegrooms headed back to Brooklyn looking up from seventh place to play their first home game against the Columbus Solons, nicknamed the "Babies" because this was their first year in the association. Its captain was Brooklyn's former first sacker, big Dave Orr. The Brooklyn fans, having had their hopes boosted to the heavens, were stunned by their heroes' stumbling start. When the Bridegrooms took the field in their home uniforms of light gray and blue, the welcome was many degrees below global warming.

"'Which is the home team, the dark blues or the light grays?' was a question asked by a stranger at yesterday's contest at Washington Park and it was not a surprising question under the circumstances, for never before did our local team receive the cold shoulder from the home crowd as they did yesterday," the *Brooklyn Eagle* reported.[9] The only love was shown to former Bridegroom Orr, who was presented with a floral horseshoe when he first came to bat. The atmosphere didn't get any warmer when Brooklyn had to settle for a 9 to 9 tie with Columbus when the game was stopped because of rain.

The cool reception infuriated the *Eagle* correspondent, 65-year-old Henry Chadwick, the great baseball writer. Chadwick was born in England but moved to Brooklyn in 1837 as a young boy. He grew up to become the most influential baseball writer in the history of the game. He invented the box score and the method of scoring still used today. After tirelessly promoting "base ball" as the national pastime for decades, he was known as the "Father of Base ball," though with his white hair and short beard these days he looked more like Father Christmas. A blatant supporter of the home team — as were most sportswriters in those days — Father Chadwick also yearned for a Brooklyn pennant. He now rose to the Brooklyn players' defense.

"Hitherto on occasions of their returns from disasters abroad, they have been received at home with an encouraging pat on the back by their club patrons, as much as to say, 'Never mind, boys, you had hard luck; go in and rally in the old Brooklyn style, as your Atlantic ancestors did in the early days of the game.' But this year an exceptional cold shoulder was given them." In words for the ages, he wrote of fickle fans: "Base ball crowds are like all other crowds; they worship at the shrine of success only, and the majority are only apt, when occasion offers, to help kick the man who is down." Chadwick predicted: "There is an innate strength in the Brooklyn team which will bring them to the front in due time, when their more fortunate rivals will be growling at their hard luck."[10]

Poor Captain Foutz became the scapegoat for the team's sagging start. A New York writer commented: "The cranks have commenced in Brooklyn already. They want Orr back. Long Foutz is not fielding within twenty points of his last year's form, as they say, and they want 'fat Dave' back in his place."[11] The criticism wore on Foutz, so he went to Byrne and McGunnigle and asked to be relieved of captain duties in order to focus on playing first base. His bosses agreed and re-appointed left fielder Darby O'Brien as captain. O'Brien was reluctant to take on the post again, but he was a fiery competitor. "He is a good coacher, a virtue possessed but sparingly by Foutz," said *Sporting Life*.[12]

Legendary sportswriter Henry Chadwick created the symbol "K" for strikeouts. Chadwick said he chose K because it was the last letter in "struck" out and "is easier to remember in connection with the word than 'S'" (National Baseball Hall of Fame Library).

The captain switch likely made little difference. More important, as Chadwick had predicted, the Brooklyn team simply had too much talent to keep losing. Like a great battleship that had chugged down the wrong channel, the U.S.S. Bridegrooms slowly began to turn in the right direction by taking three of its next four games from the visiting Baltimore Orioles, with Bob Caruthers pitching the final win "with more of his old time skill than any game he has played this year," Chadwick reported. "These four games with the strong Baltimore team have fully shown that the home team possesses that innate strength which the *Eagle* gave them credit for the day of their return from their out of town visit. They have now got into their regular pace and with fine weather and crowd attendance — for the boys like to see a 'full house' as the actors do — they will yet show their strong rivals that the pennant is not to be had without the hardest kind of struggle while the Brooklyn team is in the race."[13] The Philadelphia team followed Baltimore to Washington Park, and the *Eagle* headline told a new story: "Three Straight Games Wrested from the Athletics."

Then came the most contentious contest of the early season. The game against Philadelphia was on Sunday, and the matchup drew the biggest crowd ever at Ridgewood Park, totaling 12,614 people. Only a few thousand could sit in the grandstand, the rest standing around the field. With no fences in the outfield, ropes were strung to hold back the crowd. Under special ground rules, balls into the crowd were doubles, the reason being that the pack would step back to allow a Brooklyn hit to role past for a possible home run, but would close ranks to block a Philadelphia hit.

How different newspapers described the events of this day provided a vivid view of the biases of hometown sportswriters. Here is how the hometown *Brooklyn Eagle* reported it:

> A more orderly Sunday gathering was never seen on a ball field. In fact at no period since the grounds have been occupied by the Brooklyn Club has a better assemblage of spectators been present at the park; and yet the crowd put a stop to play in the sixth inning of the contest by rushing in on the outfield until it was impossible to proceed with the game. There was no disturbance and no excitement beyond the fact that the spectators encroached upon the field, one portion starting the move and the others following like sheep.

In the bottom of the sixth inning, with the A's up 5 to 1, the crowd began to push in behind Philadelphia outfielders Curtis Welch and Harry Stovey,

> and while Foutz was at the bat the umpire called time and notified the Brooklyn officials that the field must be cleared. The ground officers went down to induce the crowd to stand back, as they had done the previous five innings, and Mr. Byrne and O'Brien tried their best to get them back, while Stovey and Welch — as dozens of men were ready to testify — told the crowd they could move in if

they liked, and they did so, and soon the Athletic players, who had gathered back of second base in a bunch, were surrounded, and it then became impossible to place the crowd back in their former position. Umpire Holland, seeing that the ground officials and Mr. Byrne had done their best to clear the field, and also that there was no possibility of having the contest resumed, called the game back to the last even five innings, which left the game a draw, 1 to 1.

By rule, the home team had to provide police security or a game would be forfeited. "Under the circumstances no claim of forfeit will hold good, especially in the view of the fact that positive proof can be presented showing that Stovey and Welch encouraged the crowd to break in," the *Eagle* reported. "They were in a hurry to close the game, so as to catch the train, and they knew that if the crowd broke in it would be likely to end in a forfeit. That it was their game because of the lead they had secured was a nonsensical claim."[14]

To summarize the Brooklyn view, a large yet orderly crowd had gathered at Ridgewood on a fine Sunday afternoon to enjoy the pure sport of baseball, and the overflow enthusiasts in the outfield had been lured onto the field of play by trouble-making Athletics players who wanted to win by forfeit and catch the early train to Philly. Here is how the same game was reported by *Sporting Life*, which was published in Philadelphia.

TROUBLE AT RIDGEWOOD

We have reached the blood-boiling notch in the baseball thermometer in this locality, and if the circus continues, the season will close with an epidemic of emotional inanity. The loss of three games straight by the Athletics set its very enthusiastic fans heading to the game. The several roads leading to the Mecca of the Sunday base ball contests were overrun. The general impression seemed to be that the Athletics were due to win, and a big pot of money in small bits was placed that way."

[In the sixth inning] Brooklyn had one man out and a runner at the bat when there was a stir among the crowd at the lower end of the out field, then a rush and some seven thousand people, moved by some power, dashed on the diamond, swallowed the players in a maelstrom of humanity, and the game was shut off at a point most critical. The dozen or more pay coppers fought valiantly with the crowd, President Byrne and Manager McGunnigle leading the forces, but they, too, were soon lost in the rush and the attempt to resume play might as well have been made against an ocean torrent. So the players of both teams made for the dressing rooms with the crowd howling for play, [but that was no longer possible]. President Byrne was mad. Order and a dollar's worth for your dollar is his hobby, and he told the crowd that had they kept their places they would have witnessed a full game, though the crowd then besieged the press box and the cry went up that Curt Welch was to blame, as

> he had invited those standing near him to encroach on the diamond. In addition, I was personally informed by a friend who made the trip across the bay in the ferry boat on the way to the Pennsylvania depot, on which the members of both teams were after the game, that Welch, in speaking of the rush, admitted that he had called in the crowd "just for fun."[15]

Byrne, figuring his boys might have rallied to win the game, appealed the ump's decision to the American Association's Judiciary Committee. Big mistake. A week later a three-man board, meeting at the Grand Hotel in Cincinnati, came back with its verdict. "Resolved: That it is the opinion of the Board of Directors that in the game played at Ridgewood, N.Y., on Sunday, May 5, 1889 between the Athletic Base Ball Club and the Brooklyn Base Ball Club, Umpire Holland erred in deciding the game a draw; and the Board of Directors hereby reverses the decision and gives the game to the Athletic Base Ball Club by a score of nine runs to none."[16] Instead of a tie, another game was added to Brooklyn's loss column.

Brooklyn followed good advice to make up for its early ills: Go West, young men. The team boarded the train to Louisville for the start of a long western trip. All major league teams traveled by train, from as far east as Boston to as far west as Kansas City. In the 1889 season, the Brooklyn Club would ride the rails for a total of 10,695 miles. Kansas City players would cover 12,360 miles.[17] The long trips were a mixed blessing. On the positive side, the traveling allowed teammates to bond. On the negative side, the boredom could lead to fracases, especially if drinking was involved, as it usually was. The drinking also turned out to be a problem on one train trip by the St. Louis Browns when Chris Von der Ahe's wife asked her husband for a late-night beer. Chris ordered the brew, only to be told the beer was all gone. The players had downed it all.

The Bridegrooms opened their western tour by roaring to four straight wins over Louisville and the Cincinnati Red Stockings, moving the team into second place. The surging Bridegrooms next headed to St. Louis for a showdown against the first-place Browns. Just as Brooklyn was rising, the Browns had hit a rough patch, demoralized by their combative, 38-year-old owner. Before a final road game at Louisville, St. Louis second sacker Yank Robinson sent a boy back to his hotel to fetch his padded sliding trousers. When the boy tried to re-enter the park, an elderly gatekeeper, a Mr. Niehouse, refused to let him in without a ticket. When Robinson got wind of the problem, he confronted the gatekeeper in "language that made his gray hairs stand on end," the *St. Louis Post-Dispatch* reported. Niehouse went to Von der Ahe "with tears in his eyes" to complain about Robinson. Der Boss hunted down Robinson on the players' bench and in full view of spectators delivered a tongue-lashing and $25 fine.

That evening, as the team was ready to board the Chicago, Burlington & Quincy Railroad to Kansas City, Robinson wouldn't go unless Von der Ahe removed the fine. Der boss refused. Most of the players backed Robinson and refused to board the train, which left without them. All except Robinson caught a later train.[18] The Browns proceeded to lose three straight games, raising suspicions that the players were trying to "get even" with Von der Ahe. But Arlie Latham retorted that "the charge that the team did not try to play is all bosh."[19]

Such tantrums were old hat in St. Louis, and Robinson was back on the field when Brooklyn arrived in town. The Bridegrooms seemed destined to fail their first big test as St. Louis captured the first two games. Manager McGunnigle didn't panic and stayed with his four-man pitching rotation by sending Adonis Terry out to face St. Louis ace Elton Chamberlain, nicknamed "Icebox" because of his cool demeanor. The result was "one of the greatest games ever played in St. Louis," the *New York Times* exulted.[20] Brooklyn tied the game in the ninth, and the teams battled into extra innings. Then "a hit by O'Brien, two sacrifices by Collins and Burns and a hit by Visner

Handsome St. Louis Browns pitcher Icebox Chamberlain was hot stuff to women admirers who flocked to see him pitch and sent him perfumed notes (Library of Congress).

did the work in the eleventh," the *Eagle* reported, with Brooklyn winning 5 to 3.

A report on the win was telegraphed back to Brooklyn and put up on a bulletin board outside the *Eagle* office. "The large crowd which read it broke out in enthusiastic cheers. Hats were thrown in the air, and men and boys screamed with delight. The cheers could be heard several blocks away."[21] Maybe the Brooklyn boys weren't such losers after all.

The joy was soon cut short by shocking news on the home front. Shortly after midnight on May 19, a fire broke out back in Washington Park. "The large grandstand at Washington Park, from which enthusiastic admirers of the Brooklyn Base Ball Club have for several seasons cheered the local players on to victory, is a dismal, charred and blackened ruin," the *Eagle* reported the next day. "Beside the stand some two hundred feet of the high board fence enclosing the ground on the Fifth Street side and the rear fences of three houses facing on Fifth Avenue were also consumed. The origin of the fire is a mystery, nor is it positively known in what portion of the grand stand the flames broke out. It is supposed, though, that they started in the dressing rooms under the old portion of the stand, on the Fifth street side. Several engines were promptly on the scene, but the fire had gained such headway that the firemen found it impossible to save the stand, and they confined their exertions mainly to saving adjacent property."[22]

St. Louis second baseman Yank Robinson never wore a glove in his 995 games in the major leagues. He died at age 34 of tuberculosis (Library of Congress).

Club secretary Charley Ebbets was on the case. He rushed to the scene and immediately began plans to rebuild. The park was covered by a $7,000 insurance policy, but it would cost three times that amount to rebuild. Ebbets vowed to have the park ready for the big series at the end of May against the Browns. Back in St. Louis, the Bridegrooms had their own fire to put out. The bulldozing Browns and their rowdy fans were determined to show that Brooklyn was only a pretender to the championship throne. More than 15,000 people — the largest home crowd in six years — jammed into Sportsman's Park, filling the standing room space and snaking two and three rows deep around the outfield. The St. Louis fanatics were in their usual form, howling insults at the Brooklyn players and the umpire. But Brooklyn passed the test, as Caruthers carved up his former teammates with a pitching gem that gave the Bridegrooms a 2–2 split in the four-game series on the Browns' home turf.

Brooklyn's pennant express was back on track. Next stop: Kansas City, where the Brooklyn roll continued with two straight wins, though a dispatch from the Kansas City reporter gave much of the credit for the second victory to umpire Frederick Goldsmith: "Aided by their efficient tenth man, Goldsmith, and playing in the greatest luck, the Brooklyns won a game from the Cowboys today." Chadwick quickly responded: "This is the old, worn out story sent by partisan reporters when their pet

Brooklyn team secretary Charles Ebbets served four years on the Brooklyn Board of Alderman and one year in the New York Assembly before running a losing campaign for the New York state senate (*New York Clipper*).

team that they bet on is whipped. It is always the umpire. Of course, the reporters up in their box can always judge a play better than the umpire who is on the spot."[23]

It was Brooklyn President Byrne who burnished his image when the team moved on to Columbus, Ohio, to face the Babies, led by crybaby-in-chief Dave Orr. The evening was cool and rainy, and the score was knotted 1 to 1 in the bottom of half of the second inning when Joe Visner walked for Brooklyn, stole second and continued on to third, where Umpire Goldsmith called him safe in a close play. Captain Orr saw it differently and raced over from first base to loudly protest. When Orr wouldn't stop kicking, the umpire fined him, then threw him out of the game. When Columbus refused to go on without its captain, Goldsmith awarded the game to Brooklyn by a 9 to 0 forfeit. Under the rules, the Columbus management would also be fined $1,500.

At this point, the Columbus manager told his counterpart McGunnigle that his boys were ready to play without Orr. The decision to continue the game was left up to Byrne, who was traveling with the team. Spurning a sure win — and not wishing to stick a fellow owner with a $1,500 fine — Byrne gave the O.K. and the game continued. In the fifth inning, Terry socked a homer over the left-field fence and Brooklyn went on to win 5 to 2. The *Ohio State Journal* in Columbus backed the umpire and Byrne — sort of: "After Goldsmith had refused to reverse his decision, wrong though it may have been, it was the duty of Captain Orr to return to his base and resume play.... President Byrne has enjoyed considerable unenviable notoriety for some time in connection with association matters, very unjustly, we believe, but we are bound to say in this case that he did the handsome thing when he might have made trouble on a technical point."[24]

Dave Orr wasn't about to forget. "I'll bet a month's salary we will beat 'em out of the championship," he told a reporter as the Brooklyn team rolled away from the park in horse-drawn carriages. "Oh, mamma, but it does me good to do up that crowd. I'll get even, god blast 'em," he said as he shook his beefy fist at the departing carriages.[25] Brooklyn ended its most successful western trip ever by winning 11 of 14 games. Even the *St. Louis Post-Dispatch* was impressed: "They are, by all odds, the strongest team that has visited here. The Browns have been fortunate in batting the visitors' pitchers but the Bridegrooms stand up and hit the ball squarely and hard."[26]

The winning streak threw a spotlight on Gunner McGunnigle as the thinking man's manager. "McGunnigle was the first of the great sign stealers," according to Lee Allen, the former official historian of baseball at the National Baseball Hall of Fame. "He was also the first manager to signal to players by waving a scorecard on the bench. Nervous as a sitting hen, McGunnigle also gave signs by tapping bats, drumming away as if he were a telegrapher."[27] Many Brooklyn players, including Bushong, Terry and Burns, said McGunnigle was the best manager they had ever played for.[28]

Gunner was a man of eccentric habits. On road trips, he always carried a canvas grip stuffed with items he might need in case of an emergency. These included: "One screw-driver, one big pewter spoon, one spool of thread, one bottle of liniment, one ball of twine, two needles, one roll of lint, one small bundle of absorbent cotton, one paper of tacks, one bottle of cough syrup, one box of matches, and last, but not least, the monstrous gilt horseshoe that Mac considered his mascot."[29] At first, McGunnigle ordered ice tea every day for his team to drink instead of iced water. The tea parties ended when Byrne saw the bills. The Brooklyn owner, an inveterate gum chewer, urged the men to chomp gum, especially on the road, instead of drinking water.[30]

The ever-inventive McGunnigle wanted to go even further. In 1889, the Edison Company had begun installing underground electrical lines in Brooklyn, perhaps inspiring the Bridegroom manager. One of his ideas "was what the boys called his electric heel tapper," *Sporting Life* reported. Mac's idea was to put a small metal plate in the batter's box that would be hooked up via an underground electrical wire to a button on the players' bench. The batters would put one foot on the plate, and McGunnigle would press the button to send shocks to them to signal what the pitcher was about to throw. He even called in an electrician to get a cost estimate, but the electrician explained how impractical the idea was. "In the first place," he said, "you would have to use a pretty strong current to make it of any value for the purpose, and that might prove dangerous. Then, again, it would not take long for the opposing batsmen to get onto the metal plate in the box, and that would spoil the scheme."

So McGunnigle reluctantly dropped the shock scheme. Before long, the innovative manager had another idea, "which was even more startling in originality than the first." Washington Park had a big sign above the center-field fence. It was a cigarette advertisement with a huge picture of a dog's head. McGunnigle wanted to paint one eye black and one eye white. "He proposed to manipulate the eyes by electricity, for, be it understood, Mac is an Edison in embryo," *Sporting Life* said. "A straight ball coming he would let down the white eye. The black eye would indicate a curve ball. Nothing could have stopped him from putting this scheme into execution had not his players kidded him so unmercifully about it."[31]

For now, Mac was getting the job done without shocks and winking eyes. Instead of limping home in seventh place, the Bridegrooms this time returned in triumph in the second spot while moving up fast on the Browns. Brooklyn fans couldn't wait for the home series with St. Louis and the reopening of Washington Park in a morning-afternoon double-header on May 30, celebrated as Decoration Day in honor of soldiers who died in the Civil War. Despite rainy weather, more than 9,000 people showed up for the first game. The Bridgrooms came out decked in their new checkered uniforms. The uniforms, the *Eagle* said, "are the handsomest in the association. They are tasty in color, loose fitting and easy, and in every way a handsome uniform for the coming champions."[32] St. Louis won, but this was only the preliminary to the big afternoon contest.

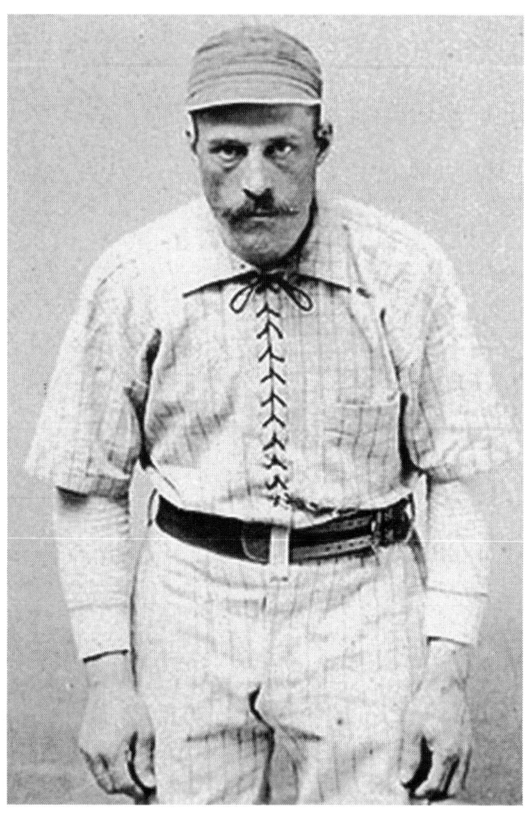

Brooklyn's Joe Visner, shown here in the club's new checkered uniforms of 1889, was the son of a fur trapper and one of baseball's first Native American players (National Baseball Hall of Fame).

The second game drew well over 20,000 people, the biggest crowd in American Association history with Brooklynites cramming into every corner of Washington Park. Even Chris Von der Ahe was impressed. "Dees is pretty near as good as St. Louis," he said, as he chuckled and rattled a couple of dimes in his pocket, "but if it vas not look so much like rain today, ve vood have plenty more."[33]

Baseball games were major social occasions, and most spectators attended games dressed in their Sunday best. Men wore suits, ties and hats. Women wore long frilly dresses and fashionable straw hats. The great Chadwick went on to describe the panorama in detail that made readers feel as if they were seated beside him:

> The scene at about 3 o'clock, looking from one end of the new grandstand, was one to be remembered. It was a regular amphitheater of over three thousand faces. But it was at 4 P.M. that the grounds presented a picture worthy of the photographer's best effort. Looking from the grandstand to the right and left it appeared as if there was but one stand surrounding the entire field, so thickly were people clustered together on every part of the grounds from whence a view of the field could be had. Standing room was at a premium in every part of the enclosure, and hundreds sat on the ragged edge of the top of the fence, while the space beyond the boundary ropes at the outfield were crowded with people thankful to get even standing room. It was unquestionably the greatest crowd on record ever seen at a ball match on this Island, and it placed the old time gatherings of the Union and Capitoline grounds completely in the background, as over thirty thousand people were present within the enclosure during the morning and afternoon.

The cranks warmly cheered the hometown boys. No cold shoulder this time, and the players rewarded the restored loyalty. With Brooklyn up 3 to 0 in the fourth inning, Foutz led off with a long hit into the crowd, which usually would be a home run but was a ground-rule double. The left-hand batting Corkhill tapped a hit to center field, scoring Foutz, who also scored on a couple of sacrifice hits. By the eighth inning, the Bridegrooms were up 9 to 6, and doing everything they could to stay ahead. When St. Louis's Tip O'Neill fouled the ball into the stands, the umpire brought out a shiny new ball, "which Burns discolored before it went to the pitcher." O'Neill then flied out. Brooklyn won 9 to 7.[34]

This was no exhibition with the Giants; this was truly the "most noteworthy" win in the history of the Brooklyn franchise up to this point. Brooklyn's record improved to 21 wins and 14 losses, good for second place behind St. Louis's 27 victories and 12 losses. All eyes turned to the final game of the series until Mother Nature intervened, big time. News of baseball was pushed from the front pages of newspapers by reports of the devastating Johnstown Flood in Johnstown, Pennsylvania, about 60 miles east of Pittsburgh. On the afternoon of May 31, 1889, the dam at the posh South Fork River Fishing and Hunting Club broke, sending 20 million tons of water from Lake Conemaugh hurtling toward Johnstown 14 miles away. About an hour later, with no warning, the water roared into the streets of Johnstown at 40 miles an hour in waves as high as nearly 40 feet. In less than 20 minutes, more than 2,000 people were killed and hundreds more injured, four square miles of downtown Johnstown were destroyed as were 1,600 homes. It was one of the worst disasters of the nineteenth century.[35] Brooklyn and other teams immediately scheduled exhibition games to raise money for the flood victims.

The flood news at first overshadowed signs of cracks re-emerging in the Brooklyn team. In the final game with St. Louis, another 11,746 people found their way to Ridgewood Park on a Sunday. To avoid a repetition of the Philadelphia debacle, Byrne had installed a low barbed-wire fence with glistening bristles around the outfield. In a well-pitched game, the Browns edged Brooklyn 2 to 1 as Silver King outdueled Bob Caruthers. The highlight of the game came in the fifth inning when Browns third baseman

Brooklyn's Washington Park drew a then-baseball record of 30,000 fans for two separate games with the St. Louis Browns on Decoration Day of 1889, with most spectators dressed to the nines (Transcendental Graphics).

Arlie Latham chased down a goat that had run onto the field and triumphantly carried it off the diamond. The loss in a well-played game wasn't alarming in itself. But for all of the hysteria over Brooklyn's Decoration Day victory, St. Louis took the series 2 games to 1.

Alarm bells did go off when Brooklyn then lost two of its next four games to visiting Kansas City. "The Browns, despite their supposed weakness in the box, have suffered no serious reverse as yet and are bravely holding their own away from home, while Brooklyn, even with the advantage of home games, has weakened and dropped back to third place, giving way to the Athletic club, which is coming up with a rush," said *Sporting Life*.[36]

The doubters were back, and this time even home-team booster Chadwick joined in. Adonis Terry was struggling to adjust to a new rule giving the batter a walk on four balls instead of five as the year before. "The new rule is damaging to all pitchers who lack command of the ball, and this happens to be Terry's one weak point," Chadwick chastised. "He has pluck and nerve in the box; is cool under trying circumstances; has great speed and effective curves at command and plenty of endurance. But with the small margin of but four balls against him, his want of command of the ball comes in very costly at times."[37]

Weak batting was a problem as well. Chadwick, an advocate of "scientific" baseball, preferred that batters try to hit grounders, or "daisy cutters," through the infield for hits rather than attempting to slug rare home runs with big swings that usually resulted in easy fly-ball "fungoes" to the outfield. Caruthers, he noted, in one game "struck at the ball as if he meant to knock it out of the lot, and this he did time and time again, even when men were on the bases. What was the result? He struck out twice and when he did hit the ball he hit a fungo and was easily retired. Robert, from being one of the most effective batsmen of the team, is now the weakest, simply from his foolish effort to slug the ball instead of trying to place it safely."[38]

What drove Chadwick crazy was Brooklyn's insistence on batting first when they won the coin toss at the start of a game. Since only one baseball — or sometimes two — was used in a game, the theory was that it was best to have "first crack" at the new ball. "In fact, there is not any advantage to be derived from going in at the bat in the first inning," argued Chadwick, who contended a team is better to have the last chance at bat if they are behind. Manager McGunnigle favored batting last, but he was overruled by team captain Darby O'Brien. "Until they get out of this stupid rut," Chadwick said, "they will not lead their rivals in the pennant race. It is simply mulish obstinacy in keeping in a familiar rut and shows weak captaincy and equally weak management in doing it."[39]

To top it off, the Bridegrooms even had to give up their good-luck monkey, "owing to bad manners," *Sporting Life* reported. It seems that the monkey "startled the city" by breaking loose and "tackling several saloons, at each of which he was royally welcomed, the result of which was that he got boiling drunk and was in the humor to smash things. The monk is a confirmed lush."[40]

When Brooklyn followed a loss to Cincinnati with another defeat at the hands of St. Louis, Chadwick was moved to poetry with a gloominess worthy of Edgar Allan Poe:

> Only a fly ball hit in the air,
> Direct to the hands of the left field player;
> Eagerly watched by thousands of eyes
> For on that catch depended the prize.
> Hands were ready to give applause
> For Darby had offtimes given them cause;
> But for once — as luck would have it — he failed.

"That is the rhymester's story of yesterday's contest, in lines brief but to the point. There is no questioning the fact that the Brooklyn team is not the favorite of Dame Fortune. At Ridgewood and at Washington Park this week the least stroke of good luck would have given the Brooklyn team a position in the pennant race which have been like taking the tide at the flood which leads on to fame and fortune. But it was not to be; and instead they have been pushed down in the list and given an uphill fight in the struggle for the pennant which will require the best efforts to enable them to recover the valuable ground lost within the past few days."[41]

The most ominous sign was that the grumbling spread from the sports stories to the *Eagle's* popular "Walks About the City" column: "Manager McGunnigle of the Brooklyn base ball team will have to inspire his boys with more ambitious energy or look disconsolately at their club name in third position from now till the end of the championship season.... The Philadelphians have taken in hand the race with St. Louis for first place, while the Brooklynites struggle alone, in their rear."[42]

McGunnigle continued to express confidence in his "boys." But as midseason approached, Gunner may well have been wondering just how far a dive it would be from the towers of the Brooklyn Bridge to the East River below. (The answer: 276 feet, 6 inches.) Maybe to get an idea, at some point McGunnigle climbed to the top of the Statue of Liberty, which had been formally opened in October 1886 in New York Harbor, between Manhattan and Brooklyn. Mac threw his derby hat out of one of Lady Liberty's windows to the water 300 feet below.[43] The hat floated away—perhaps like Brooklyn's pennant hopes.

Chapter Seven

Down to the Wire

With his Brooklyn Bridegrooms struggling in third place, manager Gunner McGunnigle decided to make a major change to try to improve the team's luck. With "much trepidation," he switched hats, exchanging his derby "dicer" for a straw hat. The Bridegrooms also found a new lucky mascot. No monkey this time. It was a big, black stray cat named "Tabby," who roamed Washington Park and slept in Charley Byrne's office.

Sure enough, by late June the Bridegrooms were on a winning streak. This had less to do with cats and hats than with a McGunnigle pitching change. Mickey Hughes, the rookie sensation of the previous season, was mired in a sophomore slump. Gunner dropped him from the rotation in order to use ace hurler Bobby Caruthers more often. Caruthers had come up with a new pitch he called the "glide." "It waltzes up towards the batsman with a smile on its countenance, but when he attempts to smote it, it 'glides' away," *Sporting Life* noted.[1]

Brooklyn headed for Philadelphia for two games with the second-place Athletics. Caruthers and his "glide" took the first game 3 to 2 for Bobby's 13th win. Then Adonis Terry hurled a 9 to 1 victory, and suddenly the Bridegrooms were back in second place, heading off for a showdown with the first-place St. Louis Browns. The streak continued in the Mound City as Caruthers pitched a 7 to 4 win. Terry lost the first game of a July 4 double-header 4 to 3 to Icebox Chamberlain in a game that featured a new double umpiring system, with Frank Gaffney behind the plate and Jack Kerins on the bases. But Brooklyn won the series with a 12 to 10 win in the second game behind Tom Lovett with Caruthers in relief.

As St. Louis continued to slip, Chris Von der Ahe, as usual, found ulterior reasons. In mid–July, he alleged that third baseman Arlie Latham and pitcher Silver King were cooperating with gamblers. Nobody ever found any evidence to back up the charges. Among those who came to the defense of the Browns players was Brooklyn president Charley Byrne: "I regard the story as an unqualified lie that was either conceived in the brain of an idiot or in that of some person who had only some malicious design in view," he said. "Were Latham, supposing for the sake of argument, inclined to be crooked he is too sharp to enter any such compact as is charged. And I can say the same for King."[2]

While St. Louis was squabbling, the Brooklyn stars were coming together as a team. The players liked each other and appreciated McGunnigle's low-key managing style. Hard-hitting Joe Visner and veteran Bob Clark took over most of the catching duties. Even bad-boy Tommy Burns was a "gentleman" and thrived under the team harmony. Center fielder Pop Corkhill was saving runs with spectacular catches. In one game at Cincinnati, a Reds batter slammed what looked like a sure homer to center. Corkhill raced after the ball "and as it passed over his head, he sprang into the air and caught it one handed."[3] Third baseman George Pinkney was becoming the first iron man of baseball, playing in every Brooklyn game since the spring of 1886. He eventually would play in 577 straight games, a record that would stand until Boston Red Sox shortstop Everett Scott played in 1,307 consecutive games between 1916 and 1925. Scott's record was broken in 1939 by the New York Yankees' Lou Gehrig, whose record of 2,130 straight games was in turn broken by the Baltimore Orioles' Cal Ripkin in 1995.

Brooklyn third baseman George Pinkney still shares the record of most singles in one game—six—achieved in a June 26, 1885, contest against Philadelphia (Library of Congress).

Brooklyn's manager also was gaining more attention. "Let me say a word of William McGunnigle, a man whose modesty tends to push his light under a bushel," said a correspondent for *Sporting Life*. "He does not court notoriety and always hugs the bench with his players. He is with his men at all times and on all occasions he is figuring at some method by which a profitable trick may be learned. Mac's mind is ever on base ball, and you can seldom switch him off it, both in and out of school. The players think a heap of him, and the close attachment existing between he and they is evidenced in the fact that he is always a welcome guest to their circle."[4]

The team was drawing huge crowds to Washington Park, including an increasing number of women, one of whom was a reporter for the *New York World* newspaper. Her report on a Ladies Day game between Brooklyn and Kansas City was probably considered cute by her male counterparts, but it gave a great description of the game at that time. She wrote

After retiring as a baseball fly catcher, Pop Corkhill switched to catching crooks as chief of police in Stockton, New Jersey (Library of Congress).

> One of the Brooklyn men put on a sort of chest protector that looked like an alligator skin such as you see hanging up in leather stores ... and one glove about ten sizes too large for him, and got off in a corner by himself. This was the catcher, it seems. He was persistently watched over by a little man who was dressed in a butternut flannel costume, with a padded-out, accordion-plaited corsage cut high and who acted as umpire, and whom nobody seemed to like.... First the "pitcher," who belonged to the Kansas City nine tried to throw the ball, but threw it in such a way that no human batter could hit it. Sometimes the man with the bat didn't even try, and again he would strike at the ball wildly, to no purpose. All the time the

> nut-brown kept calling out at the top of his lungs something about "Ball one!" "Two strikes;" "Foul!" and so on, until finally the man with the chest-protector, finding that it was too hard to catch the ball where he had been standing, put a sort of muzzle on his head and went up as close as he could get to the man with the bat. Then the little umpire put a muzzle on his head and went and stood over against him, watching everything he did with the closest attention. The reporter was in a fever of anxiety for fear one or both of them would be slain.[5]

The Bridegrooms won 14 of 18 games to move closer to first place as they returned home to face league-leader St. Louis on August 1. The Browns won the first game 6 to 2 on a muddy field as Icebox Chamberlain beat Bobby Caruthers. Adonis Terry then pitched the Bridegrooms to a 13 to 6 win. The next day was a Sunday and 17,000 people made their way to Ridgewood Park. Caruthers was in top form against his old mates, giving up only three hits as Brooklyn took the series two games out of three.

As usual, St. Louis did not take losing well. Charley Comiskey accused Byrne and his boys of being thieves in the night. "I think the Brooklyns are a very inferior club; and if it wasn't for the help of the umpires they wouldn't be where they are now," he said. "They are regular dark-lantern robbers and they have stolen more than 15 of the games that they have won. Byrne is the boss of the umpires. He fixed their salaries and whatever he says to them goes."[6] (In fact, Byrne had resigned from the umpire committee in 1889 to avoid any appearance of conflict. He once said, "If all the umpires robbed for Brooklyn, why aren't we further up in the race?") A week later, Brooklyn headed into St. Louis just a half-game behind the Browns. Finally, they could move into first place. All they had to do was beat the four-time champions in their own ball yard. More than 8,000 people crowded into Sportsman's Park to see Caruthers and Icebox Chamberlain. St. Louis took the lead with two runs in the first inning, and then in the fourth Charlie Duffee, the Browns' 5'5" center fielder, "set the crowd wild" by slugging a homer into the left-field seats. (The tiny Duffee led the team in homers that year with 16.)

But it was Duffee's glove that saved the game for the Browns. In the ninth inning, the score was tied when a Brooklyn batter slammed a ball high over Duffee's head. "Nobody expected him to get it, and when he got his hands on the sphere and clung to it, it was several seconds before the crowd could realize that he had actually caught it," reported the *St.*

Louis Post-Dispatch. "Then the shout which went up could have been heard a mile away. Even the players looked out at the center fielder in blank astonishment." When the inning ended, "Duffee received an ovation that lasted more than a minute."

The game went into the 10th inning, when Tommy McCarthy of the Browns bunted the ball foul several times (bunting foul with two strikes wasn't yet an out), and then lashed a triple to center. Tip O'Neill followed with another three-bagger over Pop Corkhill's head. Yank Robinson hit a sacrifice fly to score O'Neill, and St. Louis took the first game 4 to 2. During the contest, Chris Von der Ahe kept his field binoculars trained on third sacker Arlie Latham. Der boss decided that his play was "suspicious," and suspended Latham after the game. The *St. Louis Post-Dispatch* noted that Latham "made a sorry exhibition of himself while at the bat and certainly acted in a queer way in the field. [At bat] Latham reached out for several balls that would have taken a barber pole to corral."[7]

In the second game, the Browns pounded Adonis Terry and Dave Foutz for 18 hits, winning 14 to 4 despite 10 fielding errors by St. Louis. For the third game, attendance was the highest for season, with up to 16,000 in the stands. St. Louis won its third in row as Chamberlain blanked the Bridegrooms 11 to 0, while Caruthers "was knocked all over the cow pasture."

When the game ended, Sportsman's Park erupted in a blaze of fireworks. The Brooklyn players were stunned by the losses. Manager McGunnigle was so devastated that he sat on the bench and wept. Who said there was no crying in baseball? As the team left the park in an omnibus — a large, horse-drawn bus — Bob Caruthers sat in a front seat and stared out the window, "thinking over the uncertainties of base ball."[8] The *St. Louis Post-Dispatch* chortled that "the good people of Brooklyn are getting out telescopes to view the pennant. It has moved so far West in the last few days that it is no longer visible to the naked eye at the City of Churches."[9]

Brooklyn clawed back, winning its next three games in Kansas City. The victory string set off another clash with Chris Von der Ahe. When the ump didn't show up for the games, Kansas City manager Bill Watkins agreed to let Brooklyn's Doc Bushong umpire. (Bushong was out with a broken finger.) Von der Ahe immediately saw another Byrne conspiracy. The Brooklyn owner, Chris charged, "induced" Watkins to be his "handy tool." It was all part of a "scheme to get the hand in the Association race.

Mr. Byrne has control of the umpires, and it is time someone makes a start to see whether he has control of the Association."[10]

Von der Ahe telegraphed the American Association's board of directors protesting the three Kansas City games, but to no avail. Though it does seem odd that a player would umpire a game involving his own team, even Kansas City players agreed that Bushong had been evenhanded. The St. Louis owner certainly didn't get any sympathy back in Brooklyn. "Evidently President Chris Von der Ahe of the St. Louis club has lost his presence of mind, and he is rapidly approaching that mental condition when the services of an inquiring committee on lunacy will find their services needed," the *Eagle* said. "Not content with charging one of his most serviceable and honest players with crookedness, which he was utterly unable to prove, he gnashes his teeth in rage and goes in like a bull against a locomotive in charging all kinds of dishonesty, first against one of the straightest umpires in the national game, and lastly against the president of the Brooklyn Club, whose integrity of character stands out in the association firmament like a bright particular star. Verily, 'whom the gods would destroy they first make mad.'"[11]

Meantime, Brooklyn continued on a roll. Manager McGunnigle began using Mickey Hughes again, with good results. On August 24 at Cincinnati, Hughes, "who has been an easy mark for everybody, proved too much for the Reds," the *Eagle* reported. "Mickey wasn't faster than a narrow gauge limited express, but the Reds failed to transact business with him. The ball came floating up to the plate looking as big as a football but somehow or other the Reds could not line it out safely."[12] Bushong, making a rare appearance behind the plate — as a catcher instead of as an umpire — picked off three runners at third base. Pinkney hit a two-run homer.

The pennant drive was slowed the next day. It was Sunday, and in many parts of the country playing ball on the Sabbath was the devil's work. With Cincinnati having banned Sunday ball, the contest was moved to Hamilton, Ohio, about 25 miles to the north, where there also was a Sunday law. Before the game even started, a "white whiskered, red nosed county squire" arraigned managers Bill McGunnigle and Gus Smelz for violating the law, but allowed the game to proceed. More than 5,000 people turned out, as Bob Caruthers faced off against Cincinnati's Jess Duryea. Brooklyn was leading 4 to 2 in the bottom of the fourth inning when 18 police officers streamed onto the field — one cop for each starting player — and

At 5'6", Brooklyn's Mickey Hughes was one of the shortest pitchers in baseball history. His career also was short. He dropped out of baseball at age 24 with a drinking problem (*New York Clipper*).

began making arrests. Umpire Bob Ferguson mingled with fans to avoid possible capture. The police, acting on a complaint by the Law and Order League of Hamilton, took everyone to the Hamilton City Hall before the mayor, who fined each player $5 plus court costs, for a total of $159.50. The Cincinnati team paid the fine.[13]

Back in Brooklyn, Mickey Hughes stopped Kansas City for his fifth straight win, moving the Bridegrooms into a tie for first place with St. Louis. The next day Brooklyn took sole possession of first after the Browns lost to Columbus 6 to 5 on a home run by none other than the old Bridegroomsman himself, Dave Orr. Brooklyn then won four out of five games against visiting Cincinnati. One reason may be that Manager McGunnigle sat in the first row of the grandstand for some games to better steal the catcher's signs and tip off the Bridegroom batters.[14]

Charley Byrne was growing more optimistic by the day.

> The team has been putting up an even steady game of ball lately, and it is to that we owe our success. One thing which has helped us a great deal in crawling up toward the top is the all-around skill of our men. Most teams stand away up in one respect and away down in another, but our club ranks third in both batting and fielding. Of our pitchers, Caruthers has been doing the best work. He is often hit hard, but generally manages to win his game on account of good work when it is necessary to exert himself. He is not and never was a strikeout pitcher like Terry, and seldom wastes his arm upon a weak batter. He has the good sense to know there are always eight men playing on the team besides himself.[15]

The Bridegrooms and the Browns headed for a showdown in Brooklyn in a three-game series in early September. Charley Comiskey was chomping at the bit. "We are not afraid of Brooklyn or any other club," he said. "All we ask is a square deal from the umpires; this we may not get, but if we don't they will hear from us. We can beat Brooklyn on their own grounds, just as easy as in St. Louis. This is not a brag, but it's the truth."[16]

Then came the September 7 contest that *Sporting Life* writer J. F. Donnelley called the "Lobster and Frankenstein Game." Lines were long at the ticket window three hours before game time. By 3:00 P.M. the stands were filled, with others ringing the field behind ropes for a total of 15,143 people. Bob Caruthers was set to face Icebox Chamberlain again, with both pitchers already having won more than 25 games. The game started at 4:00 P.M. on an overcast day with Fred Goldsmith as the umpire.

The Bridegrooms went up 2 to 1, and, as skies darkened, their pace of play slowed noticeably in the hope the game might be ended, giving them a win. Chris Von der Ahe, who had been sitting in the grandstand, moved to the players' bench, his field glasses in tow. At one point, Browns batter Arlie Latham temporarily eased the tension by shouting at a nervous-looking McGunnigle, "Stop pulling on your mustache." Then St. Louis went up 3 to 2 after six innings. It was 5:40 p.m. At this point, "each member of the St. Louis team suddenly discovered that it was too dark entirely to even think of playing ball and went groping about in truly pitiable fashion," Donnelly wrote. "Comiskey called upon Goldsmith to call the game and was met with a flat refusal, the umpire telling Comiskey that it was fully light enough to play for some time, and that anyhow it would been been finished at that time had not he and his men conspired to delay play."

"Play ball," Goldsmith shouted. "Chamberlain, after many maneuvers, would suddenly think of something he had to say to [first baseman] Comiskey and the two would meet half-way and confer. As they concluded this pow-wow, O'Neill would start from the extreme left field, stroll leisurely in to first base and have his little talk, being succeeded by McCarthy, who would make his way, snail-fashion, from right field. Then a ball pitched, it all started over again." Meantime, McCarthy got into shouting matches with fans behind him in right field.

With St. Louis at bat in the seventh inning, Von der Ahe sent three well-dressed young men who were assisting him out to a local store. They returned with candles and matches, which the St. Louis owner made use of to show the umpire that there wasn't enough light to play ball. Der Boss "lit a whole row around the St. Louis bench in footlight style, around Von der Ahe. A sweet smile played about his expansive lower face and his nose glowed as it never glowed before." A ball of newspaper thrown on the field rolled into the candles and set the paper on fire, but the blaze was quickly doused.

Manager McGunnigle had the cops remove Von der Ahe's three young aides from the park, and the game continued with Comiskey delaying all the way. As Brooklyn was preparing to come to bat in the ninth inning at 6:18 p.m., St. Louis's McCarthy surreptitiously picked up the ball and dropped it into the Browns' water bucket, giving it a good soaking. Dave Foutz saw him and notified Goldsmith, who threw out the wet ball and put a new one in play. Comiskey again griped that it was too dark to play. Brooklyn's first batter of the inning, Bob Clark, swung at and missed a third strike, but catcher Jocko Milligan missed the ball. As Clark ran all the way to second, Milligan slammed down his glove, claiming that he couldn't see the ball because it was too dark. Comiskey had had enough. Even though his team was leading 4 to 2, he called in his men, who left the field amid hoots, jeers and flying objects.

McGunnigle pressed to restrain patrons from going onto the field, not to keep order but to give Umpire Goldsmith time to do his official duty. Goldsmith stared at his watch, waited the required five minutes and declared Brooklyn the winner, 9 to 0, by forfeit. Plus, St. Louis would be fined $1,500 for leaving the field before the game was over. On his way off the field, St. Louis's McCarthy got into a scuffle with a Brooklyn fan, and the police gave the player an escort to the clubhouse.[17] Von der Ahe claimed even he had been a subject of attack. "As I was leaving the players' bench to go to Byrne's office, some contemptible whelp threw a beer glass at me, and it came very near to hitting me on the head," he said. "The terrible state of affairs is due to Byrne, and he alone must be accountable for its existence"[18]

The "disgraceful" contest caused turmoil across the country, with reaction depending on whom you rooted for. "I never saw a man make a greater mistake than Von der Ahe is making," Brooklyn Manager McGunnigle said. "He is a bad loser and has lost his head because he is in danger of losing the pennant. Comiskey has had his own way all his life and thought he could bulldoze and rob us on our ground as well as he did on his own. The St. Louis men were not mobbed, not injured and not in danger."[19]

The *St. Louis Globe-Democrat* accused Byrne of riling up the Brooklyn crowd.

> When Byrne got home from his recent western trip he knew that unless he resorted to extremes the coveted pennant would not float over the Brooklyn grounds. What did he do? He rushed to the newspaper offices and started to broadcast awful stories of the treatment his players had received at the hands of the St. Louis people. The Bowery toughs, who are great friends of the Brooklyn Club, poured into the Brooklyn grounds Saturday prepared to avenge the alleged insults offered to their pets in the wild and woolly West. No one blames Goldsmith for not calling the game as he would surely have been killed by the Brooklyn and New York toughs.[20]

Charley Comiskey actually *did* blame the umpire. "Goldsmith is wholly responsible for all of this disturbance," he said. "Had he done his duty as the rules require he would have called the game when it became too dark for further playing. In Saturday's game it was very evident to us that he was afraid to call the game, as the crowd was in a very ugly mood. I tell you Goldsmith is a 'baby' and that he was afraid to do his duty."[21] Goldsmith replied that he was afraid of nothing in the line of duty.

The dispute escalated when Byrne received the following telegram: "C. H. Byrne, president Brooklyn B.B. Club; I refuse to allow my club to play any more games in Brooklyn. (signed) Chris Von der Ahe."[22] Chris wasn't kidding. The next day more than 17,000 people turned out at Ridgewood Park for the second game, but St. Louis didn't show. Umpire Goldsmith got out his watch again, and declared another forfeit for Brooklyn. Back at the Grand Central Hotel in New York, Von der Ahe asserted: "Byrne knew that I would not take my men over to Ridgewood Park where there were no police and probably have some of them so badly injured that they could not play any more this season, if they were not outright killed."[23] He added: "Why my men would not go over to play ball for $1,000 apiece. They were afraid for their lives."[24]

Byrne pooh-poohed Von der Ahe's claims. "American Association rules require us to give proper police protection and to preserve order on the grounds. This we have always done and will continue to do," he said.[25] The *New York Times* opined, "The action of Von der Ahe in disappointing the spectators was generally denounced as a disgrace to baseball. There is nothing for the Association to do now but expel him."[26]

Von der Ahe finally agreed to play the scheduled Tuesday game at Washington Park, but the contest was rained out. The two forfeits gave Brooklyn a four-game lead with a little over a month to go. But the brouhaha wasn't over. League president Wheeler Wyckoff arranged a meeting in Cincinnati on September 24 to review the entire matter. The meeting was, in effect, a trial, with the association's board of directors as jury and each side presenting their cases and questioning the parties involved.

Prosecutor Von der Ahe made Charley Byrne out to be the prime cause of the evil. "As I told him, we never had any trouble in the Association until he came in. I organized the Association and got it going. I spent $1,500 in 1881 getting it into shape. Then in 1884 this man comes in and endeavors by his schemes to get charge of the whole thing."[27] Lawyer Byrne headed the Brooklyn legal team, cross-examining Browns manager Charley Comiskey, who testified that a game at the nearby Polo Grounds the very same day had been called because of darkness. Comiskey did concede that McCarthy had soaked the baseball in water, but he claimed that his teammate "was prompted by a desire to clean the ball." Byrne then presented an affidavit by Umpire Goldsmith stating that when the Browns left the field there was ample light to continue playing, and that the St. Louis delays were "willful and in direct violation of the deponent's orders and commands to the captain."[28]

Finally, the verdict came. After a long consultation the board decided on a sort of compromise, awarding Saturday's game to the St. Louis club and remitting the fine on the grounds that Umpire Goldsmith's decision was wrong. As to Sunday's game, the board upheld the forfeit to the Brooklyn Club and imposed a fine of $1,500 on St. Louis for failing to appear at Ridgewood Park. The directors also recommended that the services of Fred Goldsmith as umpire be discontinued.[29] Charley Byrne and his partners were furious. They would not forget the slight by their American Association colleagues. "Our case was the strongest ever laid before an executive body, and we went prepared to fight for our rights to the very end," Byrne said. "But what was the result? A contemptible compromise that is not only ridiculous but makes the association the laughing stock of the base ball world."[30]

Even with the off-field decision, Brooklyn continued to move further ahead of St. Louis in the standings. The more they did, the more Von der Ahe brought his wrath down on his players. He suspended Arlie Latham again and fined Yank Robinson. But Captain Comiskey professed to be confident of winning the pennant, saying, "We have thirteen games yet to play, and we expect to win them all."[31]

Newspaper coverage of the American Association's closest pennant race in history was interrupted by sensational reports that the National Brotherhood of Base Ball Players was going to start a major league and had even lined up investors, led by Cleveland railroad magnate Albert L. Johnson. The National League dismissed the reports as rumors, and Brotherhood leaders flatly denied the story. Chris Von der Ahe scoffed: "There are not six men in the whole Brotherhood who have an ounce of business brains. They can't even take care of the salaries they are now getting. And capitalists are not going to trust their money to such hands."[32] The reports, however, had a ring of truth to them.

In late September, McGunnigle made a key decision on pitching. He decided to use only the two pitchers who were doing the best down the stretch, Bobby Caruthers and Adonis Terry, in nearly all of the 11 remaining games of the season. "I think it's folly to make a change while the men are pitching good ball," Mac argued. Caruthers won three of the next four games, including a 9 to 0 shutout of Philadelphia in Brooklyn's final home game on October 6. The Bridegrooms headed on the road with a 2½ game lead over St. Louis, with four games to play in Baltimore and three in Columbus. The road trip did not begin well. Billy Barnie's Baltimores bested Byrne's Brooklyn Bridegrooms 3 to 2 with Terry in the box for Brooklyn. Caruthers pitched the Bridegrooms to a 12 to 9 win in the second game. Then Brooklyn's pennant express was almost derailed by a blessed event.

On the morning of October 9, Caruthers's wife back in Brooklyn delivered a bouncing baby boy, and the pitcher went to Byrne to tell him the news. Byrne congratulated the new father, then assuming that Caruthers wanted to go home, said, "We cannot spare you, but nevertheless I will grant you a leave of absence." To Byrne's surprise, Caruthers declined: "The telegram says that my wife is doing well, and I know that in case I should go home and the club should then lose games, she as well I would be worried, and that might do more harm than if I remained away. I will therefore stay with the club until the season closes."[33] The new papa proceeded to pitch for the second straight day, beating Baltimore again, this time 17 to 9.

With St. Louis breathing down its neck, Brooklyn faced Baltimore for one last game with Terry pitching. The score was tied 2 to 2 until the sixth inning, when Brooklyn broke open the game to win 7 to 2, led by catcher Bob Clark, who had four hits, scored four runs and stole four bases during the game. "The team is full of ginger and left last night for Columbus," the *Eagle* reported.[34] The Bridegrooms were now leading by just two games over St. Louis, which had won 12 straight. Nevertheless, all the Bridegrooms had to do was beat sixth-place Columbus and Brooklyn would have its first American Association pennant.

A big crowd turned out in Columbus, hoping to see the locals spoil the Bridegrooms' plans. In the first game, Caruthers went up against the Babies' top pitcher, Mark Baldwin, who gave up only two hits until the fifth inning, when Brooklyn scored three unearned runs. By the eighth, the Bridegrooms were up 5 to 4. One more inning and the pennant would be close at hand. In the ninth inning, Baldwin led off with a single. The next batter, Spud Johnson, hit a fly ball to center field, an easy out. But Pop Corkhill misjudged the ball, which sailed over his head. Johnson went to third. "A scene of wild excitement ensued," the *Brooklyn Eagle* reported. "The bleachers arose as one man and showered cushions and hats into the diamond in clouds. Play had to be stopped for fully ten minutes. Never before in Columbus had such a scene been witnessed." Columbus scored to win 7 to 5.[35]

The Brooklyn loss "was a godsend for St. Louis, as it improves the Browns' chances decidedly," the *St. Louis Post-Dispatch* cheered. "They are now within .007 of the Bridegrooms, being tied with them in the matter of games lost and three games behind them in the games won."[36]

Game two at Columbus became Brooklyn's biggest game of the year. Adonis Terry was up to the challenge, pitching a 2 to 1 win. "Yesterday's contest may be regarded as one marked by the most noteworthy victories the Brooklyn team have achieved this season," Henry Chadwick wrote in the *Eagle*. "Will Terry has, by his gentlemanly conduct on all occasions, by his strictly temperate habits, determined pluck and perseverance in the face of difficulties and earnest effort to do his best for the welfare of the club, long ago earned a reputation second to that of no one in the professional fraternity. But in the effective work he did in the box in the last two critical contests in Columbus he added laurels to his wreath, which make him the star of his company in the closing of the campaign."[37] Brooklyn was now up two games, with one game to go.

Back in Brooklyn, plans began for a magnificent parade to welcome the new champions. The team was to arrive the next Tuesday night by boat at the Fulton Ferry at 5:00 P.M. A reception committee would meet Byrne, McGunnnigle and the team and take them in horse-drawn carriages to Washington Park "escorted by members of local baseball clubs in uniform, carrying torches and led by a military band, pyrotechnic displays on route being a feature." It would be the biggest celebration since the opening of the Brooklyn Bridge six years earlier. "As it will be the first event of the kind in the history of the game in this city, it should be made specifically interesting," the *Eagle* said.[38]

But Chris Von der Ahe rained on their parade. In a last-ditch effort to win the pennant, he claimed the right to play postponed games. Although the season officially ended on October 14, under the American Association's constitution "postponed games" could be played prior to October 17. St. Louis was given permission to play its four postponed games with Cincinnati and Philadelphia. The news set off a howl of righteous indignation in Brooklyn, where it was "plainly to be seen that the conspiracy which had deprived the Brooklyn Club of its rights in the case of the forfeited game lost to Brooklyn by St. Louis had been further extended to include the three days of grace given the clubs after the close of the regular season which ended yesterday," the *Brooklyn Eagle* harrumphed. "That the arrangements to play the extra games entered into by the Cincinnati and Athletic clubs have been made solely with a view to down the Brooklyn team at any cost is too apparent to be questioned for a moment, and it is but a fitting climax to the discreditable action taken by the Board of Directors at their Cincinnati meeting."[39]

Brooklyn President Byrne responded to the added games with a letter to the public from Columbus.

> The Brooklyn Club will leave for home tonight and are due in Brooklyn about 5 o'clock tomorrow afternoon. It is inadvisable to have our friends make any arrangements for our reception. Under the schedule adopted by the American Association, limiting championship games from April 1 to October 14, we have won the American Association championship. Two games are to be played by St. Louis in Cincinnati tomorrow to enable St. Louis to get to Philadelphia to play off its postponed games there. This, if done, simply makes our championship race a farce. If we are deprived of the victory we have justly earned by these methods, we must trust our cause to an honest press and public sentiment.[40]

In the final game of the season at Columbus, Adonis Terry pitched for the second straight day. Aided by several errors by Columbus shortstop Charley Marr, the Bridegrooms rolled to a 6 to 1 win as Terry won his 21st game. Brooklyn stood first in the standings with a record of 93 wins and 44 losses; St. Louis had 89 wins and 44 losses. The next day, St. Louis was scheduled to play a double-header in Cincinnati. One loss, and Brooklyn would win the pennant.

Charley Byrne, Manager McGunnigle and the Brooklyn players were on a train, heading back to Jersey City. They had no idea what had happened in Cincinnati until they arrived at the station to see a large crowd waiting for them. Then the word came. Cincinnati had won the first game 8 to 3. Though St. Louis won the second contest, it was all over. Brooklyn had won the pennant. For Charley Byrne, it was the moment he had been dreaming of since he began building the team in 1883. Upon hearing the news, "his worried face relaxed into a contented smile, and his entire nervous system underwent a change," *Sporting Life* said. "The strain had been long and severe, and the reaction was immediate. He expressed himself as being glad at the positive settlement of the championship in that it would avoid any complication that would surely have arisen had St. Louis won both games."[41]

The Bridegrooms were escorted to the boat that would take them to Brooklyn. Steamships blew whistles and crew members waved hats as the boat proceeded to the dock at the foot of Fulton Street, where an enormous crowd could be heard shouting and cheering. "Cheer followed cheer as the boat drew nigh, and when the boys proudly stepped ashore and filed through the ticket taker's gate, it was like bedlam let loose," the *Brooklyn Eagle* said. "It was all their life was worth to fight their way through the crowd that choked the street at the ferry entrance. Darby O'Brien was patted on the back by scores of cranks, Dave Foutz nearly had his arm wrung from its socket by excited admirers, Tommy Burns was hemmed in by a dozen or more, and so it went on all through the list."

Finally, the players got into 12 open carriages. "With a crack of a dozen whips the procession started off on its triumphal trip through the city. Up Fulton street, through Henry and Montague to the City Hall, the route was lined with happy, delighted citizens from the dignified business man down to the ubiquitous small boy, all bent on the one purpose to heartily welcome the champions. At the City Hall the principal officers of the city were gathered on the steps, and as the carriages were driven by another big cheer greeted the players."

Then it was on to Washington Park. In the crush at the ferry, Bob Caruthers, his brother, Manager McGunnigle and Secretary Ebbets were caught in the swirl and rushed along two blocks away from where the carriages had been gathered. When they had fought their way clear, the procession was a half-mile away. They went to the grounds in an elevated train. When the players arrived, there was a large crowd waiting. "The youngsters of the neighborhood had prepared a big bonfire in front of the grounds, and from the branches of two trees hung a banner with the legend: 'Brooklyns, Champions, 1889.'" From there, the tired players headed home. Caruthers was anxious to see his baby son for the first time.[42]

Across the City of Churches, residents let loose the joy that had been

The 1889 Brooklyn Bridegrooms, with manager Bill McGunnigle dressed in civvies in the middle. In front of him is Mickey Hughes. The front row (left to right): George Pinkney, Bob Caruthers, Hub Collins, Oyster Burns, Bob Clark and Tom Lovett. Back row: Germany Smith, Pop Corkhill, Adonis Terry, Dave Foutz, Darby O'Brien, Doc Bushong and Joe Visner (Library of Congress).

bottled up since the team began in 1883. "The success of the home team was the talk of the town in every quarter; and in nearly every theater last night was the news given out from the stage in some form or another, either by open announcement or by special reference made to the event in the topical songs or local gags," the *Eagle* said. "The spontaneous outburst of yesterday afternoon was perhaps a better reception than any formal affair would have been."[43]

The St. Louis papers took the Brooklyn victory with their usual grace. They dubbed Brooklyn "the Bogus Champions" and "Byrne's Blacklegs." Said the *St. Louis Post-Dispatch*: "Not only were the umpires favorable to Brooklyn, but some clubs played very strange ball when pitted against them. The whole thing looks very suspicious, and if the Brooklyn management were not guilty of underhand work they are certainly surrounded by an unfortunate chain of circumstances which looks decidedly bad."[44]

After six frustrating and expensive years, the team of Byrne, Abell and Doyle had finally achieved its dream. Not only did Brooklyn win the flag, but the season home attendance of 354,000 was the highest ever achieved by any team at this point in the history of baseball. The total wouldn't be topped in Brooklyn until 1916. Even better, the team the Bridegrooms would face in the World's Series would be the "boys from over the bridge"—their bitter rival, the New York Giants.

Chapter Eight

The Pre-Subway Series

The 1889 "World's Series" between the Brooklyn Bridegrooms and the New York Giants could not be called a subway series because subways hadn't been invented yet. Therefore, call it "the elevated rail series," because that's what many fans from both cities rode to the games for the first official clashes in a long rivalry.

The annual "World's Series" was arranged by the champions of the two major leagues however they wished. Planning for the 1889 series began immediately after Brooklyn won the American Association pennant. Brooklyn president Charley Byrne met with Giants owner John Day and manager Jim Mutrie at the New York office of *Sporting Times* on the afternoon of October 16. They decided to play 11 games. To avoid the fiasco of the never-ending 1887 St. Louis–Detroit World's Series, they agreed the Series would end when one team won six games. The opening game was to be played at New York's new Polo Grounds, and then the contests would alternate between Brooklyn and New York.

The two sides met again the next day and picked umpires. New York selected Frank Gaffney, while Brooklyn chose Tom Lynch. Though Gaffney was considered to be one of the finest umpires in the game, some New Yorkers were not thrilled by the choice. They feared he had a beef against Giants shortstop John Montgomery Ward, who once punched Gaffney in the eye after a disputed call. One hitch was that Lynch wanted $600 to ump the Series, double the amount offered, so he was dropped. Both teams then agreed on American Association umpire Bob Ferguson.

Mutrie's Giants were formidable opponents. The team had six future Hall-of-Fame players: pitchers Tim Keefe and Mickey Welch, shortstop John Ward, first baseman Roger Connor, outfielder Jim "Orator" O'Rourke and catcher William "Buck" Ewing. "There is only one great ball player in the country, and he is William Ewing," said Boston's King Kelly. "He stands head and shoulders above all others. The New York Captain knows more about baseball in one second than the majority of ball players will learn in a dozen seasons. [He is] what the Statue of Liberty is to a toothpick."[1]

Gunner McGunnigle's Brooklyn team, by contrast, had no future Hall-of-Fame players. It was a squad of solid players but few superstars outside of Bob Caruthers, who led the American Association with 40 wins in 1889, and Dave Foutz, whose 113 runs batted in ranked second in the Association. Only two Brooklyn players batted .300 for the season — Oyster Burns at .304 and Darby O'Brien at .300. Joe Visner and Pop Corkhill led the team in homers with eight, far below league-leading John Reilly's 19. But together, the team had scored 995 runs, the most in all of baseball.

Buck Ewing was the first catcher elected to the Baseball Hall of Fame. He had a habit of dropping his mask on home plate so runners might stumble over it and miss touching the plate (Library of Congress).

Betting was brisk, with New York the favorite at $100 to $85 for the first game.[2] The general public and even sportswriters weren't the only ones who wagered on baseball games. Pete Rose was born too late. While Pete was banished from baseball in 1989 for betting on his Cincinnati team, the practice was common for early ball players. Brooklyn's Dave Foutz was a habitual gambler on just about anything; he lost $1,800 in the 1884 presidential election when he bet on Maine Senator James Blaine to beat Grover Cleveland. Foutz reportedly cashed in $245 of winnings for the 1889 season and put $100 on Brooklyn to win the first game. He also agreed to give Bob Caruthers $50 if Caruthers won the first game, while the pitcher would fork over $50 to Foutz for a loss.[3] Caruthers was a high roller. He was known to lose $500 at one poker game and then go down the street to win it all back in another game in the same night. Like Foutz, he often bet on Brooklyn during the season. Some in the press were starting to raise red flags about player betting. "The practice is getting to be an evil," wrote one *Sporting Life* correspondent. "The public does not like the practice and will not stand much more of it."[4]

Managers Bill McGunnigle and Jim Mutrie bet each other a suit of clothes on the outcome of the Series. The 38-year-old Mutrie was more than the manager of the New York team; he basically started the club. After playing with McGunningle at Fall River, Massachusetts, in 1877, Mutrie in 1880 was player-manager of a team in Brockton, where his teammates included future Browns third sacker Arlie Latham. According to Latham, Mutrie was a "cycle bug," and after a June game against Yale University in New Haven, Connecticut, he left with the receipts and rode his big-wheeled bike down to New York.[5] Mutrie got a job at a New Jersey box factory and became a frequent sight in the New York area riding his bike with his long hair flowing in the wind. One day he saw a newspaper ad that the Polo

New York Giants manager Jim Mutrie's major league winning percentage of .611 (658 wins and 419 losses) from 1883 to 1891 is second only to New York manager Joe McCarthy's .615 (2,125 wins and 1,333 losses) from 1926 to 1950 (Library of Congress).

Grounds, a site for polo matches at 110th Street and Eighth Avenue in New York, was available for lease. "There's my spot," he said. "I'm going to get it."

One problem: Mutrie didn't have the stuff that dreams are made of—enough money. He couldn't get a bank loan. He was about to give up when he ran into Jules Rankin, a reporter for the *New York Herald*, who introduced him to John B. Day, the owner of a tobacco company. Day, a former amateur ball player, was interested. With Day's backing, Mutrie leased the Polo Grounds and hired the local Hops Bitter team, including its one-armed pitcher, Jack Nelson, to form a franchise called the New York Metropolitans. The team played its first game at the Polo Grounds against the Washington Nationals, and the Mets won 4 to 2.[6]

In late 1882, the American Association accepted the Mets for the 1883 season. In the fall of 1882, Mutrie heard that the National League's Troy, New York, team was folding, and with Day's support acquired the squad's best players, including a young catcher named William Ewing. Day used the players to form a new team, the New York Gothams, which he placed in the National League in 1883. Suddenly, thanks to Mutrie and Day, New York had two teams in the major leagues. The Mets, with Mutrie as manager, won the American Association pennant in 1884. Now, as skipper of the National League team, Mutrie had won two straight pennants and was going for his second consecutive world championship.

Mutrie also claimed to have coined the New York National League team's nickname. During the Gothams' spring exhibition games in 1885, he frequently yelled to his team, "Come on, you giants." Writers picked up on the name and began calling the team the New York Giants. "The name was a natural," Mutrie said. "We were big men physically, and the real giants of the baseball field."[7]

Mutrie was a handsome, colorful man who wore long cutaway coats and top hats. He pretty much let Captain Ewing manage the team on the field, while he served as chief promoter. To woo working-class people to the National League games, he coined the team slogan, "We are the people," which he would shout as the team rode to games on an open carriage. Mutrie was known as "Truthful James," because he stretched the truth in a charming way. He was so popular with reporters that he had his own keys to local newsrooms.

Genial Jim Mutrie never lacked for confidence, and he was eager to talk about the coming championship match against Brooklyn. "Why, my dear boy, we'll win the series from Brooklyn or any other club on earth. The Giants are world beaters," he told a reporter. "Brooklyn or the cream of all the players in the American Association can't compare with the Giants. We can outbat them, outfield them, outrun them and outgeneral them. Now, how in the name of common sense can they win? Before the series is over Brooklyn will gain some knowledge of baseball or rather the delicate points of the game. Some of our teamwork plays will open their eyes. I may be mistaken, but, my dear boy, I seldom make an error."[8]

During the Series, the usually-quiet Gunner McGunnigle also made news. He was considering resigning when the Series was over, he told reporters. "The best evidence in the world that I have performed the work allotted to me is that the club made money and won the championship," he said. "But my work has not been appreciated. Beyond that I will say nothing for the present."[9] Charley Byrne was puzzled, saying he didn't know his manager had any grievance. *Sporting Life* correspondent J. F. Donnelly speculated on the cause. "I am afraid Mac is troubled with that degree of super sensitiveness to which most good men are subject," he wrote, "and that some trifling incident has worried him and caused him to drop a word that has been magnified."[10] Gunner may have been reacting to published reports that Baltimore skipper Billie Barnie would be hired to manage Brooklyn in 1890.

The 1889 World's Series, which was set to begin in New York, had a significance that went far beyond the games. "The rivalry between New York and Brooklyn as regards to baseball is unparalleled in the history of the national game," the *New York Times* observed. "It is not confined to the players or the attaches of the clubs, but the patrons take part in it. Old men, middle-age men, beardless youths, small boys, and even members of the gentler sex have the fever, and when the champions of the two teams meet heated arguments as to the merits of the nines are sure to follow."[11]

As the first game opened on a bright, sunny day on October 18, the rival cities crackled with plenty of emotion. The crowd at New York's Polo Grounds totaled 8,848 people and would have been higher if not for transportation snags. The crowds overwhelmed the elevated rail-car systems, leaving thousands of fans stranded at downtown station platforms and unable to get to the game. Those who did reach the Polo Grounds were keyed to a fever pitch. Though Giant backers were in the majority, the visitors from Brooklyn made their presence known. "They shouted, cheered, hissed, yelled, stamped their feet, clapped their hands, and acted as only baseball 'cranks' can," the *New York Times* said. The Giants fans were equally vocal. "Buck! "Buck!" the crowed yelled at Ewing when their team entered the field. And then it was "Ward!, Ward!" for handsome Johnny Ward.[12]

Umpire Frank Gaffney was decked out in a tight-fitting brown suit. Bob Ferguson was so grateful to have been chosen as the second umpire that he yelled out, "My head is swelled already," and the crowd roared in response. With Ferguson behind the plate and Gaffney stationed behind first base. New York chose to bat first. At precisely 4:00 P.M., Brooklyn took the field with Adonis Terry in the pitcher's box.

Brooklyn fans cheered as New York's first two batters, George Gore and Mike Tiernan, hit easy fly balls to left fielder Darby O'Brien. Terry then struck out Buck Ewing. New York was down in the first, one, two, three. Now the Bridegrooms faced great right-hander Tim "Sir Timothy" Keefe, who had won 28 games during the season. Hub Collins led off with a single, and then raced around the bases to score on an O'Brien double. Oyster

New York Giants pitcher Tim Keefe became teammate John Montgomery Ward's brother-in-law in 1889 when he married Helen Dauvray Ward's sister (Library of Congress).

Burns slapped a sharp single, sending O'Brien home. Suddenly, Brooklyn was up 2 to 0. Keefe got the next two batters out. But then catcher Bob Clark measured a Keefe curve and socked a hit to send Burns home. After Terry followed with a single, Pop Corkhill slugged a double, scoring two more runs. It seemed as though Manager McGunnigle had already picked up the Giants' signals for Keefe's pitches, as the Bridegrooms seemed ready for his "peculiar slow balls." The first inning ended with the visitors from Brooklyn up 5 to 0 on the world champions.

The New York fans were stunned, but their boys were coming up for a second swat at Terry. The Giants had decided that they could steal on Clark, the Brooklyn catcher. In the second inning, John Ward walked and moved to second when Roger Connor reached first on an error. On the next pitch, Ward took off to steal third base. Clark rifled the ball to Pinkney, who tagged the sliding Ward out. New York, however, scored two runs in the inning because of an error by center fielder Corkhill, and the score was 5 to 2. The New York cranks were alive again, confident that pitcher Keefe would settle down.

In the bottom of the second inning, Collins stepped to the plate and slammed a pitch past left fielder Jim O'Rourke and into the standing crowd. When O'Rourke couldn't find the ball, Collins raced around the bases for a home run. Brooklyn was up 6 to 2. Buck Ewing opened the Giants fourth inning with a double. He, too, tried to steal third, but Clark cut him down with another strong throw. Terry walked Ward, who went to second when Connor also drew a base on balls. Again, Ward headed for third and again Clark's throw was true. Maybe this strategy of running on the Brooklyn catcher wasn't such a hot idea. The Giants weren't done, though; Danny Richardson socked a long fly to center field. Corkhill leaped for the ball, turning a complete somersault as he grabbed the sphere with a spectacular catch. But after he hit the ground, the ball dropped out, allowing New York to score two more runs. To add injury to insult, Corkhill had to leave the game with an ailing back.

The Giants edged even closer in the fifth inning when Keefe, who had walked, came home on a Ward single. The score was now Brooklyn 6, New York 5. The powerful Giants came all the way back in the seventh inning. With two out and two runners on, Johnny Ward gave the Giants a 7 to 6 lead by knocking in both men with a long hit to left field. Ward then scored from third when O'Brien dropped a fly ball. Roger Connor singled, finally was able to steal second base, and scored on a single by Richardson. O'Rourke slammed a triple, putting New York up 10 to 6. It had taken a while, but New York fans breathed easier.

The Bridegrooms didn't give up, scoring two more runs to make the score 10 to 8. The skies were darkening in the bottom of the eighth inning with two out and Brooklyn's Joe Visner on second base. Just one more out, the New York fans pleaded, and the game would end on account of darkness. Sure enough, Darby O'Brien hit an easy grounder to third baseman Richardson. But the ball rolled under Richardson into left field, allowing Visner to score. Then Collins hit a fly ball to right, but Gore had trouble seeing it. The ball dropped as O'Brien raced home to tie the score.

Oyster Burns followed with a double, scoring Collins. When the second baseman muffed Dave Foutz's grounder, Burns scored to give the upstart Bridegrooms a 12 to 10 lead. The Giants began pleading with the umpires to call the game, which would have reverted the score to the end of the seventh inning. While this was going on, Foutz intentionally stepped off second base and allowed Ward to tag him for the third out. By the time New York came to bat in the top of the ninth, it was too dark to play. The umpires called the game, and Brooklyn had won. Giants fans looked on in stunned silence, while the Brooklyn fans rushed the field, hoisted O'Brien on their shoulders and carried him off the grounds.

Brooklyn enthusiasts were even more excited for the second game at Washington Park. By 2:30 P.M., the stands were filled to overflowing, and the crowd of 16,172 people — the second largest ever at the field — spilled over into the banks of grass and grounds at the side of and behind the center-field ropes. One of the many women in the crowd was overcome with heat and fainted. "The banks were crowded and hundreds of small boys, in order to get a bird's eye view of the game, clambered to the top of the fence and watched the struggle to their heart's content," the *New York Times* said. "It was a grand sight. Thousands of human faces could be seen in all directions and save a few tilts in which dyed-in-the-wool 'cranks' took part, the best of good nature prevailed."[13]

The Giants players were excited, too. Second baseman Mike Tiernan was in such a hurry to get to the game that he forgot his stockings and had to wear the red ones of the Brooklyn players. Starting pitcher Ned "Cannon Ball" Crane had to borrow a Bridegrooms shirt. Umpire Lynch finally consented to umpire and replaced Ferguson. He would get his $600 for his work.

Brooklyn decided to take last bats, allowing New York to come up in the first. McGunnigle sent his star pitcher, Bob Caruthers, to the box, with Joe Visner behind the plate. George Gore greeted Caruthers with a sharp single, then raced to second on a wild pitch and eventually scored on a groundout to put New York up 1 to 0. "This was the signal for an outburst of applause from the Giants' admirers. They jumped to their feet, howled, shook each others' hands and gave various other evidence of their joy."[14]

In the bottom of the first, Brooklyn faced off against Crane, a stocky right-hander who had achieved only a mediocre year of 14 wins and 10 losses. Darby O'Brien walked and raced to third on a Collins single. O'Brien scored on a Dave Foutz hit. After one inning, the score was tied 1 to 1. New York's Roger Connor started the second inning with a single to left field, and Danny Richardson reached first on an error by shortstop Germany Smith. After tagging up on a long fly out and moving to third, Connor scored on a groundout. New York was up 2 to 1. In the bottom of the second, Brooklyn came right back. Caruthers walked, Pop Corkhill reached first on an error and both Bridegrooms advanced on a Crane wild pitch. O'Brien hit a hot grounder to second, scoring Caruthers to tie the game. With Corkhill on third base, Collins tried to steal second base. Giants backstop Buck Ewing faked a throw to second, but instead fired the ball to third, catching Corkhill for the third out. Cries of "Ewing! Ewing!" could be heard everywhere while the Brooklynites looked on in amazement. The inning ended tied 2 to 2.

The Giants made it 6 to 2 in the fifth when Tiernan, New York's leading hitter for the season with a .335 average, singled and stole second. Tiernan scored on a single by Ward, who promptly stole second on a poor throw by catcher Joe Visner. Sensing an opportunity, Ward purposely danced off second to draw a throw from the catcher. He did. Visner's throw sailed into center field, and Ward waltzed home. Brooklyn could do nothing against Cannonball Crane, who suddenly was living up to his name. Catcher Ewing urged his hurler on. "Ned, you must be feeling good today. You didn't leave your speed at home." When Corkhill fouled out to Connor for the last out, this time it was the visiting New York fans who swarmed the field to shake the hands of the winning Giants players. The Series was tied at one game apiece.[15]

New York Giants pitcher Cannonball Crane was known as a big drinker. After being released as an umpire in Rochester, New York, in 1896, he began drinking heavily and was found dead in a hotel room at age 34. It was either an accidental death from a prescription drug or suicide from drinking acid (Library of Congress).

Then a bizarre event took place. Right in the middle of the World's Series, the Giants paused to celebrate their National League pennant at a star-studded banquet on the evening of Sunday, October 20. The show was at the Broadway Theater at Broadway and 41st Street. Tickets went for $10 each, with proceeds benefitting the Giants players. Many would -be attendees were turned away, as the event drew a standing-room crowd of more than 2,000 of New York's high society. At 7:00 P.M., the curtain went up, revealing the National League pennant hanging above the stage, with "1888–89" in big black letters. Then another sign was lowered with manager Jim Mutrie's slogan: "We Are the People." The crowd began chanting, "What's the matter with Jim Mutrie?" "He's all right!" "Who's all right?" "Why, Mutrie!" Then there were cheers for each member of the team as they lined up on stage, resplendid in black tuxedos.

The grand opening was followed by more than three hours of entertainment consisting of 22 musical numbers and recitations. The crowd roared as Broadway's De Wolfe Hopper gave his famous recitation of "Casey At The Bat," which had been written just three years before by George Thayer. Then emcee Digby Bell drew more cheers for his telling of "The Boy on the Left Field Fence." It was 11:00 P.M. by the time Bell again took the stage, followed by Jim Mutrie and his players, who formed a semi-circle around their manager. The audience erupted when Digby declared: "Gentlemen of the New York Club, twice League champions, and very probably twice world champions, I salute you."

Mutrie stepped forward on behalf of the team. "Nine years ago I spent weeks trying to find a man who would back a professional base ball club in this city," he said. "Finally I found one John B. Day, a man whose name stands for all that is fair and honorable in base ball, as well aa in business. Then 1,000 people was considered a large attendance at one game, now we often play before ten, fifteen and twenty thousand. I think we have the confidence of the public; I think we have the confidence of the press. Such confidence will never be abused by the New York Club."

Just then New York's chances of winning the Series nearly suffered a blow. A cord holding the illuminated sign, "We Are the People," snapped. The big sign fell, just missing several Giants players. Digby Bell decided it was time to call it a night. "It's all over," he declared to the crowd. But the crowd wasn't ready to leave. So the emcee called for John Montgomery Ward, who stepped forward to deliver a brief talk about being "deeply grateful." Then shouts went up for Buck Ewing. The captain reluctantly came to the front to give his thanks. Finally, the audience dispersed as midnight neared. Fortunately for the Giants, there was no game the next day.[16]

The Giants were confident as the Series returned to the Polo Grounds the next Tuesday. "It's a hundred dollars to a toothpick that we win today," Captain Ewing declared. More than 6,100 turned out. The Giants sent out 27-game winner Mickey Welch. McGunnigle chose Mickey Hughes, who had won just nine games, and Bob Clark was back behind the plate. New York chose to bat first. With one out, Tiernan slapped a single, went to second on a wild pitch and scored on a Ewing double. Ewing proceeded to steal third base and scored on a hit by Ward. Clark again threw out Ward trying to steal second, and the inning ended with the score 2 to 0. Brooklyn came back to tie the game in the bottom of the second inning. Dave Foutz walked and scored on George Pinkney's double. Pinkney moved to third on a Ward error and scored on a Corkhill fly to left field. In the third, Brooklyn loaded the bases, and Foutz singled in two runs, putting the Bridegrooms up 4 to 2.

Brooklyn kept on coming. In the fourth, Pop Corkhill homered over the left-field fence. Hughes doubled and scored on O'Brien's single. Brooklyn was now up 6 to 2. The Giants narrowed the score to 6 to 5 on a three-run homer by John O'Rourke. But in the bottom of the inning, Brooklyn moved up 8 to 5 on hits by Clark and Corkhill. Still, the Giants wouldn't fold, closing to 8 to 7 in the bottom of the sixth inning. As New York came to bat in the eighth inning, McGunnigle decided not to take any chances with Hughes and sent Bob Caruthers to the box. The Giants went down in order. Then, displaying shades of Charley Comiskey and the St. Louis Browns, as darkness neared the Bridegrooms began stalling. The New York fans hissed and hooted. In the top of the ninth inning, New York loaded the bases. Suddenly Umpire Gaffney decided it was too dark to continue and called the game. Brooklyn had won, and went up 2 to 1 in the Series.[17]

New York fans were outraged, but it was the Giants players who actually had swayed Gaffney's decision. In the top of the ninth inning, Buck Ewing was coaching at third base and urged the batter, Hank O'Day, to "hit her on ground, Hank," because a fielder would have a hard time seeing the ball in twilight. "But Captain," O'Day called back, "I can't see the ball; how am I going to hit her down?" Explained Gaffney: "I thought that if the batsman could not see the ball that it was about time to call the game and I did so."[18]

The Giants were feeling none too kindly toward the umpires when the Series continued in Brooklyn, where cold weather held the crowd to 3,405. Cannonball Crane was back in the box for New York. Brooklyn countered with Adonis Terry. The Bridegrooms got off to a fast start in the first inning when Darby O'Brien walked, stole second and raced home when Ewing threw the ball into center field. George Pinkney singled in another run to give Brooklyn an early 2 to 0 lead. The Giants came back to score a run in the third as Ewing singled in George Gore. By the bottom of the fifth inning, however, Brooklyn had moved ahead 7 to 2 as the hometown fans cheered another potential win.

But the Giants weren't done. In the top of the sixth inning, Pitcher Crane knocked in two runs with a long triple, and then came home on another triple by Gore to make the score 7 to 5. The next batter, Buck Ewing, bunted the ball back to Terry, who threw home to nab Gore, who was then caught in a rundown. Catcher Clark's throw to third hit Gore, who was running with his arms out. Umpire Gaffney called Gore out for interference. Captain Ewing complained about the call "in anything but

Sunday school language." Then Ward singled, sending Ewing to third base. Brooklyn catcher Clark tried to pick off Ewing, but the ball flew into left field, allowing the New York captain to score. Ward, meanwhile, raced around third and also scored as left fielder O'Brien's throw hit the Giants' third base coach, who was running up the third-base line alongside Ward. The score was tied 7 to 7. Brooklyn argued that Ward should be sent back to third because of interference by the coach. Ewing had heard enough. "Mr. Gaffney," he announced, "if you decide against us, I will take my men from the field. You know perfectly well that Ward is entitled to his run. Gore, too, should have been allowed to score. I don't propose to be bulldozed any longer. One-sided umpiring has been the cause of our defeats, and it must stop right here." The arguments went on for 15 minutes as the skies darkened. Gaffney allowed Ward's run to stand.[19]

In the next inning, with two out, Brooklyn's Germany Smith and Hub Collins were on base when Oyster Burns smacked a long fly ball to left field. O'Rourke couldn't see the ball, which fell to the ground for a three-run homer, putting Brooklyn up 10 to 7. After that, Brooklyn was in no rush to finish. The game was called after just six innings, and Brooklyn moved ahead 3 games to 1. The Giants were furious. "If the Brooklyns resort any longer to the dirty tactics that have characterized them in the games already played, and if the umpires continue to favor Brooklyn, the series will end," said Owner Day. "I will not allow my team to compete against a club that insists on playing dirty ball."[20]

The *Brooklyn Eagle* naturally defended the home team. "The game was called yesterday because it was too dark to play any longer; but that was not the fault of the Bridegrooms. If they could have arrested the rotation of the earth upon its axis they would have done so gladly; but since the sun stood still for Joshua that sort of interference with the motions of the heavenly bodies has never been successful. The night came down without collusion with the Bridegrooms and because it found them three runs ahead of the Giants President Day sees fit to make a charge of trickery."[21]

Day further ratcheted up the dispute by suggesting that the umpires were "crooked." Day's attack on their honesty irked the umps, who hinted they might boycott the Series if he didn't apologize. To settle things, all agreed to meet in Charley Byrne's office. Day apologized to the umpires, the captains of both teams agreed to restrain their kicking, and both owners agreed to start the games at 2:15 P.M. so that nine innings could be played.

The fifth game was back at the Polo Grounds, and cold weather again held down the crowd, which totaled 2,556 people. When the teams took the field, Bob Caruthers was again in the box for Brooklyn. Cannonball Crane was the New York pitcher for the third time after pleading to hurl again. Bill Brown was the Giants catcher because Ewing was out sick. The game was scoreless until the third inning when the Giants started slapping Caruthers around, going up 3 to 0, with Brown slugging an RBI double. By the fifth inning, the Giants had taken a commanding 8 to 1 lead, powered by a Richardson homer over O'Brien's head in left field. In the sixth inning, Brooklyn catcher Bob Clark singled but strained a muscle while running for first. He was out for the Series. When Doc Bushong went behind the plate for the first time in the seventh inning, "loud applause greeted the veteran catcher," the *Brooklyn Eagle* reported. He seemed to give new confidence to his "old pard" Caruthers, who retired the Giants in order.[22] But it didn't last long. Battery mates Crane and Brown each homered as the Giants sailed to an easy 11 to 3 win. Brooklyn's lead in the series was cut to 3 games to 2.

That same night, another astonishing bit of scheduling took place. Brooklyn, like New York, held a pennant celebration — a dinner in the Assembly Room of the Brooklyn Academy of Music, Brooklyn's major theater. Nearly 200 people jammed into the room. They hooted, hollered and waved their white napkins when the Brooklyn players entered and marched around the room, as the ever-popular Conterno's band, half-hidden in a corner behind palm trees, played "Hail to the Conquering Heroes." The players took their places at a table next to the head table, where the seated assemblage included the Brooklyn owners, sportswriter Henry Chadwick and various local politicians. On each table was the menu for the evening's servings of "Nine Innings" of delectable French dishes "with unpronounceable names," as *Sporting Life* put it. The elegant menu card featured gold letters embossed on parchment. The cover was adorned with crossed foul-line flags, featuring the inscriptions "Brooklyns" and "Champions 1889." Above in gilt was the pennant-winning percentage, .679, while beneath was an eagle with its wings spread and clutching a pennant in its little beak while at the same time upholding two crossed bats, above which was suspended an initialed gold baseball.

After dinner, the hosts broke out the cigars and coffee as the musical sounds of "Slide, Kelly, Slide" wafted from behind the palm trees. The after-dinner speeches began. At the introduction of Brooklyn's little chief Charley Byrne, the diners broke into song with, "He's a Jolly Good Fellow." The Brooklyn magnate responded, "I am not here to talk about myself, but these brave boys who sit around this table, the brave boys who brought the pennant to this town, the greatest base ball city in the world. It has been a hard job, and from the summer of 1883 my sole purpose has led in one direction, and tonight we glorify that object. I speak of my partners as well as myself. It was only a question of time that we would accomplish that result, and, thank God, we have done it." Byrne was followed by several more speakers, including the loquacious Henry Chadwick, who proceeded to tell the history of baseball, apparently almost in its entirety.[23] The celebration went on for 4½ hours into the night, no doubt prolonged by numerous swigs of alcohol. Many of the players stayed to the end, including shortstop Germany Smith, even though the team had a game the next day. It was the pivotal game in the Series. If Brooklyn won, it would take a commanding 4 games-to-2 lead. A New York victory would even the Series.

As it turned out, the game would revolve in large part around three reserve players. New York's George Gore was out of the Series with a bad cold. Taking his place was 6'2" Mike Slattery, 23, who had played in only 12 games during the season. For Brooklyn, Joe Visner again replaced injured Bob Clark behind the plate. And Jim "Jumbo" Davis, a little-used third baseman, was sent in to replace shortstop Germany Smith, who "failed to report for duty." Translation: He had a hangover.

Only 2,901 people turned out for the game in Brooklyn as the cold, rainy weather continued. The Bridegrooms got on the scoreboard in the second inning against Hank O'Day. George Pinkney led off with a single, Visner sliced another hit to left, but Pinkney was thrown out trying to go to third. A Terry hit sent Visner to third, and he scored the game's first run on a single by Pop Corkhill. The 1 to 0 lead was enough for Terry, who was pitching one of the most magnificent games of his career, giving up only three hits. Adonis had two out in the ninth inning. Just one more out, and Brooklyn would be in the driver's seat. Up stepped John Montgomery Ward, and he would be no easy out. Unlike many players who might shrink in pressure situations, Ward lived for them. "A man who can't breath an atmosphere surcharged with excitement's electricity and thrive upon it, has no business on a ball field," he once said. "Why, of my experiences, I can recall scores of times when the chords of my neck felt as street-car cables and my heart sounded like a stone-sledge."[24]

The count went to three balls and two strikes. "If I can only hit that next ball," Ward thought to himself, "lightening won't beat me to first base." In came the pitch. Ward swung and slapped a grounder into right field for a hit. "It was not a big hit, but I reached first base on it somehow or other," Ward said later. On the next pitch, he darted for second and slid under the throw from Visner. With the very next pitch, he took off for third and again beat Visner's throw. Brooklyn fans were moaning, wondering where catcher Bob Clark was when they needed him? The next batter was Roger Connor, the leading home run hitter of the nineteenth century and New York's top RBI man. Connor hit a grounder toward replacement shortstop Jumbo Davis, who "handled the ball very clumsily," allowing the batter to reach first. Ward raced home with the tying run. "That race around the bases embraced the most exciting time of my life," Ward said. "The moment I was safe at home was the proudest of my life."[25]

The New York fans went wild. "Hats, canes, and umbrellas were thrown in the air; old men, young men, middle-aged men and small boys slapped each other on the back and a feeling of joy pervaded the atmosphere," the *New York Times* said. During the excitement somebody shouted, "Ward, Ward, Johnny Ward!" The crowd took up the refrain, "and nothing but the name of the favorite shortstop could be heard for some minutes."

The game went into the 11th inning. The left-handed-batting Slattery, in for Gore, singled with one out and went to second on a groundout. Up stepped Monte Ward again. This time he tapped a bounder toward Jumbo Davis. As Davis moved to the ball, Ward "fairly flew" toward first. Davis finally snared the ball and fired it to first baseman Dave Foutz, who stretched out his long, bony frame. "Safe," the umpire cried. In all the excitement, Foutz failed to notice that Slattery didn't stop at third and was heading home. Dave threw the ball, but it was too late. Slattery scored the winning run. But above all the shouts could be heard the chant, "Ward, Ward, Johnny Ward."[26] The Series was now tied, 3 games to 3.

New York Manager Mutrie confidently predicted that the Giants would be in the lead after the next game, which took place in the Polo Grounds before 2,584 fans. Concerned that Caruthers had been hit hard in the fifth game, McGunnigle decided to start pitcher Tom Lovett, who had compiled a 17 and 10 record during the season. This day his offerings were no mystery to the Giants batters, who pummeled Lovett for eight runs in the second inning, with little Danny Richardson slugging a two-run homer into the left field seats. After O'Rourke later sent a three-run blast over the center-field fence, McGunnigle brought in Caruthers to stop the bleeding. But it was too late. Germany Smith, back in the lineup, hit a two-run homer to close the gap, but the Giants won 11 to 7 as Cannonball Crane pitched his third win of the Series.[27] New York was now up 4 games to 3.

The next game drew 3,312 people in Brooklyn as Manager McGunnigle counted on Adonis Terry to even the Series. This time the Giants found his pitches to be easy pickings. Dave Foutz tried his hand in relief but fared no better. Meantime, Cannonball Crane was pitching his fifth game in the Series. New York won easily, 16 to 7. After falling behind 3 games to 1, the Giants were within one victory of winning the championship.

After coming this far, the Bridegrooms weren't about to give up. The ninth game of the Series drew 3,067 people to the Polo Grounds. In the first inning, Darby O'Brien led off with a walk against Hank O'Day, who had won nine games and lost one during the season. Hub Collins followed with a single. Oyster Burns then blasted a double to the center-field fence, scoring both runners. In New York's first inning, Mike Tiernan doubled off Adonis Terry, advanced to third on a groundout and scored on John Ward's triple to left field. Brooklyn clung to a 2 to 1 lead until the sixth inning, when Ward — there was that man again — led off with a single, got around to third base and scored on a fly ball out. The score was tied 2 to 2. Then in the seventh inning, New York's Slattery was on third base with Buck Ewing at bat with a count of three balls and two strikes. Ewing swung and missed for strike three, but catcher Doc Bushong muffed the ball. Slattery raced home with what turned out to be the winning run as New York won 3 to 2. Bushong's passed ball foreshadowed the 1941 World Series when Brooklyn catcher Mickey Owen missed a two-out, third-strike pitch that would have given his team a win over the New York Yankees, who went on to win the Series.[28]

With its fifth straight victory over Brooklyn, the Giants had won their second consecutive world championship. "When the time of year and the cold, rainy weather is considered, it must be admitted that this series was a financial success," *Sporting Life* said. Total attendance of 47,600 for nine games exceeded the 1888 10-game Series won by New York over St. Louis by 5,000 people, and total receipts nearly doubled the previous year's take.[29] Back in the Giants clubhouse, Owner Day tallied up his club's revenues for the Series. The net was $12,056.15. Each player received a share of $380.13 from the games, but a total of about $500 each after money was added from the Broadway fund-raiser. Curiously, the team failed to vote a share to Manager Mutrie, but saloons all along Broadway served him free drinks. The Brooklyn players gathered the next day at Washington Park. Unlike the Giants, the Brooklyn players were under contract until October 31, meaning President Byrne wasn't obligated to pay them anything extra for the Series. Even so, he generously allotted each player $359.61. The Brooklyn players voted Manager McGunnigle a full share.[30]

McGunnigle no longer talked about quitting. Any doubts likely were erased the morning of October 29. When he came into the clubhouse, he was met by his players, who presented him with a gold watch and chain and a diamond-studded locket. Speaking for the team, Dave Foutz said

> I have the honor of representing the Brooklyn Baseball Club in the performance of a duty which affords me the greatest satisfaction. Recognizing, as we do, your sterling capability as a manager, and your many sterling traits of character as a man and an associate, we desire to present you with a substantial token of our regard. In accepting this watch, chain, and charm, it is our desire that you shall feel that, though the gift is of costly material and fine workmanship, it is yet but a small memento of our regard. Hoping your heart will beat long after the machinery of this watch has rusted into dust, we remain your friends and admirers, the Brooklyn Baseball Club.

Mac "blushed like a schoolgirl" as Foutz spoke. Then, glancing at the gift, he responded with words showing that he had come a long way since he wrote that barely readable letter to the Buffalo club a decade before. Perhaps recalling his father, he told the players: "Boys, you caught me unprepared. Of course, I can't tell you how much I appreciate your kindness. It is sufficient for me to say that I value the feeling which prompted you in this act much more than I do the intrinsic expression of it. I hope each will put yourself in my place and attribute your feelings under such circumstances to me. I can assure you that whatever happens the watch will never visit 'my uncle'; that it will be kept in a chamois case and that it will always be carried in a pocket over my heart."[31]

Baseball had just ended its most exciting pennant race in the most successful year in the history of the national game. Attendance was the highest ever. Just as the national pastime was riding high, some shots heard around the baseball world were about to turn the game on its head.

Chapter Nine

Revolt of the Players

As the American Association owners prepared for their annual meeting at the Fifth Avenue Hotel in New York in mid–November of 1889, St. Louis Browns chief Chris Von der Ahe was out for blood—specifically, the blood of baseball's little Napoleon, Brooklyn president Charles H. Byrne. A few days before the scheduled meeting, Von der Ahe arranged a gathering of a rump group of owners in a Philadelphia hotel with one mission: "To down that man Byrne."[1]

The Von der Ahe "combine" also included the heads of teams from Kansas City, Louisville, Philadelphia and Columbus. They agreed to back L.C. Krauthoff of the Kansas City Cowboys as their candidate for American Association president. Von der Ahe set one requirement: The group's candidate couldn't place members of the Brooklyn, Cincinnati or Baltimore clubs on any of the association committees. When told of this condition, Krauthoff angrily refused to accept the nomination, saying he wouldn't be used as a "tool" for the dissident group. He left in a huff, and the remaining owners then chose Louisville owner Zach Phelps as their candidate.

Byrne dismissed the whole conspiracy as "silly." He also vowed to reporters that he and his partners, Gus Abell and Joe Doyle, would not stand for any move to exclude Brooklyn from the American Association's levers of powers. "Charley Byrne tells this story in the cool, suave manner characteristic of the man, while his confreres Messrs Abell and Doyle look on and nod their heads knowingly," the *New York Times* reported.[2]

The American Association began the most contentious meeting in its nine-year history on November 13 in Parlor DR of New York's Fifth Avenue Hotel with a vote on a new president. Brooklyn, Cincinnati, Baltimore and Kansas City backed Krauthoff, who had switched sides. With the Von der Ahe group supporting Phelps of Louisville, the vote was 4 to 4. After each vote, another was ordered. The two sides remained deadlocked like an old-time U.S. presidential convention after 23 votes. Finally, at 4:30 in the afternoon the men in the Byrne faction picked up their hats, overcoats and umbrellas, and left for the evening. The voting resumed at 10:00 A.M. the next morning, but with the same result. Nobody was budging. The voting continued through 34 tallies until 5:00 P.M., when Byrne and Aaron Stern, the owner of the Cincinnati team, left the room. Soon the sound of popping champagne corks could be heard down the hall from Parlor F, where the National League was holding its meeting. Byrne and Stern returned to Parlor DR to announce that their clubs were joining the League.

Byrne took the floor to explain his decision: "Gentlemen: Since my connection with the American Association you have honored me by placing me on your most important committees and trusting me to act on your most important business. I have labored assiduously for the benefit of my club and the association, but the affairs of the association have now got into such a plight that myself and my club are driven from it, and compelled to seek shelter elsewhere to protect our interests."[3]

With that, he and Stern marched back to the National League meeting in Parlor F, where three baskets of wine had been delivered for the official toasts welcoming Brooklyn and Cincinnati into the League. Charley Byrne sipped wine and accepted congratulations with his usual modesty and courtesy. "I tried my best to elevate baseball, and I think I succeeded to a great extent," he said, "but unless I can live in harmony I do not want to live at all. I am glad the Brooklyn Club will have something good to offer their patrons next season, and that there will be no possibility of their being subjected to insults by men who have no further interest than to gratify their own desires and ventilate their petty grievances in public."[4] The next day, Kansas City joined the exodus from the American Association by switching to the minor league Western League. A few days later, Baltimore also exited to join the minor league Atlantic Association.

Von der Ahe was unapologetic. "The Association is all right, and don't you forget it," he said. "Why, Byrne was a man that would not stop for anything, he wanted to be the boss cook or ruin the broth.... I'm sorry that we did not sit down on him long, long ago."[5]

Brooklyn finally was a member of the prestigious National League. Byrne insisted that he would have kept the club in the association except for the vote against Brooklyn in the forfeited games with St. Louis and the meetings behind his back to undercut Brooklyn's power. Now, he would finally be free of the endless conflicts with Chris Von der Ahe. In Brooklyn, the news was greeted with joy. As Gilbert and Sullivan's *Mikado* might say, the *Brooklyn Eagle* declared, "*See how the Fates their gift allot, Byrne is happy, Chris is not.*" The good news for Brooklyn, the *Eagle* continued, was that "we are to have no more of the rowdy tactics of the St. Louis bullies of the Comiskey and Robinson class. And how the veteran habitués of the ball grounds will be pleased to learn that we shall now have a return in the near future to a series of contests marked by the old time rivalry between New York and Brooklyn."[6]

There was little time for Charley Byrne and his fellow magnates to celebrate. They were facing their biggest threat ever: a revolt of the players. Just two weeks before, in the same Fifth Avenue Hotel, the National Brotherhood of Professional Baseball Players had announced that they had formed their own Players' National League of Professional Base Ball Clubs for the 1890 season. The announcement had been expected, but the official declaration of the Players' League hit like a bombshell nevertheless. The union's president, John Montgomery Ward, issued the manifesto, which was aimed mainly at the National League. "There was a time when the League stood for integrity and fair dealing. Today it stands for dollars and cents. Once it looked to the elevation of the sport; today its eyes are upon the turnstiles. Men have come into the business for no other motive than to exploit it for every dollar in sight," Ward said. "Players have been bought, sold and exchanged as though they were sheep instead of American citizens.... We believe it is possible to conduct our national game upon lines which will not infringe upon individual and natural rights."[7]

Tensions between the players and owners had been festering for several years. Under baseball's "reserve" rule, clubs could reserve the contracts of players from year to year. The players could not switch teams on their own, but they could be sold or traded to teams in distant cities even if they didn't want to go. Club owners "can lay a player off without pay and even, under the present iron clad contract, prevent him from signing with another club that might be glad to avail itself of his services," complained veteran ball player Jack Burdock. "That means that they have it in their power to take the bread and butter out of our families' mouths."[8]

Ward and other New York players formed the Brotherhood in late

1885 after the National League set a $2,000 cap on player salaries. Even though the cap was never enforced, and star players such as Ward still were paid more than twice that amount, the arbitrary move added to the frustrations. A turning point came in late 1888, when the National League adopted a plan by Indianapolis owner John T. Brush to classify and pay players in one of five categories based on both their on-field and off-field habits. A class "A" player would be paid $2,500, while a class "E" player would get only $1,500. Players also would have to pay for their uniforms. What's more, the League adopted these rules when Brotherhood President Ward was out of the country as part of a Spalding all-star baseball team traveling around the world. To promote America's national game, Chicago owner Al Spalding organized several international tours of games between his Chicago team and all-star squads. The 1888 trip took players to such places as England, Egypt and Australia.

When the Brotherhood sought a meeting with National League officials that spring, League officials led by Spalding cavalierly dismissed the idea, saying the issues could wait until fall. "Spalding and a few of the moneyed people may regret this step. I won't say what the Brotherhood will do, but we will move," responded New York Giants pitcher Tim Keefe, secretary of the Brotherhood.[9] The players considered going on strike on July 4, 1889, but instead Ward and others began secret negotiations with capitalists to back Brotherhood teams in nearly all of the League cities.

The Brotherhood trumpeted its new league as a blow for human rights, though they also talked about tapping into the enormous riches that they thought baseball owners were making off the sweat of the players. The Players' League would be run mainly as a cooperative with the players sharing in the profits. The boards of each club were made up of four financial backers and four players. Individual players could buy stock in the company. The initial plan was for all the clubs to share expenses and profits, but the financial backers nixed that idea. Players would sign three-year contracts at their highest previous salaries and then could switch teams if they wished. They no longer could be sold without their consent. Like the National League, the Players' League would charge 50 cents admission and wouldn't play ball on Sundays. Ward and other players saw the Brotherhood as an offshoot of a growing labor movement in the U.S., much like the Knights of Labor and the new American Federation of Labor. Some labor officials agreed. "The way we look at this matter in its present shape is that the Brotherhood is a legitimate organization of skilled workmen," said Samuel J. Leffingwell, a veteran trade unionist in Indianapolis.[10]

National League owners responded quickly and harshly to the revolt, declaring a baseball war. "To the Public: The National League of Professional Ball Clubs has no apology to make for its existence or for its untarnished record of fourteen years. It is to this organization that the player of today owes the dignity of his profession and the munificent salary he is guaranteed while playing in its ranks." Moreover, the owners argued, the Brotherhood had previously agreed that contracts and transferring players were vital, so such terms as 'bondage,' 'slavery,' 'sold as sheep,' etc., becomes meaningless and absurd." In one final and lengthy sentence of rhetorical frenzy, the owners said of the Players' League

> Its official claims to public support are glittering generalities, that lack detail, color and truth, and the National League, while notifying its recalcitrant players that it will aid its clubs in the enforcement of their contractual rights to the services of those players for the season of 1890, hereby proclaims to the public that the national game, which in 1876 it rescued from destruction, threatened by the dishonesty and dissipation of players, and which by stringent rules and ironclad contracts it developed, elevated and perpetuated into the most glorious and honorable sport on the green earth, will still, under its auspices, progress onwards and upwards, despite the efforts of certain overpaid players to again control it for their own aggrandizement to its ultimate dishonor and disintegration.[11]

The National League appointed a three-man "War Committee" led by 39-year-old Chicago owner Al Spalding. His strategy was not simply to battle the new Players' League but to destroy it in a "fight to the finish." Despite the bluster, the owners were shaking in their spats. The Players' League formed teams in nearly every National League city and signed many of baseball's top players. Many of the champion New York Giants not only signed with a Players' League team by the same name managed by Buck Ewing, but the new team also leased a field next door to the Polo Grounds. Boston's King Kelly took many of his mates to the Players' League Boston Reds. John Montgomery Ward would manage a new Brooklyn entry that would include former Bridegroom Dave Orr. Even Charley Comiskey deserted Von der Ahe to manage a team in his hometown of Chicago, the Chicago Pirates. The other Players' League teams were the Philadelphia Quakers, Pittsburg Burghers, Cleveland Infants and Buffalo Bisons.

Charley Byrne's generous treatment of his players over the years paid off as Brooklyn was one of the few teams that wasn't decimated by the revolt. Indeed, Brooklyn lost only one player, Joe Visner, who signed with Pittsburgh. Second baseman Hub Collins, who turned down an offer from the Players' League, spoke for many of his teammates when he said: "Mr. Byrne treated me like a king, and I never hesitated about signing my contract for next season at the first opportunity that was offered."[12] Byrne even was able to hire new catcher Tom Daly, whom the Brotherhood quickly labeled as a traitor. "I don't want to be called a deserter," the 24-year-old Daly protested. "I attended the meeting of the Brotherhood and failed to see any of the cash spoken of, and I thought it advisable to join a club with a sound financial backing. Base ball is my profession, and I have a family to support."[13]

Even with his championship team intact, Byrne faced a huge economic hurdle. His club would have to compete for fans not only with Ward's new Brooklyn team, but with a third team, the Brooklyn Gladiators, added as one of the new clubs in the American Association. The Gladiators would play at Ridgewood Park since the Bridegrooms no longer would be playing Sunday games there. With two teams also in New York City, the New York area would have five squads hustling for the fans' dollars. The Bridegrooms also were at risk because of Spalding's hardball tactics reguarding schedules. Historically, in cities or regions with more than one team, schedules were drawn up so that one team would play at home when the other was on the road to avoid conflicting demands for fans. This time, Spalding made sure that most League home games

Brooklyn catcher Tom Daly had a weak throwing arm, so the team switched him to second base, where he became an outstanding player for years (*New York Clipper*).

would compete directly with the contests of the Players' League. The goal was to sabotage attendance at Players' League games, but for teams such as the Bridegrooms, the strategy was a two-edged sword.

Brotherhood president John Ward was taken aback by the aggressive scheduling tactic. "In making out its eight club schedule the National League seems to have declared war to the knife against our league," he said. "It will therefore be a fight, if not for the survival of the fittest, at least for a fair division of the public patronage."[14] Ward had other problems to deal with. His wife, the actress Helen Dauvray Ward, had left him and was planning a return to the stage. "My wife had to choose between me and the stage," Ward told a friend. "She has made her choice." Mrs. Ward saw it differently. "I go back to the stage because I am separated from my husband," not vice versa.[15]

Ward was snubbed again when he sought to join in a new baseball ritual of baseball clubs taking their teams south in the spring to train for the coming season. Chicago's Spalding had arranged to take his team — now called the Chicago Colts because of its new, young players — to the old Spanish town of St. Augustine, Florida. Spalding refused Ward's request to allow his new Brooklyn team to share the facility, forcing the Brotherhood chief to settle for inland Gainsville, Florida. Ward also took his team to Texas and Cuba.

Meanwhile, Al Spalding did invite Charley Byrne's Brooklyn Bridegrooms to Chicago's St. Augustine facilities. So at about 2:00 P.M. on a snowy afternoon on March 2, 1890, the Bridegrooms boarded the steamship *Iroquois* at Pier 29 of the East River under the New York end of the Brooklyn Bridge for the trip south. The boat would take them via Charleston, South Carolina, to Jacksonville, Florida, where they would travel by horse-drawn carriages to nearby St. Augustine. The landlubber Bridegrooms left shore with fears of seasickness dancing in their tummies. Manager Gunner McGunnigle "has sworn to lock himself in his stateroom at the first symptom," the *Brooklyn Eagle* reported, so that "no one may behold him in an attitude which would detract in the least from one of due respect and dignity."[16]

Five days later the team arrived in St. Augustine, which had become a winter playground for many of the wealthy of the northern East Coast, including Brooklyn co-owner Gus Abell. When the visitors weren't looking for the fountain of youth, they could enjoy the posh Ponce de Leon Hotel and watch baseball on an adjoining field. While most of the Chicago players had been put up in boarding rooms, the Bridegrooms stayed at the fashionable Cordova Hotel, where the manager was a former Brooklyn resident.

With the Chicago team winding up its spring training, Byrne quickly arranged an exhibition game with his usual flair, according to a dispatch from team co-founder George Taylor, who had returned to the newspaper business. "President Byrne secured the services of Brooks' military band for the occasion and a large crowd turned out," Taylor wrote. "The grand stand was filled with tourists, and the enthusiasm was intense. Whenever double plays, two-baggers or stolen bases were made, the many millionaires and their ladies present showed their approval in a way that would have done credit to the bleaching boards at the Polo Grounds."[17]

The Bridegrooms didn't fare well against Chicago, but that didn't matter. This was a time for the players to get in shape, some by biking or riding horses. After Manager McGunnigle and outfielder Darby O'Brien went trotting on two spirited steeds, Charley Byrne observed: "O'Brien's agility in covering every position in the field was wonderful, and McGunnigle did more sliding in his half hour's experience in the saddle than he ever did around the diamond."[18] This also was a time to have some fun in the sun. When somebody gave McGunnigle a monkey, the mischievous manager shipped the creature to a friend, patrolman Peter Davis, back in Brockton, Massachusetts, as an anonymous gift. The monkey proved to be an embarrassment for the law enforcer when it got loose and broke into houses to steal valuables.[19]

After three weeks in St. Augustine, the team headed home, this time on the Clyde steamer the *Yamasee*. The ship hit rough waters, which was especially stressful on the stomach of Dave Foutz. The ever-playful Darby O'Brien, knowing Foutz was ill, had a big dish of fat pork cooked up and set the "unsavory mass, smoking hot" before the seasick player. Foutz vowed to "get square with O'Brien if it takes all summer."[20]

The team was gearing up for its first season in the National League. They were still called the Bridegrooms, though some observers thought that as more of the players became married fathers, they should at least make it the "Grooms." The team had 11 married men along with five bachelors: Dave Foutz, Darby O'Brien, Mickey Hughes, Bob Clark and new catcher Tom Daly. "It is rumored that three of the five bachelors are 'dead gone,'" the *Eagle* reported.[21] Brooklyn basically was going with the same team that won the American Association the year before, with the addition of catcher Daly. McGunnigle would rely on the same four pitchers: Bob Caruthers, Adonis Terry, Mickey Hughes and Tom Lovett. Charley Byrne was optimistic. "The outlook for a successful season in the National League was never so promising as at the present time," he said. "We have a body of men who have had the manhood to stand by their employers, and I have reason to believe our patrons respect them for it."[22]

Under the dueling schedules, the Brooklyn squads of both the National League and the Players' League opened their 1890 seasons in Boston. Nearly 4,000 people showed up at South End Grounds on a chilly day to see the National League's Boston Beaneaters host the Bridegrooms. Caruthers went to the box against John Clarkson, a pitcher Chicago's Spalding had sold to Boston for $10,000. Clarkson had spurned the Players' League to stay with Boston at a hefty salary. The winner of 49 games in 1889, Clarkson was one of the great right-handers in baseball history. When pitching, one observer noted, Clarkson "faces second base first, then quickly whirls around and throws the ball over the plate, startling the batter. He is a swift thrower."[23] The Bridegrooms got to the great Clarkson for three quick runs, but Boston had an equally easy time with Caruthers, who gave up five runs before Terry was sent in to relieve him. In the end, the Bridegrooms lost their first National League game 15 to 9.

Pitcher John Clarkson won 328 games, including 53 in 1889. After baseball, he returned to Bay City, Michigan, where he ran a cigar store. He suffered a nervous breakdown and was declared insane. He died at age 47 (Library of Congress).

"Nine blushing bridegrooms walked disconsolately from the South

End Grounds yesterday and were hurriedly driven in hacks to the Quincy House," the *Boston Daily* reported after the loss. "Manager McGunnigle, glorious in a silk tie and immaculate shirt bosom, buttoned his new spring overcoat round his glittering diamond and mournfully joined in the procession that dragged its weary length along the pitiless cobble stones on Tremont Street. President Byrne wore a sad sweet American Association smile, crimson blushes stole furtively through his polished mustache and lost themselves in the curling smoke of a fragrant Havana he poised between his sunburnt fingers."[24]

The big event of the day, however, was the opening game of King Kelly's Players' League Boston Reds against John Montgomery Ward's team from Brooklyn, dubbed "Ward's Wonders" because one investor was the company that sold Wonder bread. Nearly 10,000 people, double the attendance at the League game in Boston, turned out at the new grounds on Congress Street. The two squads met first at the United States Hotel and in full uniform rode through the city in carriages led by a 30-piece brass band. After they arrived at the field, the teams posed in a semi-circle for photographs. The squads then marched across the diamond as the band played and the crowd cheered. Boston was dressed in new white knickerbockers, shirts and caps with red stockings. Across the chest in big scarlet letters was the word "Boston."

The first batter of the game, Boston third baseman Hardy Richardson, knocked a sharp line drive over the head of shortstop John Montgomery Ward. If as on cue, the Brotherhood president leaped high and snared the ball for the first out as even the Boston fans cheered.[25] Boston won 3 to 2, but Ward's Wonders came back to win the second game the next day before a smaller crowd of 3,320 in cold windy weather as Ward hit a three-run homer. The Bridegrooms also notched their first National League win the same day before a crowd of about 1,500 people, but lost the next two games before heading home. Ward's Wonders returned home with a 2–2 split.

Rain postponed the home openers of the Brooklyn teams three times. Finally, on April 28, the Bridegrooms opened at Washington Park in their first appearance since winning the American Association championship. Conterno's band was there again, the American Association pennant was raised, but only 2,509 paying customers showed up. They saw the home team win as Bob Caruthers was in top form, blanking the Philadelphia

Phillies 10 to 0. But it seemed that the city was waiting for the debut of the new rival, the Brooklyn Players' League team. Ward's Wonders actually played its first home game the same day, beating the Philadelphia Quakers 3 to 1. But in an attempt at one-upsmanship to avoid head-to-head opening days, Ward's team held its "official" starting game two days later.

On April 30, 6,240 people (more than twice the crowd at the Bridegrooms' opener) turned out at the new Eastern Park for the Players' League Brooklyn team's "official" opening against New York. Eastern Park had been built for a staggering cost of $150,000 amid a crisscross of rail and trolley tracks. The club's owners were led by streetcar executive Wendell Goodman, who saw baseball as a way to gain more riders. The park was horseshoe shaped with a high tower on one end. The first-day ceremonies began with Foh's 23rd Regiment Band playing the inspiring strains of *Der Freischutz*. The Brooklyn team, dressed in white and blue uniforms, formed in line behind the band and marched around the diamond to where the New Yorkers stood. The two nines then raised their caps to each other and shook hands heartily. Then all 28 players marched behind the band twice around the diamond as the crowd cheered. This was followed by much speechmaking.

Finally, the game started. When Monte Ward went to bat for the first time, the crowd went wild as the manager was presented with two large floral horseshoes. The Players' League used two umpires in every game, and the rules were designed to produce more offense. The league used a livelier ball and moved the pitching box back one-and-a-half feet, to 57 feet. Sure enough, the game was a slugfest as Wards Wonders won 10 to 5.[26]

The Players' League, with its players generally better known to the fans, drew more people to its early games than the National League. The Brotherhood teams "have scored the first blood and first knockout," cheered *The Sporting News*, which backed the players' rebellion.[27] National League president Nick Young cautioned that "the attendance at the games of both the league and the brotherhood clubs since the season began has been dwindling perceptibly, and it has clearly demonstrated the impossibility of two big base ball organizations making money. Divided attendance means diminished gate receipts, and somebody must go to the wall. In my opinion the league is better fitted financially to stand the strain."[28]

Brotherhood president John Ward quickly responded. "It is noteworthy that all this talk about no interest, the absence of local pride and meager attendance comes from National League sources. Not a single Players' League club has yet made any complaint," Ward said. "I honestly believe that rather than see the Players' League succeed the old league would prefer the national game dead and would gladly inflict the blows."[29]

The teams settled into their respective pennant races. The Bridegrooms competed for the National League flag with Cincinnati, which also had retained many of its players, along with Boston, the Chicago Colts and the Philadelphia Phillies. The other teams were the Pittsburg Alleghenys, Cleveland Spiders and Jim Mutrie's New York Giants. In the Players' League, Ward's Wonders battled the Boston Reds and that league's New York Giants. The third Brooklyn team, the Gladiators, soon sunk from sight in the American Association and eventually was replaced by Baltimore.

A bad omen for the Bridegrooms — a player injury — popped up in a May 1 game against Boston. A sliding Boston runner accidentally spiked third sacker George Pinkney, who "limped off the field with a bleeding foot." Pinkney missed the next two games, ending his record streak of consecutive games at 577 and more than 5,000 straight innings, dating to September 21, 1885.[30] On May 10 at Philadelphia, 32-year-old center fielder Pop Corkhill made history in his hometown by becoming the first Brooklyn batter to hit a home run in the National League. The count was three balls and two strikes when Phillies pitcher Tom Vickery "put the sphere over the plate just where the old man wanted it," the *Brooklyn Eagle* reported. "Corkhill hit the ball squarely and it went sailing twenty feet over the center field fence and seemed to be bound for Saratoga on a summer vacation. It was the longest and cleanest hit made on the grounds in a long term of years and the tall Brooklynite was loudly applauded."[31] Brooklyn won 6 to 4 behind Mickey Hughes.

By late May, Brooklyn was on the rise, knocking off Cincinnati in two of three games in Brooklyn. In the first game, which the Bridegrooms won 19 to 4, Brooklyn made the first triple play in its National League history. With runners on first and second in the third inning, the Reds batter hit a grounder to second baseman Hub Collins, who threw the ball to shortstop Germany Smith, who touched second for one out and threw the ball to first for the second out. First baseman Dave Foutz then zipped the ball home to catcher Tom Daly, who tagged out a third Reds runner. "It was the prettiest bit of fielding of its kind ever seen on the home field. The applause it elicited was loud and long," the *Brooklyn Eagle* said.[32]

Brooklyn was still trying to prove it belonged in the National League when Chicago came to town. The Bridegrooms were steaming over the remarks of Chicago player-manager Cap Anson during spring training. "The Brooklyn team played good association ball but they were not up to the standard of the League clubs," Anson had said. Chicago jumped to a 2 to 0 lead against Tom Lovett. Brooklyn tied the score on triples by Oyster Burns and Pop Corkhill, and then went on to win 8 to 4. What's more, the same three fielders who turned Brooklyn's first triple play a week before against Cincinnati duplicated the trick against Chicago. "'Well, well, if that is not league championship ball playing I should like to know what is' was the remark of an occupant of a seat in the grand stand at Washington Park yesterday as he arose at the close of the contest," the *Eagle* reported.[33]

Chicago player-manager Cap Anson stubbornly refused to wear a glove as a first baseman despite making a large number of errors. He later became vice president of the American Bowling Congress (Library of Congress).

The Bridegrooms began to make their move in mid–June. More than 1,100 people turned out for a Ladies Day game against the Giants. President Byrne's personal guest was Mrs. Ella Black of Pittsburg, *Sporting Life's* only female reporter. "She expressed herself as delighted with the fine exhibition of ball playing, the fine appearance of the grounds and the high character of the assemblage of spectators," the *Brooklyn Eagle* said.[34] Brooklyn won 4 to 2 as Caruthers bested Mickey Welch, one of the few Giants players who did not desert to the Players' League. The Bridegrooms beat the Giants four straight games to move back into second behind Cincinnati. McGunnigle wasn't present for the June 17 game; he briefly was called home to Brockton where his pregnant wife was ill.

Next Philadelphia came to town, led by 23-year-old pitcher Bill "Kid" Gleason and 24-year-old Billy Hamilton, who regularly stole more than 100 bases a year. The game was another Ladies Day contest. McGunnigle debated whether to start Tom Lovett as pitcher or Adonis Terry, "but as the admirers of the Adonis were out in full force" Terry got the nod. It was bad news. The Phillies pounded the Adonis so badly that Lovett replaced him in the third inning. But Philadelphia's pitcher, the returning Phenomenal Smith, was an easy target and Brooklyn "got onto Smith's curves in fine style" to win 8 to 6 for its seventh straight victory. At the end of June, the Bridegrooms headed for a showdown with first-place Cincinnati, and took the first game 8 to 6 behind Terry. But Cincinnati, led by veteran first baseman "Long John" Reilly, won the next three, sending Brooklyn sliding all the way to third place.

Fortunately, the next four games were two double-headers against last-place Pittsburg. Pittsburg's one decent player was speedy outfielder Billy Sunday, who played baseball by day and in the evening preached at local YMCAs. Sunday, "a painstaking Christian," eventually became the most famous evangelist in America. But Pittsburg didn't have a prayer this time. Bob Caruthers and Adonis Terry won the first two games on July 4 in Pittsburg. The next day back in Brooklyn, Terry and Lovett pitched two more wins, moving the Bridegrooms back into second place. Over in the Players' League, Ward's Wonders were in a four-way battle for third place.

At this point, though, the question in the major leagues wasn't who won or lost, but how many people attended the game? The Brooklyn Bridegrooms, after averaging more than 5,000 people a game in 1889, now often drew under 2,000. Ward's Brooklyn team was faring even worse. Attendance was lagging in all three leagues. "It begins to look as though the base ball managers and players have killed the goose that laid the golden egg," the *Brooklyn Eagle* declared.[35] "In a few short months, base ball as a sport has dropped to second, if not to third, place in the favor of the amusement seeking public," the *Eagle* lamented. "It is certainly subordinate to horse racing, and there is room to believe that it has been surpassed, for the time, at least, by boating and other aquatic pleasures. All of this, of course, is the result of a well defined cause, viz, The desire of some of the players to set up business for themselves."[36]

The primary problem was that there were too many teams and too many leagues to keep up with. "People who followed the games last year were able to keep the whole situation of the base ball struggle before them by a daily glance at the figures in the papers," the *Eagle* said. "No amount of genius and skill in base ball reporting now, however, can make the situation clear to anybody but an expert."[37] The baseball press began calling for a ceasefire. "To carry on the war is only proving financially disastrous," said *The Sporting News*. "With conflicting dates all over the country the crowds to one or the other must be diminished as the season progresses. Have not the rival forces had enough of the losing fight to change their dates and avoid any further trouble?"[38] Added the *New York Times*: "It took nearly thirty years to work up the enthusiasm for the national game that made so profitable a business in 1889. Already that has very much cooled. Without an

Outfielder Billy Sunday became an internationally famous evangelist. He once claimed to have converted 65,000 people to Christianity at a single New York appearance. A later study found that only 200 were "permanent converts" (Library of Congress).

amalgamation of the rival organizations, the baseball public will virtually have disappeared by 1891."[39]

Neither side budged. The conflicting schedules continued. Fewer fans showed up to watch the games. As he looked around at the empty seats in the Polo Grounds at the National League New York Giants games, manager Jim Mutrie raised a question. Instead of his motto, "We are the people," he said, this season it was "*Where* are the people?"[40]

Chapter Ten

Pennant Fever and Labor Pains

As the Brooklyn Bridegrooms pressed for the National League pennant in the second half of the 1890 season, Gunner McGunnigle was called on to do his most creative managing. Suddenly, the boys of summer were the boys of sickbay. Center fielder Pop Corkhill was out indefinitely with a sore throwing arm. Adonis Terry was sick in bed with heat exhaustion. And in an early July road trip to Chicago, team captain Darby O'Brien swung by his hometown of nearby Peoria. "While out with the boys, he put his fist through a show case and cut his wrist, severing an artery and otherwise damaging his member," the *New York Clipper* reported. Darby would be out for weeks.[1] The talkative Tom "Oyster" Burns was installed as interim captain. At about the same time, Mickey Hughes, the winner of 25 games two years before, was suspended for "insubordination and intoxication." Because of his drinking, Hughes had been used little since early in the season. He was released in midseason with a record of 4 and 4. At age 23 he was finished and would end the season pitching for a sandlot team.

Manager McGunnigle suddenly had to do more juggling than a clown at the P.T. Barnum Circus. Dave Foutz moved into O'Brien's spot in left field. Catcher Tom Daly took over first base, where he proved to be a surprisingly nifty fielder. Bob Clark filled in behind the plate. Ireland-born Patsy Donovan, 25, was obtained from the Boston Beaneaters to take Corkhill's place in center field.

Despite the makeshift lineup, the Bridegrooms continued their early July winning streak, rolling up seven straight wins as first-place Cincinnati came to town. In the first game, McGunnigle sent Bob Caruthers to the box because he was the team's only remaining hurler. Terry was ill, Hughes was out, and Tom Lovett had to rush home to Providence because his wife was sick. No problem. Burns slugged a three-run homer, and Caruthers pitched the Grooms to a 5 to 3 win. The next day, Lovett was back and twirled the Bridegrooms to a 9 to 2 victory for Brooklyn's ninth consecutive victory.

Brooklyn fans had high hopes for the third contest of the series because it was Ladies Day, and the Bridegrooms always did well in front of the fair sex. President Charley Byrne was all smiles, wearing a "natty sailor hat" and sitting in his private box explaining the game to two Southern women who were attending their first baseball contest. One was the granddaughter of former United States Senator from Virginia. Shortstop Germany Smith was jittery early in the game, so Manager McGunnigle used the crowd as an incentive. "Just look up into that grandstand, George," he said. Smith settled down to his usual fine fielding with Bob Caruthers again pitching. In the seventh inning, Brooklyn tied the score at 3 to 3—and "how the fair ones in the grand stand did enjoy that rally"—as George Pinkney came to bat with Hub Collins on third base. "One more run now, boys, and the game is ours," chirped Captain Burns. Pinkney's single sent Collins home. "Four to three and the country safe. Ladies day did it," the *Brooklyn Eagle* reported.[2] Brooklyn won 5 to 3 and now was within percentage points of first place. Manager McGunnigle was given Sunday off to go home to Brockton to be with his pregnant wife.

Outfielder Patsy Donovan became a scout for the Boston Red Sox. While in that post, he helped recruit George Herman "Babe" Ruth through his connections with the Averian Brothers, who coached Ruth at a Baltimore orphanage (*New York Clipper*).

Brooklyn rolled up its 11th straight win over the visiting Chicago Colts before Chicago finally ended the streak in the second game of the series. But that wasn't the worst of it. In the third inning, Adonis Terry, back in action and playing left field, and center fielder Patsy Donovan, who was still filling in for Pop Corkhill, ran for a high fly ball hit by Cap Anson before ramming into each other. Donovan was knocked silly and had to be carted off the field. He would be out of action for at least a week. McGunnigle had to reach deep to find a replacement. His answer was catcher Doc Bushong, who played center field. In one game, McGunnigle even decided to send Corkhill, injured throwing arm and all, back to center. Corkhill responded with a key hit as Brooklyn won 7 to 2 behind Tom Lovett, who struck out Chicago manager Cap Anson for only the third time in 69 games. The Bridegrooms at last were in first place.

The win streak may have been McGunnigle's finest moment as a manager.

> According to *Sporting Life*: Considering the disadvantages under which the Bridegrooms are playing, they are putting up magnificent ball. "It's a genuine pleasure to note the rushing fashion in which they go at their opponents and the sturdy work they do all around. There's Caruthers and Lovett doing great work in the box, and wielding the stick most handily. There's Terry working like a Trojan in left field and ready for twirling at any moment, and Doc Bushong buckling down behind the bat and then going out to play centre field. Daly, a king among ball players, is causing universal wonder by his marvelous backstop play and causing people to stare at his doings at first base. Dave Foutz, though, *is* his same old self at the initial station. His long legs are covering big territory and his hitting is always timely. He's a good fourth corner to that invincible trio, Collins, Smith and Pinkney. But what of the captain, the erstwhile governor, Tom Burns? To be truthful, the bluff right fielder is simply turning himself inside-out in his efforts to lift the club away up high, so that when Darby O'Brien returns the latter cannot reproach him for being remiss. Poor Donovan was making a most solid impression and establishing himself as a big favorite when he and Terry ran amuck on Tuesday chasing a short hit of Anson's.[3]

Despite the Bridegrooms' victorious ways, Philadelphia was winning even more often. With a July 17 Ladies Day loss by Terry, the Philadelphia Phillies moved into first place after taking 10 of their last 11 games. The Phillies, which is the oldest, continuous nickname for any baseball team in the same city, were managed by George Wright, one of the original members of the old Cincinnati Red Stockings. Meantime, over in the Players' League, Ward's Wonders won nine in a row to move into second place behind Boston. Things were looking up for manager Ward.

His wife was back, and was "an enthusiastic spectator and rooter at Eastern Park."[4] But the reconciliation would not last long.

The news on the Bridegrooms' injury front grew worse as the team headed on a western road trip. A Philadelphia paper reported that Pop Corkhill had a "dead arm" and "cannot throw across the street without excruciating pain."[5] Byrne was forced to release the veteran player, who had made so many contributions to Brooklyn's 1889 championship. But with the left-hand-hitting Patsy Donovan back in center field, Brooklyn continued to win. On August 1, the Bridegrooms won both games of another double-header against Pittsburg; in the second game, Oyster Burns became the first Brooklyn player to hit for the cycle in the National League as the Bridegrooms pummeled Pittsburg 20 to 1. The next day, the Bridegrooms topped Pittsburg 9 to 2 behind Terry to move back into first place ahead of the Phillies. There was even better news for the scribes in the Washington Park press section, as the *Brooklyn Eagle* noted: "The dead dog under the official scorer's desk was removed on Saturday morning and the atmosphere is improved."[6]

But the pennant races took a back seat to the continuing baseball war. The Players' League charged that National League teams were having such a tough time drawing fans that they were giving away boatloads of free tickets at barbershops, saloons and elsewhere. Chicago's Al Spalding even instituted an "entertainers" day, giving free entrance to anybody involved in the theatrical business or ball playing. But in Brooklyn, secretary Charley Ebbets indignantly denied any such activities by the Bridegrooms. "No, sir, we are not papering our grounds and I would like you to follow me through these books while I give you the strongest kind of evidence that what I say is true."[7]

As head of the National League's War Committee, Al Spalding sought to undermine the Players' League's charges. He sent his own agents to the games of the Chicago Players' League games to count the people going into the park. Using contacts in the press, he then had the results published, which showed that the actual numbers were far less than the reported attendance. When the Players' League reported attendance of 39,159 from July 21 to August 2, the actual was 12,648, according to the Spalding spies.[8] Whether the Spalding numbers were accurate or not, he succeeded in his goal to raise doubts about the truth of the Players' League numbers and to divert attention from the League's small crowds.

"The lying that has been going on as to the attendance at the Brotherhood games has been simply outrageous," said Chicago's Spalding, who candidly conceded: "We have done some lying ourselves, but nowhere near as strong as the other fellows. The base ball business is dead in this city. I don't hesitate to say that the National League club here is losing money, and a good deal of it, and that we are giving out false returns of our attendance. We had to do it. It wouldn't do for us to say we had 700 people and the Brotherhood come out with 3,000, when they didn't really have more than we did. We had to put our figures somewhere near theirs."[9]

Indeed, attendance numbers often were created out of thin air. At one League game in Chicago, Spalding was talking to his club secretary, John A. Brown, when a reporter came up and asked for the attendance number. The club secretary immediately replied: "Twenty-four eighteen."

"Brown, how do you reconcile your conscience to such a number?" Spalding asked after the reporter had left.

"Why, don't you see? There were 24 on one side of the grounds and 18 on the other. If he reports twenty four hundred and eighteen, that's a matter for his conscience, not mine."[10]

Albert Goodwill Spalding brought a competitive zeal to his role as the baseball war general. At this point he was the most successful baseball man in the history of the game. Although Brooklyn's Charley Byrne had already established himself as one of the National League's most influential executives, Spalding stood out in the war against the players. "President Albert G. Spalding of Chicago has forced himself to the front as the leading base ball strategist of the day," *Sporting Life* said. "He has been ably aided by President Charles H. Byrne, of Brooklyn, but his large interests in the game, combined with an ability to teach the Players' League capitalist a trick or two" easily places him in the top position.[11]

Spalding had been the game's top player in the 1870s for Boston in the old National Association of Professional Ball Players and the Chicago White Stockings in the National League. As a pitcher he won 252 games in just seven seasons and hit .313. In Chicago, he became the first prominent first baseman to wear a glove. Spalding said the first man he ever saw wearing a glove at the position was his Boston teammate, Charlie Waite, in 1875. Waite's glove was flesh-colored, making it harder to see. "He confessed that he was a bit ashamed to wear it, but had it on to save his hands," Spalding said. When Spalding moved from pitcher to first base in Chicago,

"I did not select a flesh-colored glove, but got a black one" and put pads in it, he said.[12] As a star player of the day, nobody made fun of Spalding, and use of the glove quickly spread among first basemen. It no doubt wasn't any coincidence that in 1876 the ball player and his brother had started the A.G. Spalding Sporting Goods company, which began selling ball gloves and also made Spalding a very rich man. In a blatant conflict of interest, Spalding's company provided the official National League baseball and sold uniforms, bats and other equipment to baseball clubs. Spalding retired from playing while still in his twenties and moved into the Chicago White Stockings front office. When owner William Hulbert died in 1882, Spalding took over the entire club at the age of 32.

Now, the old ball player would stop at nothing to win the baseball battle. He determined that one way to destroy the opposing league was to persuade one of its top stars to desert. So he invited his former player, King Kelly of the Players' League Boston team, to meet him at a Chicago hotel room. Spalding placed a check for $10,000 on the table and said: "Mike, how would you like that check for $10,000 filled out payable to your order?"

Chicago owner Al Spalding had a "no liquor" policy for his team and hired detectives to follow his players. He fined seven violators, including star Mike "King" Kelly (*New York Clipper*).

"Would Mike Kelly like $10,000? I should smile," Kelly responded.

"But that's not all, Mike. Here's a three years' contract, and I'm authorized to let you fill in the amount of salary yourself."

Kelly's face blanched. "What does this mean? Does it mean that I'm to join the League? Quit the Brotherhood? Go back on the boys?"

"That's just what it means," Spalding said. "It means that you go to Boston tonight."

"Well," Kelly said, "I must have time to think about this."

"There is mighty little time, Mike. If you don't want the money, somebody else will get it. When can you let me know?" Kelly responded that he needed an hour and a half, and he left the room. He returned on time. "I've been taking a walk. I went 'way up town and back. I was thinking," he told Spalding.

"Have you decided what you're going to do?"

"Yes, I've decided not to accept. I want the ten thousand bad enough; but I've thought the matter over, and I can't go back on the boys." And, he added, "Neither would you."

"Involuntarily, I reached out my hand in congratulation to the great ball player for his loyalty," Spalding later wrote.[13] Despite rumblings of discontent among some Players' League members, including New York's Buck Ewing, none were ready to return to the other side. Still, Brooklyn's Charley Byrne predicted: "The end is near at hand. The Players' League may make a few desperate bluffs to try to last out the season, but I think it will die inside of the next few weeks."[14]

Back on the field, Manager McGunnigle increasingly relied on 26-year-old pitcher Tom Lovett rather than Bob Caruthers to hold the Bridegrooms' slim first-place lead. The stocky Lovett was a tricky twirler. Batters did not "know whether to expect a swift pitched ball cutting the center of the plate or an outcurve that could not be reached with a paddle," McGunnigle said. "There is another good thing about Lovett, he never forgets the batter. He studies batters as a cat does a mouse, finds their points of weakness. If a batter cannot hit a low ball, that batter will never get a high one from Mr. Lovett."[15]

King Kelly while playing right field for Chicago reportedly once caught a fly ball with one hand while holding a mug of beer in the other (Library of Congress).

Then in the first week of August came another bad break. Lovett was pitching in the fourth inning against Boston, which was rising rapidly in the standings, when a batter hit the ball back to the box. When Lovett, who like all pitchers did not wear a glove, tried to field the ball, he split the finger on his pitching hand (to this day, it isn't known if Lovett was a right-handed or left-handed pitcher). Despite the possible loss of the club's top pitcher, the *Brooklyn Eagle* was optimistic that Lovett's finger would heal soon. "Lovett is temperate and his flesh cuts heal rapidly; not so with drunken players, who find it very different in this respect," the *Eagle* explained.[16]

McGunnigle now had to rely on Caruthers and Terry as his only two pitchers. The good news was that on August 18 in Brooklyn, captain Darby O'Brien returned to the team and moved into center field, replacing the light-hitting Donovan. McGunnigle alternated pitchers Terry and Caruthers in left field. The home crowd cheered wildly as Darby batted for the first time. Except for Lovett, the team was now intact again. The Bridegrooms lost the first game of a four-game series with Philadelphia but won the next three, with Terry pitching all three games, including both ends of a double-header. Lovett came back for the next game against Chicago, pitching a 4 to 0 shutout with his "puzzling curves." He followed up with a 3 to 0 win over Cincinnati. Lovett "has not done more skillful work in this notable season," *the Eagle* said. By the end of August, Brooklyn was up three games on second-place Boston when Manager McGunnigle was again called home to Brockton. This time it was good news. It was a boy, Edward, Gunner's seventh child.

Stocky Tom Lovett pitched the first no-hitter for Brooklyn in the National League on June 22, 1891, beating New York 4 to 0 (Library of Congress).

McGunnigle was back when Brooklyn went to Cleveland, where the Bridegrooms rolled up three more wins, two by Lovett and one by Terry. In the box for Cleveland in the second game was a promising rookie pitcher, Cyrus Young, a former rail-splitter. The new pitcher was described as a big, strong country boy who threw faster than about anybody in the league and had a drop ball that was a "killer."[17] The Bridegrooms weren't impressed, pounding the newcomer as they roared to a 10 to 6 win. (Young would go on to win 511 games, the most in baseball history, and become the namesake for the current Cy Young Award given annually to each league's top pitcher.)

Brooklyn made history in a September 1 clash with the Pittsburg Alleghenys, also known as the Innocents. To upstage a double-header by Ward's Wonders at Eastern Park, the Bridegrooms played baseball's first documented triple-header. Brooklyn won all three games. Tom Lovett pitched a 3 to 2 win in the morning game; Adonis Terry won the first afternoon game 8 to 4; and Bob Caruthers pitched a 5 to 4 win in the second afternoon game. Brooklyn second baseman Hub Collins had 12 putouts, 14 assists and only one error for the three games.[18] (There have been only three triple-headers in the history of baseball. The second was on September 7, 1896, when Baltimore won three games from the Louisville Colonels, which was managed by none other than Bill McGunningle. The third was October 2, 1920, when Cincinnati won two of three against Pittsburgh.)

Cyrus "Cy" Young won 30 games in a season five times and 20 games 15 times over a 22-year career (Library of Congress).

The next day Lovett beat Boston 13 to 9 for his seventh straight win since coming off the injury list. The Bridegrooms were sitting pretty. Terry pitched Brooklyn to another Ladies Day win over visiting New York by a 7 to 3 score, with even the Giants' female fans cheering the Adonis. It was the ninth straight win for McGunnigle's men. The National League pennant surely was theirs. Or was it?

Immediately following their winning streak, the Bridegrooms began to slip. The Giants broke Brooklyn's win streak with two straight victories before Brooklyn headed on a 12-game road trip, starting in Philadelphia. In the first game, Lovett lost a 4 to 3 squeaker. In the second game, the Phillies bombed Terry so hard that Caruthers was sent in to pitch in the third inning. But he, too, was shelled, as Brooklyn lost 13 to 6. In the third game, all seemed right as Lovett was again in top form, holding the Phillies to only one hit going into the seventh inning with Brooklyn up 3 to 1. "Then, however, Lovett went all to pieces and no less than ten hits were made of his pitching in that and the following innings," *the Eagle* reported. Philadelphia scored nine runs to give Brooklyn its third straight loss.[19] Suddenly, the Bridegrooms were only 3½ games ahead of Boston. What's more, Caruthers' ankle was hurting, and the pitching burden fell to Lovett and Terry.

Brooklynites were beginning to get nervous. The *Brooklyn Eagle* commented:

> Terry, the Grooms' great twirler, knocked out of the box and the only Caruthers batted all over the field—what can it mean? Have the Brooklyn boys been overcome by the subtle charms of Morpheas, who inhabits the sleep precincts of the old Quaker town, or are they on the toboggan? Come, throw off the lethargy, ye Grooms, if such is your ailment, and be up and doing, for everything depends on your present showing, for even the Beatats are keeping you company, those wily Westerns are showing up dangerously well. Again, ye local cranks, root with all your might and main, for if you would have your favorite land the flag, root and root continually. Perhaps your confidence in Brooklyn's lead of last Wednesday has made you careless but the present outlook bids you to be up and doing. The pennant must come to Brooklyn.[20]

The pressure was on Brooklyn to win. The Bridegrooms ought to be called the "Happy Husbands," said *Sporting Life,* "considering that they are the highest salaried team in the League, their salaries for the season aggregating over $47,000. If they should fall down and be passed by some very much lower priced team high salaries, always a bug-bear to the League magnates, would receive a black eye in the League at least."[21]

Manager McGunnigle remained unruffled, outwardly at least. "The Brooklyn boys have been in pretty fair sight of the pennant for a while past and think they have a good show to float it, but got in the track of a cyclone in Philadelphia," Gunner said. "The only explanation is that we were clearly outplayed by the magnificent work of the Phillies. I never heard of such a race as the league clubs are having this year, and you can rest assured that the club that wins will only do so by the finest kind of ball playing."[22]

Brooklyn rebounded with a win over the New York Giants, and then headed for Boston for one game with the second-place Beaneaters on September 16. Boston went up 1 to 0 on a muddy field in the first inning against Lovett, but Brooklyn quickly came back to take a 4 to 1 lead. Lovett "got down to his telling work in the box," while the Bridegrooms batters kept slashing as Adonis Terry, playing left field, made "five excellent catches." Brooklyn won going away for a 12 to 4 win that "virtually settles Boston's hopes of winning the pennant."[23] Brooklyn was now up 5½ games with only nine games to play. Finally, the pennant was nearly theirs. Manager McGunnigle fired off a telegram to Boston sportswriter William Harris, who wrote under the name "Mugwamp" for *Sporting Life.* Gunner had bet Harris a hat that Brooklyn would win the National League pennant. "You had better give it up as we are almost under the wire with nobody to stop us. You know my size," Gunner wrote.[24]

Another *Sporting Life* writer, F. W. Arnold, attributed Brooklyn's success in both 1889 and 1890 to several factors other than the players' talents. These were "first, the great generalship of that prince of magnates, President Byrne, the most excellent judgment of Manager McGunnigle and of Captain Darby O'Brien, a trinity of elements that must carry success with it all times."

After spending a day on the bench in the final road series against Cleveland, when Brooklyn won all four games, Harris was especially impressed with the Brooklyn manager.

> There isn't a Brooklyn player who works harder to win a game than does Billy McGunnigle," Arnold wrote. "He is here, there and everywhere sliding from one end of the bench to the other, always with a bat in his hand and one at his feet, and as nervous as a sweet girl graduate just before firing off her essay. This combination of manager and bats may seem a trifling matter, but as a fact it is a deep scheme between Mac and Captain Darby O'Brien out in centre field and forms a single, yet effective system of telegraphy between the two, so

> that no matter how far the manager and captain may be separated they are talking, by aid of the bats and eyes, as intelligently as if they were cheek to cheek or mouth to ear.
>
> As the game I witnessed progressed, I noticed that the only noisy man on the ground was Mac, and he coached as vigorously from the bench as if he had up on the lines, and I marveled at the fact that the umpire permitted it, but not an objection was raised. I notice that McGunnigle wins his men to him by kindness, yet he is firm and his orders are strictly obeyed. One excellent feature of his superior ability lies in the fact that he thoroughly understands the game and knows just what to do at every stage, and his men, having confidence in him, know just what to do at every stage, and readily obey him.[25]

Tom Lovett had the honor of pitching Brooklyn to the win that clinched the pennant, a 6 to 5 victory over Cleveland. For the second straight year, Brooklyn prepared an elaborate welcome-home parade for the champion Bridegrooms. For the second straight year, it didn't happen. As J. F. Donnelly reported from Brooklyn in *Sporting Life*: "Call it any kind of luck you like, but the Bridegrooms were cheated of a big slice of glory and Brooklynites of a procession and big hurrah time to-night, and all because a cow got on a track somewhere between here and Cleveland. There was a smash-up and Byrne's boys reached Jersey City three hours late," arriving half past midnight. Bands, carriages, fireworks and big crowds had been waiting, but by the time the train rolled in, only a few faithful fans and reporters were on hand. The players mainly seemed puzzled. "Darby O'Brien caressed his now full blown moustache and worried Will McGunnigle; Bob Caruthers nursed his grip and took on a reflective air; Terry was preoccupied; Lovett smiled, but held aloof," Donnelly wrote, and all pretty much departed quietly, "with the exception of George Smith, who had his usual delegation of good fellows awaiting his coming, and Daly and Burns, who were chipper and willing to talk." Manager McGunnigle "stepped from the train in a natty walking suit, light trousers and a cutaway coat and minus anything in the shape of an overcoat. He appeared as though he had just walked around the block.... The homecoming was in striking contrast to that of last year" when the city went "crazy."[26]

But the team had two final home games to play against Pittsburg. Let the celebration begin. On October 2, the new National League champions took the field at Washington Park. The Brooklyn fans applauded, but as *the Eagle* noted, "the old time enthusiasm was lacking." The baseball war clearly had sucked much of the energy out of the pennant races, even in

Brooklyn. Adonis Terry pitched the first six innings in a 9 to 1 win before giving way to Dave Foutz, who made a rare hurling appearance. Foutz also pitched Brooklyn to a 10 to 4 win in the season's final game. Down the stretch, Brooklyn won its last six games. Lovett became the first and only pitcher in the franchise's National League history to win 30 games, against 11 losses. Terry picked up three wins in the final games to bring his record to 26 wins and 16 losses. Caruthers was able to win one more game, ending the season with 23 wins and 11 losses. Oyster Burns carried the offensive load, leading the league in homers with 13 and runs batted in with 128. Darby O'Brien hit .314, Pinkney batted .309 and Dave Foutz hit .303. Brooklyn finished in first with a record of 86 wins and 43 losses, 6½ games ahead of Cap Anson's surprising Chicago Colts. The Boston Beaneaters dropped all the way to fifth. Over in the Players' League, John Ward's Brooklyn team came on strong to edge out New York for second place, 6½ games behind the pennant-winning Boston Reds.

There was talk of the Bridegrooms facing the Players' League champion Boston in a post-season series, but that's all it was — talk. There was no way that Charley Byrne or the League would allow it. Instead, the World's Series would be between Brooklyn and the surprise American Association champions Louisville, which had gone from last place the year before to beat out Chris Von der Ahe's St. Louis Browns for the pennant. Byrne was not excited by the match-up. "The prospects for making much money out of a series with Louisville are not very good," he said. "The team has no drawing powers down East, and while we may have good crowds in Louisville, yet we won't do much away from there."[27] Still, the Series was arranged, with Brooklyn a heavy favorite.

The Series got off to a promising start in Louisville on October 18. The game drew the largest weekday crowd in the West for the season, totaling 5,563 people who paid the League price of 50 cents admission instead of the association's 25 cents. Hometown boy Hub Collins led off the game for Brooklyn to so many cheers that he twice had to doff his cap. Collins singled over the second baseman's head and eventually came around to score on a hit by Oyster Burns. The Louisville players were clearly nervous, and two errors brought in two more runs as Brooklyn went up 3 to 0. That was all Adonis Terry needed, though Brooklyn continued to score to roll up a 9 to 0 victory. The only down side was that catcher Bob Clark split his thumb and was out for the Series.[28]

Brooklyn won the second game 5 to 3 behind Tom Lovett, who struck out seven batters. In the third game, Brooklyn took a 6 to 2 lead after five innings, but Louisville got to Terry for five runs in the next three innings. The score was tied 8 to 8 when the umpire called the game because of darkness. Brooklyn remained up two games to none. By the following game, Louisville was over its "stage fright," jumping on Lovett for three early runs. Brooklyn tied the score, but Louisville claimed its first game 5 to 4. The Bridegrooms were now up two games to one.

The two teams took the train to Brooklyn for the next contests. The Bridegrooms were met at the Jersey City train depot at 8:10 A.M. the next day by a small group of friends, and then were escorted by carriage to Brooklyn. Meantime, the Louisville team went to the Grand Central Hotel in New York. The teams had to wait several days to play as the next game was postponed because of rain and cold weather. Finally, the Series resumed on a gloomy Saturday. Only about 1,000 people showed up at Washington Park. The National League pennant was run up the flag pole by players of both teams as the crowd cheered. After the game started promptly at 3:00 P.M., Oyster Burns got Brooklyn off to a flying start with a homer to put the Bridegrooms up 2 to 1. The Bridegrooms added two more runs in the fourth, led by Dave Foutz's triple. Doubles by Adonis Terry and Tom Daly put Brooklyn up 7 to 2. Lovett shut down Louisville, not allowing a single hit in the final four innings as the Bridegrooms won 7 to 2 to go ahead three games to one.

Only 300 people showed up for the next game on a cold and rainy day. Terry was in the box again for Brooklyn, but this time Louisville scored a 9 to 8 win. Brooklyn shortstop Germany Smith made the play of the game, racing to stop a ground ball about 40 feet behind third base and throwing the runner out at first base. Louisville manager John Chapman said it was "without exception, the best play he ever saw."[29] After Louisville won the next game 6 to 2 to tie the Series before another tiny crowd, Byrne met with Louisville officials before the teams boarded the train for Kentucky. They made a surprising decision: the rest of the Series was canceled. One reason was the cold, rainy weather, but the other was simply public apathy. Neither team had covered its expenses since the first game in Brooklyn. The clubs said they would continue the Series the next year, but it never happened. In the end, the 1890 World's Series was canceled for lack of interest.

Brooklyn president Charley Byrne had to settle for winning his second straight pennant while the financial picture was darkening for all of major league baseball. As the *Brooklyn Eagle* noted: "Last year there was profit as well as honor in the title, but this season, owing to the baseball war, the victors will have to be satisfied with the glory."[30] Now baseball's real battle was about to begin — the battle for survival.

CHAPTER ELEVEN

Final Inning

For the Brooklyn Bridegrooms, the period following the 1890 season was a time of celebration and consolidation. Brooklyn had become the first — and still the only — major league baseball team to win two consecutive pennants in two different leagues. Finally, Brooklyn's quiet skipper got his due. Bill McGunnigle, said Brooklyn president Charley Byrne, "is one of the cleverest and hardest working managers in the business. He is kind to the men and they adore him, and it is by kindness that he gets such admirable control over them. He realizes as I do, that ball players are all right if they are treated right, with the proverbial exception now and then, although I know of no exceptions on my team."[1]

Few baseball men could match McGunnigle's record, *Sporting Life* noted:

> A great deal has been said at odd times of various players and managers who have been connected in their time with many champion teams, but one man, with a more remarkable record than any of the other many mentioned, has been entirely overlooked, simply because he is altogether too modest for the pushing baseball world and never blows his own horn. That man is Manager McGunnigle of the Brooklyn Club. Here is his unequaled record, which speaks for itself:
>
> With Brockton, Massachusetts League, First 1874; With Fall River, New England League Second, 1875; With Fall River, New England League, First 1876; With Fall River, New England League, Second 1877; With Buffalo, International League, First 1878; With Buffalo, National League, Third 1879; With Saginaw, Northwestern League, First 1883; With Bay City, Northwestern League, First 1884; With Brockton, New England League, First 1885; With Brockton, New England League, Fourth 1886; With Lowell, New England League, First 1887; With Brooklyn, American Association, Second 1888; With Brooklyn, American Association, First 1889; With Brooklyn, National League, First 1890
>
> If there is any man with a better record as a winning team leader, we have

One of Brooklyn skipper Bill McGunnigle's characteristics, the ***Brooklyn Eagle*** said, "is never failing faith in any team he may manage. If faith is the base of Christianity, Mac ought to be a Bishop instead of a baseball manager" (National Baseball Hall of Fame).

> yet to hear of him. Even Anson doesn't approach McGunnigle's record of handling winning teams by a long shot. Nine firsts and three seconds in 14 years is simply phenomenal.[2]

For Charley Byrne, the National League pennant capped seven years of tireless work to build the Brooklyn franchise from scratch. This time the club celebrated its pennant at the Grand Opera House, an appropriate setting for the opera-loving club president. Brooklyn backers packed the opera house for the occasion. The stage was set in a baseball scene with a baseball diamond, albeit with only two bases. Overhead hung the championship pennants of 1889 and 1890. The proceedings began with a solo by opera singer Florence Mathews, followed by a string of entertainers, including Dranee the juggler who wowed the crowd with his "butterfly trick." Then came the banjo player. Finally, Hyde & Behman's full orchestra struck up "See the Conquering Heroes," as all of the Brooklyn players marched on stage dressed in their uniforms. The well-dressed patrons in the orchestra cheered, and the bleacher crowd in the second-floor gallery went wild. Manager McGunnigle accepted a white championship banner, then introduced club president Charley Byrne.

"The mention of Byrne's name was like putting the match to a dozen cannons," *Sporting Life* reported. "As the little president stepped from the wings he faced a cheering, shouting gathering that sent their combined greeting at him like a cyclone. He looked wonder-eyed over the foot-lights, his legs wobbled and it was evident he was suffering a slight stroke of stage fright. But he had lots of time to get over it for the cheering was taken up again and again, lasting several minutes."

Byrne struggled to regain his composure as he began to read his prepared remarks. The words of the usually articulate baseball man seemed stiff, and then a page of his written speech fell to the floor. Byrne "colored up" and continued talking as he stooped to try to retrieve the paper, never taking his eyes off the audience. Finally, as he got to the end of a sentence, he managed to grab the missing paper. After only the slightest pause, he crumpled the paper up in his hand, stuffed the rest of his speech in his pocket and began speaking from the heart.

> Like a born orator, he started in and electrified his hearers. There was no limit to his eloquence and the good, solid English he hurled at the big gathering worked all to a pitch of enthusiasm that burst bounds when he told them in language unmistakable that he was in a position to say that Brooklyn had in all probability seen the last of the base ball war and that next season would

> mark a return to old principles, and that Brooklynites would have only one club and one championship, and interest being undivided, another good spell of times would be quite a surety. This declaration was the windup of the night, and was received with a general and united shout[3]

"The players of the Brooklyn club have stood by us through the past year and I want to say that they are going to stand by us loyally again," Byrne said. "Our ambition has been to bring about a cessation of the present base ball war. I think we shall go back to the old way and Brooklyn will have but one team in 1891. The standard we have raised will never be diminished so long as the Brooklyn people stand by us."[4]

Byrne was correct. The great baseball war was coming to a close. Despite brave claims by both sides, every team except the Players' League Boston club lost money in 1890. Financial backers of Players' League teams were in a panic. They anxiously sought to meet with National League owners, to the dismay of the players. "I am surprised that our capitalists are having anything to do with the magnates," said Brotherhood secretary Tim Keefe. "The more they go near these people, the worse it is apt to be for the Players' League. It doesn't pay to fool with a buzz saw, and the capitalists in this city ought to know that."[5]

Both sides were bluffing, but the Players' League financiers blinked first in a meeting with the National League's Al Spalding and John Day. According to Spalding, he had demanded "unconditional surrender" by the Players' League backers. "To my surprise the terms were greedily accepted."[6] The players' New York team capitulated to Day's National League New York Giants. Then Spalding accepted an offer to buy the Players' League Chicago team for $25,000. According to some sources, the losses by the Players' League actually were less than for the National League.[7] In fact, the National League had shored up John Day's New York team with an $80,000 subsidy.

Brotherhood leaders blamed spineless financiers for the defeat. Said John Ward: "The cause of the Player League troubles can be summed up in three words: Stupidity, avarice and treachery."[8] But the players, most of whom were now scrambling to rejoin their old teams, also were done in by their own greed as they sought to reap what they thought was the easy money of ownership. In the end, "the Players' League failed because it was built upon an impossible foundation," said Brooklyn's Charles Ebbets. "It was supposed to be a co-operative scheme in which a number of players, working for their own benefit, were also associated with capitalists who were looking out for profits."[9]

The National League won the baseball war, but it was a Pyrrhic victory. After baseball's greatest season ever in 1889, the national game in 1890 was so wounded that it would take a decade to recover. The war was the final nail in the coffin of the American Association, which went out of existence following the 1891 season after consolidating with the National League. The National League was left with a monopoly and an unwieldy 12-team league. Baseball didn't really begin to recover until a new competing organization, the American League, was formed in 1901 by organizers that included former St. Louis Browns star Charles Comiskey.

Much of the damage was self-inflicted by the National League owners' high-handed ways leading up to the players' revolt. Many of the players' complaints were legitimate as owners sought more and more control both on and off the field. Some observers speculated that an owner with more vision could have headed off the players' revolt. Brooklyn manager Bill McGunnigle suggested that "if the National League was run by such the man he worked for on the Brooklyn team, there would be no Brotherhood, there would be no cause for one, and it would be impossible to form one."[10] That man was the highly admired Charley Byrne. But the Brooklyn president was distracted by his running feud with St. Louis owner Chris Von der Ahe. When his club joined the National League before the 1890 season, the baseball war had been declared, and Byrne was a loyal team player. The diminutive executive became the "little general" with Spalding in leading the battle against the Players' League. "There is no dodging the statement that Mr. Spalding and Mr. Byrne accomplished the downfall of the Players' League," concluded one *Sporting Life* correspondent.[11]

Yet there also is evidence that Byrne had no qualms about opposing the National League's cavalier methods — and might have done so had he been in the League sooner. When some Players' League players moved to sign contracts with American Association teams rather than return to their old National League squads, Spalding called for such turncoats to be blacklisted. Only one National League owner "had the courage to put himself boldly on record in opposition to the boss on this point," the *New York World* said. "President Byrne of Brooklyn, undoubtedly the ablest man in the National League, is the magnate who has taken issue with Spalding, stating: 'I don't care if there are ninety nine clubs in the League and the

The 1890 Brooklyn Bridegrooms, National League champions, with manager Bill McGunnigle's new straw hat. Top row (left to right): Oyster Burns, Bob Caruthers, Adonis Terry, Darby O'Brien, Dave Foutz, George Stallings, Tom Daly. Middle row: George Pinkney, Mickey Hughes, Bill McGunnigle, Germany Smith, Charlie Reynolds, Hub Collins. On ground: Bob Clark (San Diego Genealogical Society).

Brooklyn Club makes up the even hundred, I shall fight against the blacklisting or expulsion of any players.'"[12]

Byrne was now focused on healing his wounds. The predatory schedules during the baseball war slashed Brooklyn's attendance from the record 354,000 in 1889 to only 121,000 in 1890, and the club lost at least $25,000.[13] Byrne began negotiations with the principal owners of the Players' League Brooklyn team on consolidating the clubs. Wendell Goodwin ran the Kings County Elevated Railroad company and George Chauncey headed the Ridgewood Land and Improvement Company, which owned Eastern Park and property around it. Both had invested in the players' team not for the money from baseball, but to benefit their own businesses. Charley Byrne's club had won the battle, but it badly needed the two men to invest in the consolidated team. So in late December the proud and increasingly graying Byrne went hat in hand to see Goodwin in his office at No. 2 Nassau Street. "Mr. Byrne sat meekly in a chair beside Mr. Goodwin's desk. His hands were clasped and his eyes peered submissively into those of the dashing railroad man," *Sporting Life* reported. "During the fifteen-minute talk, Mr. Byrne may have spoken fifty words. The rest of the time was filled in by Mr. Goodwin. At the parting, Mr. Byrne shook hands warmly with his would-be partner and disappeared toward the Brooklyn Bridge."[14]

One demand by Goodwin and Chauncey was that the Bridegrooms play in Chauncey's Eastern Park, which was ringed by Goodwin's trolley and rail lines. Byrne and his partners strongly resisted. Eastern Park was remote compared with Washington Park, and hard to get to despite the rail lines. But Byrne finally relented. Eastern Park would be the team's new home field.

During the lengthy negotiations, rumors began to appear in print that Manager McGunnigle would not be returning for the 1891 season despite winning two straight pennants. "I have said nothing to Mr. McGunnigle or anyone else on the subject of leaving," Byrne told the *New York World*, "and as these reports are likely to prove harmful to his prospects, I wish to say in his behalf that I could not have a more honest or trust worthy man."[15] But Byrne did offer up the old saw that Mac had hinted he might want to spend more time with his family.

A more troubling notice appeared regarding pitcher Bob Caruthers. While shooting pool at a "well known resort," Caruthers said, "If McGunnigle manages the team next season, I will not play on it. If a new manager takes hold, I will play, and play the game of my life. I like Mr. Byrne and the rest of the Brooklyn people, but I don't want any part of McGunnigle."[16] The reports didn't say why Caruthers was upset, and McGunnigle said he knew of no complaints. But *Sporting Life* noted that during the season "Caruthers was guilty of a most aggravated offense of insubordination, while a championship game was in progress, and the fact that McGunnigle fined him $100 then and there has probably changed his opinion" of his manager."[17]

In the end, McGunnigle was let go, but not for any of the speculated reasons. The change was made because Wendell Goodwin and George Chauncey, as part of the deal to invest in the Brooklyn Bridegrooms, insisted that John Montgomery Ward be made the manager. Charley Byrne was a man of great loyalty and gratitude — all of which he probably felt toward McGunnigle. But as a businessman, his top priority was the bottom line. As a result, he threw Gunner under the bus. In early February of 1891, he signed Ward for $5,000, twice McGunnigle's pay. The next day, instead of diving in to learn about his new team or prepare for the coming season, Ward headed off on the steamer *Umbria* to England, where he would stay until mid–March in an effort to work things out with his estranged wife, who was appearing in a play in London. He had no more success with her than he did with the Players' League.

Byrne's spin was to say nothing about McGunnigle but to celebrate the addition of Ward as a great player. "We needed such a man badly, as we have never been able to secure for our club what might be called a first class player-manager or an infield captain," Byrne said. Although as Brotherhood president Ward was in a way responsible for the financial dilemma of Byrne's club, the Brooklyn president added: "We all admire a plucky fighter, even if he does not win; and I think John Ward has won the admiration of Brooklyn's base ball patrons, as he has won mine."[18]

By this time, Bill McGunnigle had already left quietly and with praise from the press. "The good will of the National League club is certainly with one man, and that individual is Manager Will McGunnigle," *Sporting Life* said. "He left this city with the best wishes of the men who employed him, and his break of his connection with the Brooklyn Club was wholly voluntary. There was no hint given him that he had outlived his usefulness, or that he would not be the man for next season. In plain Christmas language, he sighed for a change, and like a man went to the front and said so, and he today boasts the friendship and good will of the men who paid him his salary last season."[19] The report has all the earmarks of a story planted by the Brooklyn management. The suggestion that McGunnigle was anxious to leave baseball and go home was undercut by the fact that in the middle of the 1891 season he jumped at the chance to take over as manager of the last-place Pittsburg National League team. McGunnigle never spoke publicly about why he left Brooklyn.

In the end, making Ward manager sealed the deal that allowed Charley Byrne, Gus Abell and Joe Doyle to retain majority control of the Brooklyn baseball club that they had started in 1883. The group led by Goodwin and Chauncey paid $30,000 in cash to become minority owners of the team.[20] Byrne continued as president of the Brooklyn Club, which would struggle to win games as well as fans in Eastern Park. But the little general rose to even more influence in the National League. Byrne "was ever battling with somebody on and for his own account," said Charley Ebbets, "but, strange to say, he was the great pacificator and diplomat, whose ability to straighten out serious tangles made him a commanding figure in both major circuits."[21]

The 1889 and 1890 pennant-winning seasons were the pinnacles for the baseball careers of Bill McGunnigle and Charley Byrne. McGunnigle would never again be given an opportunity to manage a pennant-contending team. Byrne would not live to see Brooklyn win another flag. But together the two men left a championship legacy for a team that would live on as one of baseball's most storied franchises in the City of Churches through the 1950s and then across the country in the City of Angels to this very day.

It was the team that became the Dodgers.

* * *

How the Dodgers finally got their name is an interesting story.

The Brooklyn baseball team that started in 1883 had no nickname until 1888, when sportswriters began calling the club the "Bridegrooms" after several players got married just before the season opened. The name stuck until well into the 1890s. The moniker "Trolley Dodgers" also began appearing after 1891 when the team moved to Eastern Park, where patrons had to dodge a jumble of trolley cars around the stadium. The team also was called "Ward's Wonders" when John Montgomery Ward managed the team in 1891 and 1892. With Dave Foutz at the helm from 1893 to 1896, some called the team "Foutz's Fillies" and, as the losses piled up, "Foutz's Follies."

When Brooklyn in 1899 and 1900 won its first pennant since 1890 under Ned Hanlon, the team nickname became the "Superbas" after the name of a popular stage extravaganza put on by the Hanlon family, who were no relation to the Brooklyn manager. Wilbert Robinson managed the team so long — from 1914 to 1931— that the newspapers called the squad the "Robins." But that handle no longer fit once Robinson finally left.

In early 1932, Brooklyn president Charles Ebbets decided it was time the team had an official name. He left the decision up to the Brooklyn Chapter of Baseball Writers, who decided on "Dodgers" over the "Kings," the only other name that came up.[22] The rest is baseball history. The 1932 team took the field in uniforms with Dodgers written in big, blue letters across the chest. In Brooklyn and Los Angeles, it has been Dodgers ever since.

Epilogue

CHARLEY BYRNE played leading roles in the consolidation of the National League and American Association, and in writing a new National League charter. But his Brooklyn club struggled at its new location at Eastern Park. His health began to fail in 1897, and "the Napoleon of Baseball" died of Bright's disease in January 1898 at his home in New York at age 55. He "was easily the greatest magnate of them all," *Sporting Life* said. Charley Byrne built the Dodgers franchise from scratch, worked tirelessly for baseball in general and made many important contributions to improve the game. He deserves to be in the National Baseball Hall of Fame.

CHRIS VON DER AHE became an even more extravagant showman, adding horse racing and an amusement park around the Sportsman's Park outfield. But the Dutchman fell on hard times. His wife divorced him, and his son, Eddie, never spoke to him again. His second marriage also ended in a bitter divorce when he was caught seeing his young housekeeper, who became his third wife. After the collapse of the American Association, Von der Ahe had to sell his St. Louis Browns because of heavy debts. He ended up tending bar to make ends meet. He died of cirrhosis of the liver in 1913 at age 62.

JOHN MONTGOMERY WARD managed Brooklyn for two years, finishing sixth and third. His marriage to Helen Dauvray ended in a 1893 divorce after Ward's affair with another actress. After retiring from baseball in 1894, Ward became a prominent New York lawyer and a champion golfer. He died from pneumonia while on a hunting trip in Augusta, Georgia, in 1925 on his 65th birthday. He was elected to the Baseball Hall of Fame in 1964.

DAVE FOUTZ managed the Brooklyn team from 1893 to 1896, never finishing higher than fifth. He retired after two games of the 1896 season because of bad health. Foutz suffered from asthma and died at his mother's house outside Baltimore in March of 1897 at age 40.

GEORGE TAYLOR never returned to the baseball business, but wrote for the *New York Herald Tribune* for more than 30 years. He died at his New York home in October of 1911 at age 57.

JOE DOYLE had a falling out with Gus Abell in 1892 and sold his shares in the Brooklyn team, but the two men parted as friends. Doyle became owner of New York's Elberon Hotel, where he died of pneumonia in 1906 at age 67.

GUS ABELL eventually took over control of the Brooklyn club and in 1899 consolidated with the Baltimore Orioles team and its manager, Ned Hanlon. As a result, Brooklyn won the National League pennant in 1899 and 1900, its first championships since 1890. In 1902, Abell sold his stock to Charley Ebbets and returned to his Cape Cod home, where he died in 1913 at age 80.

CHARLES EBBETS became president of the Brooklyn Club in 1898 following Charley Byrne's death. After buying stock from Abell, he became majority owner in 1902. Ebbets secretly began buying land in a run-down section of Brooklyn's Flatbush area called "Pig town." There he built a new baseball stadium called Ebbets Field, which opened in 1912. He continued as club president until his death from heart problems in 1925 at age 66.

BOB CARUTHERS never won 20 games again and returned to St. Louis, where he mainly played the outfield. After retiring, he became an umpire but was a "nervous wreck" due to his heavy drinking. He died in 1911 at his home in Peoria, Ilinois, at age 47.

DOC BUSHONG retired after the 1890 season and opened a dental practice in Brooklyn and Hoboken, New Jersey. Three of his sons also became dentists. Bushong became known as one of Brooklyn's leading bowlers. He died from cancer in 1908 at age 54.

ADONIS TERRY won 26 games for Brooklyn in 1891 before moving on to Pittsburg and Chicago until 1897. He had one more 20-game season — 21 wins for Chicago in 1895. Terry umpired for a while and also pitched in the Western League in Milwaukee, where he went into business. He died of pneumonia in Milwaukee in 1915 at age 50.

HUB COLLINS was badly injured in an 1891 game at Eastern Park when he collided with Oyster Burns while both players were running to catch a fly ball. Neither man could hear the other call for the ball over the noise of a passing train. Collins never recovered and died of typhoid fever in 1891 at age 28.

Oyster Burns continued as one of Brooklyn's best hitters until 1896, when he was traded to the New York Giants in his final year in baseball. His career batting average was .300. Burns was a longtime employee of the Brooklyn municipal government. He died in 1928 at age 64.

Germany Smith was traded to Cincinnati, where he played for six seasons before ending his major league career in St. Louis in 1898. While working as a railroad crossing watchman in Altoona, Pennsylvania, Smith was hit and killed by a swerving car in 1927 at age 64.

George Pinkney was traded to St. Louis in 1892 and ended his major league career in Louisville in 1893. He returned to his hometown of Peoria, Illinois, where he died in 1926 at age 67.

Darby O'Brien suffered from tuberculosis and never recovered his old playing skills. When he showed up for spring training in 1893, he was too ill to play and died later that year in his hometown of Peoria, Illinois, just before his 30th birthday.

Pop Corkhill played part-time for several teams before retiring in 1893 after he was hit in the head by a pitch thrown by Cannonball Crane. He ran a grocery store in Stockton, New Jersey, and at age 62 died at his home in Pennsauken, New Jersey, in 1921 following an operation.

Tom Lovett won 23 games for Brooklyn in 1891. He held out for the entire 1892 season and never regained his form. In 1894 he pitched for the Boston Beaneaters, his last season in the majors. In 1928, he fell unconscious on the street in his hometown of Providence and died at age 64.

Bob Clark played three more seasons in the major leagues for Cincinnati and Louisville. He returned to his hometown of Covington, Kentucky, where he was killed in a fire in 1919 at age 56.

Joe Visner played a half season more in the major leagues and later played in the minors for the Minneapolis Millers in his hometown. The Native American inherited 400 acres on the White Earth Indian reservation in Minnesota, where he and his wife and nine children lived until 1907, when Visner left home for 30 years. He died in 1945 in Fosston, Minnesota, at age 85.

Tom Daly switched from catcher to second base and was a top player for Brooklyn for 11 seasons before ending his career in Cincinnati in 1903. He died in Brooklyn in 1938 at the age of 62.

PATSY DONOVAN was traded to Pittsburg, where he became a .300 hitter and began managing. For several decades he managed major league, minor league and high school teams, including Phillips Academy in Andover, Massachusetts, where one of his players was future President George H. W. Bush. He died on Christmas Day in 1953 at age 88.

CHARLES COMISKEY returned to the St. Louis Browns in 1891 but moved to the National League's Cincinnati team in 1892 and 1893. In 1894 he became player-manager and owner of the St. Paul, Minnesota, team in the Western League. He moved the team to the south side of Chicago in 1900 and in 1901 helped form the American League with his Chicago White Sox as one of the entries. As owner he built Comiskey Park in 1910 and won five pennants, though his tenure was tarnished by the Black Sox scandal of 1919, when several Chicago players took money to throw the World Series. Comiskey died in 1931 at age 72. He was elected to the Baseball Hall of Fame in 1939.

ARLIE LATHAM played for Cincinnati until 1896, when he made a brief return to St. Louis. The colorful Latham performed on the stage and went to England during World War I to organize baseball games for soldiers. He lived in England for 17 years. After returning to the U.S., he became a press box attendant at home games of the New York Yankees and New York Giants. He died in 1952 at age 92.

DAVE ORR suffered a paralyzing stroke shortly after the 1890 season while playing an exhibition game in Renova, Pennsylvania, just after his 31st birthday. He never returned to baseball. He did odd jobs and was a caretaker at Ebbets Field. Orr died of heart disease in Long Island in 1919 at age 55.

JIM MUTRIE managed only one more year for the New York Giants, when he was ousted by new investors in the team who insisted on naming their own skipper. He managed a minor league team in Elmira, New York, where he also ran a hotel. In 1921 the *New York Evening Telegram* found him living in near poverty with his wife in Staten Island. The Giants gave him a pension, and he made one final appearance at the Polo Grounds in 1936. He died in 1938 at age 82.

JOHN DAY had used up much of his tobacco-business fortune to keep the New York Giants going and was removed as the team's president in 1893 by the new owners. For a while he was inspector of National League umpires. He died penniless from a stroke in 1925 in New York at age 77.

BUCK EWING continued as one of the game's star players with the New York Giants until 1893, when he moved to Cleveland and then Cincinnati before retiring in 1897. Ewing became a wealthy property owner. He died of diabetes in Cincinnati in 1906 at age 41. He was elected to the Baseball Hall of Fame in 1939.

TIM KEEFE moved to the Philadelphia Phillies in 1891 and pitched until 1893. He returned to his hometown of Cambridge, Massachusetts, where he was "Professor of Baseball Science" at Harvard University. He died in Cambridge in 1933 at age 76. He was elected to the Baseball Hall of Fame in 1964.

KING KELLY played only three more seasons, ending up with the Giants briefly in 1893 before drifting to the minors and vaudeville, his skills diminished by heavy drinking and obesity. In 1894 he took a boat to Boston to appear with the London Gaiety Girls Theatrical Company. He caught a cold on the boat and died of pneumonia in a hospital emergency room at age 36. He was elected to the Baseball Hall of Fame in 1945.

FLEET WALKER, also known as Fleetwood, played in the minor leagues until 1890. In 1908 he published a book called *Our Home Colony: A Treatise on the Past, Present, and Future of the Negro Race in America.* He and his second wife ran a movie house near Steubenville, Ohio, where he invented improvements in film-reel changing. He died in 1924 at age 64.

HENRY CHADWICK continued as baseball's most famous and most prolific sportswriter into his 80s. He promoted the theory that baseball began in England as the children's game of rounders. He died in Brooklyn in 1908 at the age of 86. He was elected to the Baseball Hall of Fame in 1938.

ALBERT SPALDING survived the baseball war as a wealthy man from his sporting goods company and the sale of property in Chicago. He left baseball in 1892 to pursue other interests. Irked by Chadwick's claim that America's game began in England, Spalding in 1905 established a commission that concluded Abner Doubleday invented baseball in Cooperstown, New York. There was no real evidence to support the claim. Spalding died in 1915 in San Diego, California, at age 65. He was elected to the Baseball Hall of Fame in 1939.

BILL MCGUNNIGLE returned to Brockton, where he started a new team in 1891 in the New England League. In the middle of the season, the

National League's last-place Pittsburg Pirates hired him as manager. Mac got caught on the wrong side of an ownership dispute and was let go at the end of the season. But he left his mark. One of his players, Connie Mack, noticed McGunnigle signaling with bats and scorecards. Mack later became manager of the Philadelphia Athletics for 50 years and was famed for signaling his players with a scorecard.

McGunnigle also was ahead of his time at Pittsburg during a rainy double-header against Brooklyn in September of 1891. In the second game, when pitcher Mark Baldwin couldn't control the slippery baseball, "McGunnigle sent for and got some rosin," a powdery substance that absorbs moisture, the *New York Sun* reported. "Baldwin had his pocket filled with it," and rubbed rosin on the ball as he pitched Pittsburg to a win. In 1926, major league baseball officially began allowing pitchers to use a rosin bag to dry sweaty fingers, though they can only rub the rosin on their fingers, not on the ball.

Mac returned to the National League again in 1896 as manager of the last-place Louisville Colonels. During a stop in Washington, D.C., he took his players to the White House, saying he knew President Grover Cleveland. The players assumed it was another of Mac's practical jokes. At the White House, President Cleveland greeted McGunnigle, "Why, Mac, how are you? We haven't met in years." The president explained to the startled players that he had seen McGunnigle play in Buffalo in the late 1870s. McGunnigle made worldwide news by asking Cleveland if he planned to run for re-election. For the first time publicly, Cleveland said, "No third term for me. Really, I couldn't stand it." Despite a verbal two-year contract, Louisville fired McGunnigle after one season. He sued and won a small settlement out of court.

Gunner McGunnigle (Transcendental Graphics).

Gunner returned to Brockton where he opened a pub and pool room on East

Elm Street across from city hall. On the night of July 22, 1897, he was returning home with several others in a horse-drawn carriage that was struck by one of Brockton's new electric trolley cars. Mac was thrown to the street and badly injured. Ironically, the man who once managed a team that became known as the Trolley Dodgers was done in by a trolley. He never recovered his health and died on March 9, 1899, at his home at 35 Arch Street at age 44. Among friends who attended his funeral were heavyweight boxing champions John L. Sullivan and Jim Corbett. McGunnigle, one obituary said, "seldom talked of his record and achievements, and the details of one of the most interesting careers in the baseball world passes with its subject."

In 1915, prominent *Boston Globe* sportswriter Tom Murnane predicted that "some day there will be an institution to honor the pioneer heroes of the diamond and also the modern stars. When that day arrives, Billy McGunnigle, because of outstanding playing ability, sagacious leadership and aggressiveness, should be one of the first enshrined therein." The National Baseball Hall of Fame opened in 1936 in Cooperstown, New York. Murnane was elected to the Hall's writers wing in 1978. But the innovative McGunnigle has never been remembered.

Gunner McGunnigle is the only manager in baseball history to win consecutive pennants in two different major leagues. His Brooklyn record is 267 wins and 139 losses, with two pennants and one second-place finish. McGunnigle's winning percentage of .658 remains the highest for any manager in the history of the Dodgers franchise.

Chapter Notes

Chapter One

1. *Brooklyn Eagle*, July 27, 1887.
2. *Atlanta Constitution*, May 19, 1916.
3. *Sporting Life*, Oct. 11, 1890.
4. *Sporting Life*, Aug. 25, 1895.
5. *Sporting Life*, March 16, 1885.
6. *Brooklyn Eagle*, Jan. 8, 1913, from *History of Baseball in Brooklyn,* by Charles H. Ebbets with Thomas E. Rice.
7. U.S. Census, 1880.
8. Walt Whitman, *Leaves of Grass.*
9. *Sporting Life*, Sept. 9, 1896.
10. *Sporting Life*, March 17, 1900.
11. Andy McCue, "Charles H. Byrne," *Baseball's First Stars*, SABR, p. 19.
12. *Brooklyn Eagle,* Nov. 3, 1887.
13. Albert Spalding, *America's National Game*, p. 190.
14. *New York Clipper,* Jan. 20, 1883.
15. *Brooklyn Eagle*, Jan. 23, 1883.
16. *Brooklyn Eagle*, March 31, 1883.
17. *Brooklyn Eagle*, May 10, 1883.
18. *Brooklyn Eagle,* May 13, 1883.
19. *Brooklyn Eagle*, May 25, 1883.
20. *New York Times,* May 25, 1883.
21. *Brooklyn Eagle*, July 2, 1883.
22. *Sporting Life,* Aug. 29, 1888.
23. *Brooklyn Eagle,* June 1, 1883.
24. *Brooklyn Eagle,* July 24, 1883.
25. *Morning Journal,* quoted in *Brooklyn Eagle,* March 23,1884.
26. *Brooklyn Eagle*, Sept. 30, 1883.
27. *Cincinnati Commercial*, quoted in *Brooklyn Eagle,* March 23, 1884.
28. *Brooklyn Eagle*, May 6, 1884.
29. *Sporting Life*, Jan. 27, 1906.
30. *Sporting Life,* April 18, 1888.
31. *Brooklyn Eagle,* June 29, 1884.
32. *Washington Post*, June 7, 1884.
33. *Washington Post*, June 10, 1884.
34. *New York Clipper*, Jan. 27, 1883.
35. *New York Age*, n.d.
36. National Baseball Hall of Fame, Cooperstown, N.Y.
37. *Brooklyn Eagle,* Oct. 5, 1884.

Chapter Two

1. *St. Louis Globe-Democrat*, March 11, 1877.
2. *St. Louis Post-Dispatch*, Feb. 17, 1905.
3. *St. Louis Globe-Democrat*, July 31, 1881.
4. *St. Louis Post-Dispatch* Feb. 17, 1905.
5. Latham file, National Baseball Hall of Fame.
6. *Sporting Life*, Jan. 13, 1886.
7. *Sporting Life,* June 14, 1886.
8. Ibid.
9. Latham file, National Baseball Hall of Fame.
10. *Sporting Life,* July 17, 1889.
11. *Sporting Life,* Feb. 8, 1913.
12. *New York Times*, Jan. 6, 1885.
13. *Brooklyn Eagle*, Jan. 26, 1913, from *History of Baseball in Brooklyn,* by Charles H. Ebbets with Thomas E. Rice.
14. *Brooklyn Eagle*, Jan. 11, 1885.

15. *Brooklyn Eagle*, Feb. 1, 1885.
16. *Brooklyn Eagle*, April 12, 1885.
17. *Brooklyn Eagle*, June 6, 1886.
18. *Brooklyn Eagle*, April 26, 1885.
19. *Sporting Life*, April 11, 1896.
20. *Brooklyn Eagle*, June 18, 1885.
21. *New York Times*, Sept. 8, 1885.
22. *Sporting Life*, Oct. 14, 1885.
23. *Sporting Life*, Dec. 2, 1885.
24. *Brooklyn Eagle*, March 13, 1886.
25. *Brooklyn Eagle*, July 25, 1886.
26. *Sporting Life*, June 14, 1886.
27. *Sporting Life*, June 21, 1886.
28. Ibid.
29. *Sporting News*, Aug. 8, 1887.
30. *Brooklyn Eagle*, July 16, 1886.
31. *Cincinnati Enquirer*, in *Brooklyn Eagle*, July 18, 1886.
32. Sporting *Life*, July 12, 1886.
33. Albert G. Spalding, *America's National Game*, p. 525.
34. *Sporting Life*, June 8, 1887.
35. *Sporting News*, Aug. 8, 1887.
36. *New York Times*, Aug. 5, 1887.
37. *Brooklyn Eagle*, Aug. 4, 1887.
38. *Buffalo Commercial*, in *Brooklyn Eagle*, March 11, 1888.
39. *Sporting Life*, Oct. 19, 1887.
40. *New York Times*, May 20, 1887.
41. *Sporting Life*, Oct. 5, 1887.
42. *Brooklyn Eagle*, Feb. 4, 1913, from *History of Baseball in Brooklyn*, by Charles H. Ebbets with Thomas E. Rice.

Chapter Three

1. *Sporting Life*, Sept. 19, 1896.
2. Jay P. Dolan, *The Irish Americans*, p. 74.
3. Mike Shotwell and Christian G. Samito, "An Irish-American at Gettysburg," *Gettysburg Magazine*, January 1999, p. 105.
4. *Schools and School Boys of Old Boston, 1894.*
5. *Brockton Enterprise*, April 8, 1990.
6. *Brockton Times*, Feb. 9, 1915.
7. Letter from son, William McGunnigle, to the National Baseball Hall of Fame, Aug. 29, 1966.
8. Robert A. Kane, "Baseball's Forgotten Pioneers," *The Baseball Research Journal*, p. 17.
9. Ibid.
10. *Reach's Official 1895 Baseball Guide*, p. 103.
11. *New York Sun*, April 27, 1890, *New York Times*, Jan. 24, 1915.
12. *Sporting News*, July 26, 1886.
13. *Cleveland Plain Dealer*, May 12, 1888, reprinted from *Philadelphia Press.*
14. Frank McGrath, *Fall River Baseball History.*
15. *Portland Argus* in *Brooklyn Eagle*, Jan. 2, 1887.
16. *Fall River Daily Herald*, Aug. 3, 1877.
17. *Fall River Daily Herald*, Oct. 25, 1877.
18. *Brockton Enterprise*, April 8, 1990.
19. *Buffalo Express*, May 4, 1878.
20. *Buffalo Express*, Aug. 13, 1879.
21. *Boston Globe*, Dec. 29, 1910.
22. *New York Clipper*, May 30, 1879.
23. *Buffalo Express*, July 12, 1878.
24. *Buffalo Express*, Sept. 24, 1878.
25. *Chicago Daily-Tribune*, July 13, 1879.
26. *Buffalo Express*, Aug. 14, 1879.
27. *Buffalo Express*, Sept. 18, 1879.
28. *New York American* in *Washington Post*, Dec. 18, 1910.
29. *New York Clipper*, Feb. 2, 1889.
30. *Saginaw News*, March 14, 1883.
31. *Saginaw News*, April 16, 1883.
32. *Saginaw News*, June 27, 1883.
33. *Saginaw News*, June 10, 1883.
34. *Saginaw News*, June 11, 1883.
35. www.saginawgolds.com/files/history/pdf.
36. Letter from son, William McGunnigle, to National Baseball Hall of Fame, Aug. 29, 1966.
37. *Brockton Weekly Gazette*, April 25, 1885.
38. *Brockton Weekly Gazette*, July 25, 1885.
39. *Boston Globe*, July 24, 1885.
40. *Boston Globe*, Aug. 1, 1885.
41. Letter by McGunnigle's grand-

daughter, Margaret Schottdorf, June 7, 1999.

42. *Brockton Times*, March 10, 1899.

43. Robert A. Kane, "Baseball's Forgotten Pioneer," *The Baseball Research Journal*, p. 17.

44. *Boston Globe,* Oct. 6, 1887.

45. *Sporting Life*, July 27, 1887.

46. *Sporting Life*, Nov. 16, 1887.

47. *Brooklyn Eagle,* Feb. 4, 1888.

48. *Sporting Life*, Nov. 9, 1887.

Chapter Four

1. *New York Times,* April 13, 1885.
2. *Brooklyn Eagle*, Oct. 27, 1887.
3. *Brooklyn Eagle*, Feb. 4, 1913.
4. *Washington Post,* Sept. 15, 1895.
5. *Sporting Life*, Nov. 18, 1887.
6. *New York Times,* Jan. 24, 1915.
7. Joe Gunson letter to National Baseball Hall of Fame, May 2, 1939.
8. *Brooklyn Eagle,* Oct. 13,1887.
9. *Sporting Life,* June 12, 1889.
10. *Sporting News,* Aug. 27, 1887.
11. *Louisville Courier-Journal,* quoted in *Brooklyn Eagle,* Nov. 26, 1888.
12. *Brooklyn Eagle*, Nov. 30, 1887.
13. *Louisville Courier-Journal,* quoted in *Brooklyn Eagle*, Nov. 26, 1888.
14. *Sporting Life*, Dec. 3, 1887.
15. Ibid.
16. *Sporting Life,* Nov. 30, 1887.
17. *Brooklyn Eagle,* Dec. 16, 1887.
18. *Brooklyn Eagle,* Dec. 14, 1887.
19. *Brooklyn Eagle,* Dec. 7, 1887.
20. *Sporting News,* Dec. 3, 1887.
21. *Philadelphia Record,* in *Sporting Life,* Dec. 14, 1887.
22. *Sporting Life*, Dec. 14, 1887.
23. *Sporting Life*, Sept. 14, 1887.
24. Ibid.
25. *Sporting Life*, Dec. 8, 1887.
26. *St. Louis Post-Dispatch*, June 10, 1887.
27. David Nemec, *The Beer & Whiskey League,* p. 96.
28. *Sporting Life*, Sept. 3, 1887.
29. *New York Times,* April 19, 1888.
30. *Sporting News,* Dec. 3, 1887.
31. *Sporting News,* Nov. 23, 1887.
32. Alfred H. Spink, *The National Game,* p. 130.
33. *Sporting Life,* Feb. 8, 1888.

Chapter Five

1. *Brooklyn Eagle,* Jan. 15, 1888.
2. *Brooklyn Eagle*, Feb. 26, 1888.
3. *Brooklyn Eagle,* March 6, 1888.
4. *Sporting Life,* April 11, 1888.
5. *Brooklyn Eagle*, April 6, 1888.
6. *Brooklyn Eagle*, June 5, 1888.
7. *Brooklyn Eagle*, Jan. 29, 1888.
8. *Brooklyn Eagle*, Feb. 4, 1888.
9. *New York Times,* April 19, 1888.
10. *Washington Post*, Nov. 4, 1896.
11. *Brockton Daily Gazette*, March 15, 1888.
12. *Brooklyn Eagle*, April 19, 1888.
13. *Brooklyn Eagle,* April 15, 1888.
14. *Sporting Life*, May 1, 1889.
15. *Brooklyn Eagle*, May 11, 1888.
16. *Brooklyn Eagle*, May 28, 1888.
17. *Brooklyn Eagle,* June 3, 1888.
18. *Sporting Life,* July 1888.
19. *New York Times,* July 4, 1888.
20. *New York Times,* July 22, 1888.
21. *Sporting Life,* July 27, 1888.
22. *Sporting Life*, July 18, 1888.
23. *Sporting Life*, July 25, 1888.
24. *Sporting Life,* July 18, 1888.
25. *Brooklyn Eagle*, July 16, 1888.
26. *Sporting Life,* Aug. 15, 1888.
27. *Sporting Life,* Aug. 8, 1888.
28. *Sporting Life,* Aug. 29, 1888.
29. *Sporting Life,* Aug. 15, 1888.
30. *Brooklyn Eagle*, Feb. 4, 1913, from *History of Baseball in Brooklyn,* by Charles H. Ebbets with Thomas E. Rice.
31. *Brooklyn Eagle,* Aug. 23, 1888.
32. *New York Clipper,* Sept. 15, 1888.
33. Alfred H. Spinks, *The National Game,* p. 300.
34. *Sporting Life,* Oct. 10, 1888.
35. *Cincinnati Enquirer*, quoted in *Brooklyn Eagle*, Sept. 27, 1888.
36. *New York Clipper,* Oct. 13, 1888.
37. *New York Clipper,* Sept. 22, 1888.

38. Alfred H. Spinks, *The National Game,* p. 228.
39. *Sporting Life,* Oct. 31, 1888.
40. *Brooklyn Eagle,* Oct. 24, 1888.
41. *New York Clipp*er, Nov. 10, 1888.

Chapter Six

1. *New York Clipper,* April 6, 1889.
2. *Sporting Life,* April 10, 1889.
3. *Sporting Life,* April 3, 1889.
4. *Brooklyn Eagle,* April 10, 1889.
5. U.S. Census, 1890.
6. *Brooklyn Eagle,* April 14, 1889.
7. *Sporting Life,* May 1, 1889.
8. *Sporting Life,* April 27, 1889.
9. *Brooklyn Eagle,* April 26, 1889.
10. *Brooklyn Eagle,* May 3, 1889.
11. *Brooklyn Eagle,* April 23, 1889.
12. *Sporting Life,* May 1, 1889.
13. *Brooklyn Eagle,* May 2, 1889.
14. *Brooklyn Eagle,* May 6, 1889.
15. *Sporting Life,* May 9, 1889.
16. *Sporting Life,* May 15, 1889.
17. *Brooklyn Eagle,* May 25, 1889.
18. *St. Louis Post-Dispatch,* May 3, 1889.
19. *St. Louis Post-Dispatch,* May 7, 1889.
20. *New York Times,* May 19, 1889.
21. *Brooklyn Eagle,* May 19, 1889.
22. *Brooklyn Eagle,* May 20, 1889.
23. *Brooklyn Eagle,* May 22, 1889.
24. *Ohio State Journal,* in *Brooklyn Eagle,* May 29, 1889.
25. *Sporting Life,* July 5, 1889.
26. *St. Louis Post-Dispatch,* June 1889.
27. Lee Allen, *The Giants and The Dodgers,* p. 25.
28. *New York Clipper,* March 23, 1889.
29. *Sporting Life,* April 11, 1891.
30. *Sporting Life,* April 7, 1889.
31. *Sporting Life,* July 18, 1891.
32. *Brooklyn Eagle,* June 3, 1889.
33. *Sporting Life,* June 5, 1889.
34. *Brooklyn Eagle,* May 31, 1889.
35. Johnstown Flood Museum, Johnstown, Pa.
36. *Sporting Life,* June 5, 1889.
37. *Brooklyn Eagle,* June 4, 1889.
38. *Brooklyn Eagle,* June 6, 1889.
39. *Brooklyn Eagle,* June 3, 1889.
40. *Sporting Life,* June 19, 1889.
41. *Brooklyn Eagle,* June 19, 1889.
42. *Brooklyn Eagle,* June 16, 1889.
43. *Boston Sunday Globe,* 1959.

Chapter Seven

1. *Sporting Life,* Aug. 14, 1889.
2. *Sporting Life,* July 24, 1889.
3. *New York Clipper,* July 20, 1889.
4. *Sporting Life,* Aug. 7, 1889.
5. *New York World,* in *Sporting Life,* Aug. 7, 1889.
6. *Sporting Life,* Aug. 10, 1889.
7. *St. Louis Post-Dispatch,* Aug. 11, 1889.
8. *Sporting Life,* Aug. 21, 1889.
9. *St. Louis Post-Dispatch,* Aug. 13, 1889.
10. *Sporting News,* Sept. 7, 1889.
11. *Brooklyn Eagle,* Sept. 6, 1889.
12. *Brooklyn Eagle,* Aug. 25, 1889.
13. *Brooklyn Eagle,* Aug. 26, 1889.
14. *Sporting News,* Sept. 7, 1889.
15. *New York Evening Telegram,* Aug. 23, 1889.
16. *New York Times,* Sept. 4, 1889.
17. *Sporting Life,* Sept. 18, 1889.
18. *St. Louis Post-Dispatch,* Sept. 11, 1889.
19. *Brooklyn Eagle,* Sept. 8, 1889.
20. *Sporting News,* Sept. 14, 1889.
21. Ibid.
22. *Washington Post,* Sept. 8, 1889.
23. *Brooklyn Eagle,* Sept. 8, 1889.
24. *New York Times,* Sept. 9, 1889.
25. *Sporting Life,* Sept. 18, 1889.
26. *New York Times,* Sept. 9, 1889.
27. *St. Louis Post-Dispatch,* Sept. 21, 1889.
28. *Sporting Life,* Oct. 2, 1889.
29. *New York Times,* Sept. 24, 1889.
30. *Brooklyn Eagle,* Sept. 26, 1889.
31. *St. Louis Post-Dispatch,* Sept. 27, 1889.
32. *Washington Post,* Oct. 25, 1889.

33. *Brooklyn Eagle*, Oct. 10, 1889.
34. *Brooklyn Eagle*, Oct. 11, 1889.
35. *Brooklyn Eagle*, Oct. 13, 1889.
36. *St. Louis Post-Dispatch*, Oct. 13, 1889.
37. *Brooklyn Eagle*, Oct. 15, 1889.
38. *Brooklyn Eagle*, Oct. 12, 1889.
39. *Brooklyn Eagle*, Oct. 15, 1889.
40. Ibid.
41. *Sporting Life*, Oct. 23, 1889.
42. *Brooklyn Eagle*, Oct. 16, 1889.
43. Ibid.
44. *St. Louis Post-Dispatch*, Oct. 16, 1889.

Chapter Eight

1. *New York Times*, Oct. 18, 1889.
2. *Brooklyn Eagle*, Oct. 18, 1889.
3. *Brooklyn Eagle*, Oct. 18, 1889.
4. *Sporting Life*, Nov. 21, 1889.
5. Latham file, National Baseball Hall of Fame.
6. *New York Evening Telegram*, Sept. 18, 1921.
7. Ibid.
8. *New York Times*, Oct. 14, 1889.
9. *New York Times*, Oct. 17, 1889.
10. *Sporting Life*, Oct. 23, 1889.
11. *New York Times*, Oct. 19, 1889.
12. Ibid.
13. *New York Times*, Oct. 20, 1889.
14. *Sporting Life*, Oct. 30, 1889.
15. *New York Times*, Oct. 20, 1889.
16. *Sporting Life*, Oct. 24, 1889.
17. *New York Times*, Oct. 23, 1889.
18. *Sporting News*, Nov. 4, 1889.
19. *New York Times*, Oct. 24, 1889.
20. *New York Times* Oct. 25, 1889.
21. *Brooklyn Eagle*, Oct. 25, 1889.
22. Ibid.
23. *Sporting Life*, Oct. 30, 1889.
24. *Washington Post*, July 13, 1890.
25. Ibid.
26. *New York Times*, Oct. 26, 1889.
27. *New York Times*, Oct. 27, 1889.
28. *New York Times*, Oct. 30, 1889.
29. *Sporting Life*, Nov. 6, 1889.
30. *New York Clipper*, Nov. 2, 1889.
31. *New York Times*, Oct. 31, 1889.

Chapter Nine

1. *Sporting Life*, Nov. 20, 1889.
2. *New York Times*, Nov. 14, 1889.
3. *Sporting Life*, Nov. 20, 1889.
4. Ibid.
5. *Sporting Life*, Nov. 27, 1889.
6. *Brooklyn Eagle*, Nov. 18, 1889.
7. *New York Times*, Nov. 5, 1889.
8. *New York Clipper*, Oct. 15, 1887.
9. *New York Clipper*, July 13, 1889.
10. *Brooklyn Eagle*, Nov. 4, 1889.
11. *Sporting Life*, Nov. 27, 1889.
12. *Brooklyn Eagle*, Feb. 17, 1890.
13. *Sporting Life*, Nov. 20, 1889.
14. *Sporting Life*, April 19, 1890.
15. *Sporting Life*, Feb. 26, 1890.
16. *Brooklyn Eagle*, March 3, 1890.
17. *Brooklyn Eagle*, March 12, 1890.
18. *Brooklyn Eagle*, March 14, 1890.
19. Letter from son, William McGunnigle, to National Baseball Hall of Fame, Aug. 29, 1966.
20. *Brooklyn Eagle*, April 1, 1890.
21. *Brooklyn Eagle*, April 13, 1890.
22. Ibid.
23. *New York Clipper*, Dec. 28, 1889.
24. *Boston Daily*, April 23, 1890.
25. *Brooklyn Eagle*, April 20, 1890.
26. *Brooklyn Eagle*, May 1, 1890.
27. *Sporting News*, April 6, 1890.
28. *Brooklyn Eagle*, April 26, 1890.
29. *Brooklyn Eagle*, May 11, 1890.
30. *Brooklyn Eagle*, May 2, 1890.
31. *Brooklyn Eagle*, May 3, 1890.
32. *Brooklyn Eagle*, May 11, 1890.
32. Ibid.
33. *Brooklyn Eagle*, May 22, 1890.
34. *Brooklyn Eagle*, June 14, 1890.
35. *Brooklyn Eagle*, April 27, 1890.
36. *Brooklyn Eagle*, July 6, 1890.
37. *Brooklyn Eagle*, April 27, 1890.
38. *Sporting News*, May 10, 1890.
39. *New York Times*, July 17, 1890.
40. *Brooklyn Eagle*, July 20, 1890.

Chapter Ten

1. *New York Clipper*, July 12, 1890.
2. *Brooklyn Eagle*, July 11, 1890.

3. *Sporting Life,* July 16, 1890.
4. *Brooklyn Eagle,* July 18, 1890.
5. *Brooklyn Eagle,* July 27, 1890, quoting "a Philadepia paper."
6. *Brooklyn Eagle,* Aug. 5, 1890.
7. *Brooklyn Eagle,* July 22, 1890.
8. *Brooklyn Eagle,* Aug. 5, 1890.
9. *Sporting Life,* Aug. 9, 1890.
10. Albert G. Spalding, *America's National Game,* p. 287–288.
11. *Sporting Life,* Jan. 10, 1891.
12. Albert G. Spalding, *America's National Game,* p. 475–476.
13. Ibid., p. 295–98.
14. *Sporting Life,* Aug. 9, 1890.
15. *Sporting Life,* Aug. 10, 1890.
16. *Brooklyn Eagle,* Aug. 9, 1890.
17. *Sporting Life,* Aug. 16, 1890.
18. *Brooklyn Eagle,* Sept. 2, 1890.
19. *Brooklyn Eagle,* Sept. 11, 1890.
20. *Brooklyn Eagle,* Sept. 10, 1890.
21. *Sporting Life,* Aug 16. 1890.
22. *Brooklyn Eagle,* Sept. 11, 1890.
23. *Brooklyn Eagle,* Sept. 17, 1890.
24. *Sporting Life,* Sept. 20, 1890.
25. *Sporting Life,* Oct. 4, 1890.
26. *Sporting Life,* Oct. 11, 1890.
27. *Sporting Life,* Oct. 4, 1890.
28. *Brooklyn Eagle,* Oct. 19, 1890.
29. *New York Times,* Oct. 28, 1890.
30. *Brooklyn Eagle,* Sept. 28, 1890.

Chapter Eleven

1. *Sporting Life,* Oct. 11, 1890.
2. *Sporting Life,*Oct. 4, 1890.
3. *Sporting Life,* Nov. 8, 1890.
4. *Brooklyn Eagle,* Nov. 3, 1890.
5. *New York Clipper,* Oct. 25, 1890.
6. Albert G. Spalding, *America's National Game,* p. 286–288.
7. *Sporting Life,* Nov. 22, 1890.
8. *New York Clipper,* Dec. 16, 1890.
9. *Brooklyn Eagle,* Feb. 20, 1913, from *History of Baseball in Brooklyn,* by Charles H. Ebbets with Thomas E. Rice.
10. *Sporting Life,* Nov. 3, 1890.
11. *Sporting Life,* Jan. 10, 1891.
12. *New York World,* in *Sporting Life,* Feb. 1891.
13. *Sporting Life,* Oct. 11, 1890.
14. *Sporting Life,* Dec. 27, 1890.
15. *New York World,* in *Sporting Life,* Jan. 3 1891.
16. *Sporting Life,* Dec. 13, 1890.
17. *Sporting Life,* Dec. 27, 1890.
18. *Brooklyn Eagle,* Feb. 6, 1891.
19. *Sporting Life,* Nov. 28, 1890.
20. *Sporting Life,* April 19, 1891.
21. *Brooklyn Eagle,* Jan. 30, 1913, from *History of Baseball in Brooklyn,* by Charles H. Ebbets with Thomas E. Rice.
22. *Brooklyn Eagle,* Jan. 23, 1932.

Bibliography

Books

Allen, Lee. *The Giants and the Dodgers.* New York: G. P. Putnam & Sons, 1964.

Axelson, G. W. *"Commy": The Life Story of Charles A. Comiskey.* Chicago: Reilly & Lee, 1919.

Baseball Encyclopedia, 10th Edition. New York: Macmillan, 1996.

Bevis, Charlie. *The New England League: A Baseball History 1855–1949.* Jefferson, NC: McFarland, 2007.

Caillaut, Jean-Pierre. *A Tale of Four Cities: Nineteenth Century Baseball's Most Exciting Season.* Jefferson, NC: McFarland, 2003.

Cash, Jon David. *Before They Were the Cardinals.* Columbia: University of Missouri Press, 2002.

Curry, Richard. "Saginaw, Michigan Ball Clubs of 1883 & 1884 Return to Life." n.d. http://saginawoldgolds.com/ files/ History.pdf.

Dolan, Jay P. *The Irish Americans.* New York: Bloomsburg Press, 2008.

Graham, Frank. *The Brooklyn Dodgers: An Informal History.* New York: G. P. Putnam & Sons, 1945.

Hetrick, J. Thomas. *Chris Von der Ahe and the St. Louis Browns.* Lanham, MD: Scarecrow Press, 1999.

James, Bill. *The New Bill James Historical Abstract.* New York: Free Press, 2001.

Leitner, Irving A. *Baseball Diamond in the Rough.* London: Abelard-Schuman, 1972.

McNeill, William F. *The Dodgers Encyclopedia.* Champaign, IL: Sports Publishing, 2003.

Morris, Peter. *But Didn't We Have Fun?: An Informal History of Baseball's Pioneer Era, 1843–1870.* Chicago: Ivan R. Dee, 2008.

Morris, Peter. *Catcher: How the Man Behind the Plate Became an American Folk Hero.* Chicago: Ivan R. Dee, 2009.

Nemec, David. *The Beer & Whiskey League: The Illustrated History of the American Association — Baseball's Renegade Major League.* Guilford, CT: The Lyons Press, 2004.

_____. *The Great Encyclopedia of 19th Century Major League Baseball.* New York: Donald Fine, 1997.

Okkonen, Marc. *Minor League Baseball Towns of Michigan.* San Diego: Thunder Bay Press, 1997.

Pearson, Daniel M. *Baseball in 1889 Players vs. Owners.* Bowling Green, OH: Bowling Green State University Press, 1993.

Schiff, Andrew J. *"The Father of Baseball": A Biography of Henry Chadwick.* Jefferson, NC: McFarland, 2008.

Seymour, Harold. *Baseball: The Early Years.* New York: Oxford University Press, 1960.

Spalding, Albert G. *America's National Game.* New York: American Sports Publishing, 1911.

Spink, Alfred H. *The National Game.* Carbondale: Southern Illinois University Press, 2000.

Stout, Glenn. *The Dodgers: 120 Years of*

Dodgers History. Boston: Houghton Mifflin, 2004.

Terry, James. L. *Long Before the Dodgers: Baseball in Brooklyn 1855–1884*. Jefferson, NC: McFarland, 2002.

Travers, Stephen. *Dodgers Past and Present.* Minneapolis: MVP Books, 2009.

Periodicals

Boston Globe
Brockton Daily Herald
Brockton Gazette
Brockton Times
Brooklyn Eagle
Buffalo Express
Fall City Journal-Herald
New York Clipper
New York Times
St. Louis Globe-Democrat
St. Louis Post-Dispatch
Sporting Life
Sporting News
Washington Post

Websites

Baseball Almanac
http://www.baseball-almanac.com
Baseball Chronology
http://www.baseballchronology.com
Baseball Library
http://www.baseballlibrary.com
The Baseball Page
http://www.thebaseballpage.com
Brooklyn Ball Parks
http://www.covehurst.net/ddyte/brooklyn
Brooklyn Eagle
http://www.eaglebrooklynpubliclibrary.org
The Deadball Era (obits)
http://www.thedeadballera.com
LA84 Foundation (Sporting Life)
http://www.la84foundation.org/index/SportingLife.htm
Los Angeles Dodgers
http://www.losangeles.dodgers.mlb.com
Major League Baseball
http://www.mlb.com
Minor League Baseball
http://www.milb.com
19th Century Baseball
http://www.19cbaseball.com
Old Fulton Post Cards (old newspapers)
http://www.fultonhistory.com
Society for American Baseball Research
http://www.sabr.org

Photograph Credits

Library of Congress
National Baseball Hall of Fame Library
San Diego Genealogical Society
Transcendental Graphics

Index

Numbers in ***bold italics*** indicate pages with photographs.